the New Believers

the New Believers

RE-IMAGINING GOD

Rachael Kohn

HarperCollins*Publishers*

HarperCollins*Publishers*

First published in Australia in 2003
by HarperCollins*Publishers* Pty Limited
ABN 36 009 913 517
A member of the HarperCollins*Publishers* (Australia) Pty Limited Group
www.harpercollins.com.au

HarperCollins*Publishers*
25 Ryde Road, Pymble, Sydney NSW 2073, Australia
31 View Road, Glenfield, Auckland 10, New Zealand
77–85 Fulham Palace Road, London W6 8JB, United Kingdom
2 Bloor Street East, 20th floor, Toronto, Ontario M4W 1A8, Canada
10 East 53rd Street, New York NY 10022, USA

National Library of Australia Cataloguing-in-Publication data:

Kohn, Rachael.
   The new believers: re-imagining God.
   ISBN 0 7322 7531 8.
   1. Religion. 2. Faith. 3. Spiritual life. I. Title.
210

Cover design by Marcia Grace
Internal design by Louise McGeachie
Typeset in 11 on 15pt Bembo by HarperCollins Design Studio
Printed and bound in Australia by Griffin Press on 80gsm Bulky Book Ivory

5 4 3 2 1   03 04 05 06

To Tom,
with whom I enjoy a continuing conversation
on matters scientific and spiritual

CONTENTS

Religion blushing, veils her sacred fires, and
unawares, Morality expires.
Alexander Pope, *The Dunciad*, Book IV, line 649

Nothing is so fatal to religion as indifference …
Edmund Burke, *Reflections on the Revolution in France*

INTRODUCTION

Religion has the singular effect of dividing people, yet its aim is the exact opposite. It's meant to give direction to the lost soul, yet it throws many people into confusion. The experience of faith is intended to provide comfort, yet the mere mention of it arouses the deepest suspicions of the spiritually alienated. The very same things could be said about love. But we would not on that account give away the possibility to love, nor be derelict in rescuing it when it has fallen into ruin. Equally, the human race has not given up on faith in something greater than the material riches of life even if some of the conventional indicators of belief, such as formal religious worship, have diminished. The analogy goes further. For as many variations as there are on the secret to true love so there are myriad views on what constitutes the spiritual essence of life, which since time began has found expression in the form of religion. This book presents some of the most important recent trends in the quest for that essence, which has proved remarkably adaptable and resilient despite the extreme pressures on religion to disappear.

Despite its longevity, religion — like love — is never without its distractions, challenges and creative urges. One could choose almost any moment in the past and remark that at no time was religion under greater stress by the forces of history. If it was not war that threatened to undermine central principles of the creed, then it was peace that tempted the indulgence in newfangled ideas. If it was not poverty that forced a grinding existence, heedless of moral decency, then it was prosperity that was forgetful of the virtues of charity and simplicity. If it was not science that challenged the foundation of religious doctrine then it was magic that converted sublime faith into a host of practical spells and esoteric knowledge. If it was not a prediction of the immediate onset of the Last Days and the Day of Judgment, then it was the lack of belief in an apocalyptic end to history that produced exactly the same outcome, a total abandonment of the traditional practice of religion. All of these have been continuous features of religious history up to and including the present, and yet today one often hears the cant that religion has never before been so tested and found so wanting.

This is bunk, of course. Religion has always been tested and always found wanting, which is why it has never stood still, but has been a hotbed of controversy, innovation and striving like every other aspect of human endeavour. Sex crimes by the clergy may be red-hot news today, but in the late Renaissance when there was no lack of official inquiries into the sexual misconduct of priests and nuns, the guilty were summarily dispatched in public hangings, castrations and imprisonment. Lack of belief in Christian doctrine may seem epidemic today, but until the Spanish Inquisition was abolished in 1834, the Roman Catholic Church had its hands full pursuing unbelievers and heretics who could be imprisoned, tortured, expelled, burned at the stake or publicly executed for their lack of faith or 'mistaken' beliefs. In the past, there has been as much ink spilt by zealous believers as by adventurous questers on finding the truest interpretation of the scriptures, the most inspired poetic description of the numinous, and the tightest philosophical argument for the existence of God. Today's multitude of publications on similar topics, including encomiums to the Goddess and arguments for a universal biological process that is nothing more nor less than the Higher Power behind all life, merely continues a long tradition. It seems there is a never-ending desire to capture the transcendent reality beyond the mundane limitations of daily life, and yet just as urgently the immanent, indwelling and pervasive sense of the divine presence immediately begs to be included in any discussion of divinity. The eyes cast heavenward are also and always drawn downward to look into everyday life, finding there the God of small things.

Underlying all the reinterpretations of matters spiritual, however, is the pivotal question, 'What is religion for?' For everyone who gives priority to a socially constructive expression of the religious life and a world-reforming agenda, there is another who prefers an inward journey of purification and personal atonement, a refuge from the material world and a direct path to divinity. These are two sides of the religious coin without which it can be said there is no valid currency in spiritual life. And yet, the last thirty years of religious innovation have witnessed a distinct preference for the inward, self-focused spiritual awakening associated with the mystics over the socially constructive and politically directed expressions of the churches. The reasons for this have been manifold and an increasing number of books, such as David Tacey's recently published *Spirituality Revolution*, have sought to explain and justify the non-institutional expressions of spirituality, particularly among young people as both a protest against formal creeds and crystallised forms of worship and a genuine attempt to create a spiritually vibrant consciousness within the broad experience of their lives.

They are the new believers whose vague spiritual aspirations are being shaped by the movements and issues outlined in this book. The language of their dreams was a long time in the making, however, and owes much to my generation. Indeed, nothing was more perplexing to me as a teenager and confirmed Beatlemaniac than seeing the most original Englishmen of my generation don Eastern dress and follow around an Indian holy man, Maharishi Mahesh Yogi, the founder of Transcendental Meditation, known simply as TM. It seemed to my besotted eyes that everything the Fab Four represented — love, impishness, fun and, above all, everything English — disappeared in an instant. But in the late 1960s nothing could have been more inevitable. By the early 1970s a tide of student activists was turning toward spiritual leaders, who were increasingly making appearances on college and university campuses in the hope of recruiting intelligent devotees from middle- and upper-class families. I would soon encounter a fair swag of them in my university career, where I participated in the general surge toward religious enthusiasm by combining a study of contemporary religious movements with textual studies of Judaism and Christianity, as well as Chinese and Japanese Buddhism. While this was the time of the greatest burgeoning of comparative religion studies in universities across North America and England, popular culture itself was awash with the new religious consciousness and it was finding its voice in the music of the times. Songwriters were not just churning out memorable tunes, it seemed everyone from Bob Dylan, who assumed the persona of an Old Testament prophet, to Van Morrison, who would strike an increasingly mystical note, articulated the new spiritual aspirations of a generation. Their songs would become the unofficial anthems of the most spiritually experimental generation modernity had produced.

This book would be a memoir if that phenomenon had been a mere aberration in an otherwise constant religious establishment. But the spiritual revolution of the 1970s, despite its litany of disastrous communal experiments and some tragic cultic abuses, had enormous consequences and, it could be said, unleashed a process of globalisation in the religious traditions of the West that continues to present us with a bewildering array of choices and some long overdue religious renovations. Indeed, it is surely time to lay down the blunt nineteenth-century instruments of prognostication, which saw society in a struggle between the forces of religious and moral values on the one hand and the inexorable slide into secularism on the other. That dilemma is not as interesting as it once was because it no longer describes the situation we are in. The spiritual innovations occurring within the received mainstream traditions and the invention of new religions take their inspiration, direction and even language from the secular world itself, that is, from the hard and soft sciences, political movements like environmentalism, and even the arts. The new believers are not only incorporating secular notions into their spiritual outlook, which it has to be said occurred in the past, when, for example, popes employed the 'science' of astrology and sought to harmonise it with Christian beliefs or churches came over to the view that the black races were as fully human as the white races. But the new believers are also fascinated by the apparent similarities between religious traditions, and in their most idealistic moments hope that this discovery will lead to a new era of religious co-operation.

Today one is more likely to consider teachings of the Dalai Lama as compatible with the teachings of Christ and the Bal Shem Tov than to condemn the leader of Tibetan Buddhism to the unsaved world of the heathens. Today one is more likely to encounter Jews who meditate or do yoga than who know nothing about these Eastern practices. Today one is more likely to find individuals who do not formally practise their family or inherited tradition, yet who emphatically state that they are spiritually aware and interested in the higher aspirations and values that religion teaches. Today one is more likely to find dedicated religious practitioners who freely criticise and doubt particular teachings and their exponents. Yet the blind and mute followers of rigidified tradition and charismatic cult leaders remain as an ever-present reminder that in the religious life there are also those who believe that true faith is marked by slavish obedience and unquestioning submission. Today one is as likely to encounter casualties of the new religions as of the Church. And yet for a great many people who believe that the spiritual urge is a deeply humanising leaven in an otherwise hyper-materialist world, it is also true that its riches are not always easily available to them. They are the spiritually questioning and exploring listeners of *The Spirit of Things* program on religion and spirituality, which I produce, with my colleague Geoff Wood, and present on ABC Radio National. They never fail to write to me or call me to express a view, but most often they just want to register their gratitude for keeping the doors of perception wide open, because they believe, as I do, that cultivating spiritual wisdom and ardour begins with an open and inquiring mind.

The religious trends that comprise the chapters of this book are approached in the spirit of inquiry that has sustained me for many years, both as a university academic and a radio broadcaster. In a field that has no lack of fraudsters, egomaniacs, pontificators and the mentally ill parading as prophets, messiahs and enlightened beings, my research and interviews have sometimes yielded bizarre results. They have included everything from the so-called enlightened beings, who behave like control freaks surrounded by slaves tending to their every need, to the confident young housewife who invited me to examine the 'scoop marks' behind her knees left by the extraterrestrial that visited her bedside one night. Spiritual celebrities can turn out to be some of the strangest people to meet, which is why their views, regardless of how seductively they are packaged in bestselling paperbacks and CDs, deserve to be considered and subjected to the same critical analysis that is regularly visited on the established traditions.

Fortunately, there are some very fine and deep-thinking individuals who occupy the spiritual firmament. They are obliged to share the stage with some of the indomitable popularisers who for better or worse extend the conversation to a broader public. Both the scholars and the popularisers have managed to speak to a generation of men and women who are yearning for a specific type of religious experience or vocation that has been forgotten in the mists of time or has not been available thus far. It is the convergence of academic and popular thought that has resulted in our current spiritual revolution, which is the subject of this book. Not all of the thinkers here would necessarily see themselves as leaders of the revolution, especially those who publish their work as scientific findings and draw cautious inferences from it about the spiritual dimension of the natural world. But all are aware of how much their work is changing the way we think about what it is to be human, and that fundamentally is what the religious life is about.

Those who might have been expecting a litany of cases drawn from the cultic fringe will have to wait for a future book. However, those who do come under the lens here are not beyond reproach or criticism. But that is only a sign of respect in the religious life, whose leaders, theologians, researchers and philosophers have not ascended to their level of influence without themselves questioning the ideas and world-views that have been passed down to them.

Of course, the answers given do not have to be complete, and it is this which divides the new believer from the true believer. The latter is most at home in ideological and theological constructions that are watertight and are guarded by punitive gatekeepers, who spout self-assured formulas of their faith at the drop of a hat. Their apologists know only how to make excuses for their shortcomings and they denounce their critics and keep them at bay, lest they infect the faithful. The new believers, on the contrary, are not certain of their boundaries, largely because they are still exploring the territory and expanding their field of vision or paring it down to size. Feminists and eco-spiritualists have overlapped their interests in recent years, and scientists have found common cause with the latter, while psychologists have roamed into the mystical spiritualities of East and West. Even the arch-reformer, John Shelby Spong, admits that he does not have all the answers for his new wave Christianity, especially around the issue of evil. Very likely, in years to come, his followers will close those gaps and claim a certainty that Spong himself does not claim in all matters — but that is a familiar theme. It is the process whereby the exploratory new believer is turned into the convinced true believer, the process that continually shapes and reshapes the world of religion.

With apologies to those who know this to be obvious, it must be said that there is no intrinsic merit in the argument of the new believer. It is a well-rehearsed conceit that most contemporary religious change is coursing upward in the inevitable evolutionary spiral toward a better spiritual expression. Too many catastrophic religious experiments, which openly harnessed modern ideas and technology in their methods and rhetoric, should put the lie to that. But it is also true that the current attempts to reshape received traditions and mint new spiritual practices to accord with the improved social situation of women, the latest discoveries in science, the fresh encounters with exotic traditions and the awakened ecological awareness of our planet's needs reflect genuine efforts to sanctify and give meaning to a changed world.

1. RE-INVENTING THE SELF
The Lesson of Oz

One of the most compelling moral tales of the modern world is *The Wizard of Oz*. Dorothy, a young girl from Kansas, dreams that she is in a strange enchanted land, where she meets three delightful companions — a scarecrow, a tin man and a cowardly lion — who each are in need of a quality to make them complete. Together they follow the yellow brick road, through dangerous territory, in order to come to a wizard who can grant them their wishes. They discover the wizard is just an old man who manipulates lights, whistles and smoke behind a curtain to make people believe he has the power to bestow on them qualities which, in fact, they have possessed all along. All they need to do is believe in themselves. Dorothy, too, learns a lesson. Throughout the adventure she expresses a desire to go home, but in the end she is told by Glinda, the Good Witch of the North, to concentrate on her wish and it will happen. Waking up from her dream, Dorothy announces to her family and friends gathered around her, 'There's no place like home.' That place 'over the rainbow' where skies are blue and dreams come true is right here on earth — and right in your own back yard. And most importantly, it is in your own power to make it real.

It is no wonder that this story, first published in 1900, became an American icon. Translated into most major languages it would certainly be a popular alternative to the dark and forbidding themes of Grimm's fairytales. It encapsulates bred-in-the-bone Yankee optimism and the downhome values that owed more to the power of positive thinking and the late nineteenth-century 'Freethought' movement than to church-oriented Christian piety. In fact, the author of *The Wonderful Wizard of Oz* (the book upon which the famous movie was based) was consciously writing a tale that fully reflected the scientific rationalism which had seriously questioned the received beliefs in a personal God, and it's a view that has remained one of the most influential in our own time. L. Frank Baum was a Theosophist, who championed a new world of human spirituality which saw the merging of science and religion, nature and philosophy, in an awareness of a higher truth that placed the human with limitless capacities at its centre. If we take the wizard to be but a metaphor for the old Father God of the Bible, who was hidden from view but was responsible for our salvation if only we provided him with the right petitions and prayers, then Baum's story reveals him to be nothing more than an old fogy, believed in only by children and halfwits.

In his place was a humanity that saw through the fraud and believed in itself. The great new revelation was that anything was possible. The greatest intellect, the purest body and finest social order could be crafted from an ethic of human perfectibility. The scarecrow could have a brain, the tin man could have a heart and the cowardly lion could indeed gain his courage, while Dorothy and her little dog, Toto, could find happiness at home with Auntie Em. It was not only simple, it was in conformity with nature itself.

Frank Baum, the son of an oil industrialist, was the quintessential freethinker of his generation. Married to the feminist Maud Gage, Baum wrote throughout his varied career for several local papers, and in an editorial for the *Aberdeen Saturday Pioneer*, written ten years before he published America's most famous children's story, he mused about the decline of faith, by which he meant a growing unbelief in the doctrines of Christianity. But he was quick to point out that a new source of hope would be found in nature, although not in the way that led some scientists to atheism:

> The age of Faith is sinking slowly into the past; the age of Unfaith becomes an important problem of to-day. Is there in this a menace to Christianity? This unfaith is not the atheism of the last century. It is rather an eager longing to penetrate the secrets of Nature — an aspiration for knowledge we have been taught is forbidden.[1]

The extraordinary scientific discoveries in the nineteenth century may have compelled some to turn their backs on faith in God altogether, but for others, like the Theosophists, who were followers of Madame Blavatsky, science offered great hope as the means by which the individual would break through her apparent physical, mental and spiritual limitations. As with all students of esoteric wisdom, Theosophists believed that the expanding knowledge of the material world would finally unlock the secrets of other worlds where the so-called 'Ascended Masters' resided, that lost continents, such as Lemuria and Atlantis, would be found, and above all the divinity itself would be glimpsed.

While these mysteries remained largely elusive (when they were not conjured in the charged atmosphere of Madame Blavatsky's seances), the 'secret doctrine' of the universal religion could be discovered underlying the traditions of India and the Far East. This 'secret doctrine', which Helena Petrovna Blavatsky spelled out in a fanciful and complex work of 1500 pages of the same name, promoted the idea that certain psychic and physical powers were part of human nature, but had been allowed to die, smothered by the confining patriarchal tenets and structures of the church. The key to their revival lay in the apprehension of the spiritual practices of Hindu yogis and sages, of whom the Theosophists, like Baum, were in awe, not least because of the ease with which they lived with nature.

The Theosophists, in fact, are the dissatisfied of the world, the dissenters from all creeds. They owe their origin to the wise men of India, and are numerous, not only in the far famed mystic East, but in England, France, Germany and Russia. They admit the existence of a God — not necessarily a personal God. To them God is Nature and Nature God.[2]

Baum preferred to believe in a universal God that was not bound to institutional religion but found expression in all religions, with the obvious omission of Judaism. In this he reflected the view of the esoteric wisdom schools of the nineteenth century which were largely hostile to or simply forgetful of the religion that was responsible for the Bible and gave birth to Christianity. Perhaps because Judaism is theologically bound to a people, and therefore has certain ethnic or national connotations, in the roster of the great founders of religion, Moses rarely makes an appearance. In the editorial for the *Aberdeen Saturday Pioneer*, this is how Frank Baum summed up the universal God who appeared throughout history in different guises to different peoples.

Many ages ago Budda came to enlighten the civilization of the East.

The pure and beautiful doctrines he taught made ready converts, and to-day his followers outnumber those of any other religion.

To the fierce and warlike tribes of Arabia, Mohammed appeared. His gentleness and bravery tamed their fierce natures. They followed him implicitly, as millions of their descendants follow him still.

Confucius with ready sophistry promulgated a 'religion of reason.'

His works are to this day the marvel of all intelligent people; his myriads of disciples have never wavered in their faith.

The sweet and tender teachings of Christ, together with the touching story of his life, have sunk deeply into the hearts of those nations which rank highest in modern civilization.

In their separate domains all these religions flourish to-day. Their converts are firm and unflinching, their temples cover the land, and each in its own way sends praises to a common Creator — a Universal God.[3]

Baum's perspective is recognisable today as the New Age outlook. The great religions are seen as fonts of wisdom, containing truths that can be learned in the same way as scientific truths are discovered, and then utilised for one's own enlightenment. His harmonious vision of the different traditional believers all singing praises to the one Creator sends a clear message to his readers that various religious truths can co-exist and are not worth fighting over, since at bottom they are entirely compatible, if they are not actually the one truth. This is why Baum assured his readers that: 'If Christianity is Truth, as our education has taught us to believe, there can be no menace to it in Theosophy.'[4]

A lot rested on that conditional 'if', for Baum and other Theosophists and Freethinkers saw problems in conventional Christianity. Its claim that it offered an exclusive path to salvation by a personal savior God was inconsistent with the Theosophical belief in the indifferent power of a divinity identified with nature and accessible to all people who were willing to be searchers after Truth. Christianity was also taken to be wrong in presuming that man's nature was fallen and sinful and in need of redemption. Quite the contrary! The higher powers of man were thought to be buried within his nature, which lay almost forgotten under the rigid edifice of organised religion. It was not hope for salvation from a sinful nature, but rather the unerring search for the Truth at the core of one's original nature, which was the Theosophical aim, and it had a noble scientific ring to it. The only barrier to recognising this Truth was the limited application of one's intellect and will. It was not surprising that the complete apprehension of this Truth, this Divine Wisdom, was attainable only by the few.

Theosophy is not a religion. Its followers are simply 'searchers after Truth.' Not for the ignorant are the tenets they hold, neither for the worldly in any sense. Enrolled within their ranks are some of the grandest intellects of the Eastern and Western worlds.[5]

This description of the Theosophists' self-image of the 1890s by Frank Baum could be transferred without alteration to the contemporary New Age movement. Today, adherents of New Age spirituality not only believe that supreme truth surpasses the confines of any one religion, but they also are inclined to view the New Age perspective as significantly more sophisticated or 'evolved' than the exclusive beliefs of the ordinary Christian. There is another important difference between the New Age approach to spiritual truth and the Christian's. From its origins to the present, the Church has allotted to itself the role of the saviour of lost souls, with the onus on the Church to cast its nets as widely as possible and draw in the whole world lest it die in sin. The New Age aim of enlightenment of humanity, on the other hand, puts the onus on individual seekers, who are obliged to spread their own nets as widely as possible in search of divine wisdom, which, it is believed, is not guarded or promoted by any one religion or particular institution. The truly enlightened being therefore must study the esoteric arts and plunge into a bewildering array of world mythologies in the hope of finally awakening the full power that lies within the self.

If *The Wonderful Wizard of Oz* was the vehicle for Baum's heroic theosophical tale, where the potential to be more than what you think you are lies within, then its contemporary version is the movie *Star Wars*, an equally compelling story of heroic self-discovery. The inspiration for this at once futuristic and medieval tale of a young man's awakening to his own power, the 'Force', to avert evil was another true believer in the world's religious myths, Joseph Campbell. This close friend of *Star Wars* film director George Lucas was a largely self-taught comparative religionist, who is singularly credited with popularising the world's religious myths as a source of personal empowerment. The culmination of his numerous books on the topic, which brought his ideas to millions of television viewers in 1985–86, was the series produced by Bill Moyers, 'Joseph Campbell and the Power of Myth', which was shot largely at George Lucas's ranch.

Campbell's influence on popular thought, and particularly the New Age, is enormous, but not for the reasons that might be supposed. The desire to learn about other people's religious beliefs is not the attraction of Campbell's work. Hundreds of anthropological texts on the same topic have languished on library shelves for more than a century. It is quite simply Campbell's way of presenting the mythic stories of the world's religions as a means of travelling inward and finding the divine self, the place where all religious and spiritual truths originate.

> Read myths. They teach that you can turn inward and you begin to get the message of the symbols. Read other people's myths, not those of your own religion, because you tend to interpret your own religion in terms of fact — but if you read the other ones, you begin to get the message. Myth helps you to put your mind in touch with this experience of being alive. Myth tells you what the experience is.[6]

Campbell's *The Hero with a Thousand Faces* was first published in 1948. It presented the sacred stories of peoples as diverse as the Greeks, the Mayans and the Norse, not as accounts of tribal origin or national significance — after World War II nothing could have been more distasteful — but as paradigms for personal development. With the help of concepts drawn from the work of psychologist Carl Jung, such as the collective unconscious wherein universal personality constructs or behavioural patterns reside, Campbell was able to provide disparate national myths and rituals with a primal, shared and personally redemptive significance they would not otherwise appear to have for Western readers. With one stroke Campbell managed to popularise the theories of the then little-known Swiss psychologist while laying to rest the negative critique of myth associated with the founder of psychoanalysis, Sigmund Freud, for whom the world's myths had quite the opposite significance. For Freud, whether it was the story of

Oedipus or the biblical account of Moses, they were equally the memory banks of the human race and its primal neurotic, not its redemptive, tendencies. It followed that rituals were merely stultifying artefacts, nothing more than reminders of an archaic myth. This highly rationalist and ethical perspective had its roots in Kantian philosophy. Nothing could be further from the Campbell–Jung approach to ritual as a means of recreating and directly experiencing the power of myth. Call it romantic or utilitarian, there were elements of both in Joseph Campbell's unabashed appropriation of the world's myths and rituals as a means of furthering the personal quest for heroic adventure and spiritual transformation.

Campbell, who died in 1987, is still the most popularly quoted comparative religionist, but it is not because he represents the academic discipline which goes by that name. Scholars who study the world's religions are keen to note their very important distinctions, which an immersion in their sacred language and history inevitably reveals. Campbell, on the other hand, represents a variation on a far older, one might say 'imperialist' trend of comparative religious writing, which is perhaps best exemplified by another highly influential writer of Scots origin, Thomas Carlyle. A historian of some repute, he catapulted to fame and fortune with a series of lectures delivered in May 1840 on 'Heroes, Hero-Worshipping and the Heroic in History'.

Carlyle was born in 1775 and trained for the ministry, but under the influence of the Scottish Enlightenment he decided against a future as a Presbyterian parson. Instead he wrote with enthusiasm about religion as a universal phenomenon, in which man practically believes and acts in ways that make him feel spiritually related to the 'unseen world'.

> We see men of all kinds of professed creeds attain to almost all degrees of worth or worthlessness under each or any of them. This is not what I call religion, this profession and assertion; . . . But the thing man does practically believe; . . . the thing a man does practically lay to heart, and know for certain, concerning

his vital relations to this mysterious Universe, and his duty and destiny there, that is in all cases the primary thing for him, and creatively determines all the rest. That is his *religion*.[7]

Carlyle went to great lengths to describe 'this mysterious Universe' as a 'Force', which is everywhere and also within us, a never-resting whirlwind in creation, 'high as Immensity, old as Eternity … an unspeakable Godlike thing towards which the best attitude … is awe, devout prostration and humility of soul; worship if not in words, then in silence'.[8]

To act in keeping with 'this mysterious Universe' was the mark of a 'Great Man' or 'Hero', who would in turn be worshipped as a god. 'May the Force be with you!' would become the most memorable line of the film *Star Wars*, in which Luke Skywalker overcomes the evil Darth Vader, and by virtue of his bravery assumes the role of a 'Hero'. If Carlyle had lived a century and a half later, he would have identified Luke Skywalker as akin to Christ himself.

> Hero-worship, heartfelt prostrate admiration, submission, burning, boundless for a noblest godlike Form of Man — is not that the germ of Christianity itself? The greatest of all Heroes is One — whom we do not name here! … you will find it the ultimate perfection of a principle extant throughout man's whole history on earth.[9]

For Carlyle the dynamic relationship which the hero sustains with 'the Force' is not merely some private preoccupation or personal obsession, but, like the gods of all civilisations, it has manifest social implications. Loyalty to the hero is nothing other than faith itself: 'Faith is loyalty to some inspired Teacher, some spiritual Hero. And what therefore is loyalty proper, the life-breath of all society, but an effluence of Hero worship … Society is founded on Hero-worship.'[10]

While Carlyle's argument fitted beautifully with the Victorian love of Greek myths and Arthurian legends, ravishingly depicted in art by the

Pre-Raphaelite Brotherhood and the Aesthetic Movement, its romantic appeal would founder on the rocks of a Dickensian society groaning under the distresses of poverty and social disarray. The importance of the hero for the wellbeing of society was being seriously questioned by architects of social progress in the mid nineteenth century. The great political philosopher, John Stuart Mill, for example, admired the French, whom he believed were more deeply egalitarian than the hierarchically minded and complacent English. Mill was more interested in improving the conditions of society at large than in identifying a heroic leader. Although he recognised the importance of an intellectual elite, he believed that society's progress should be secured through pragmatic political change, not determined by the unpredictable and capricious acts of great men.

Although good friends, Mill and Carlyle were intellectual opponents, which is perhaps why the first volume of Carlyle's *The French Revolution* was accidentally used to light a fire while on loan to Mill!

The two men had very different motives for their interest in the great political upheaval across the English Channel, with Carlyle championing the hero as 'the spiritual Captain' of the people and as 'the Uniter of them with the Unseen Holy'. In his lecture on 'The Hero as Divinity', Carlyle bemoans the decline of hero-worship in an age that he is aware denies the existence of great men, and instead subjects history's towering figures, like Luther, to such scrutiny that it runs them all into 'a little kind of man!', merely a 'creature of the Time'.[11]

Nothing so distresses a person of faith as the sober rationalist's charge that they are merely caught in the wheels of time, in the inevitable flow of events, which willy-nilly determine their fate. Faith in a God who intervenes in history, or answers one's prayers, or strengthens one's resolve to overcome evil is precisely the kind of faith that can overturn the inevitable and vanquish the odds stacked up against one. But where is this God to be found, and what will be our duty by Him? As we can see, the theosophical and deist musings of the nineteenth century had largely done away with the Father God of the Bible, who split the Red Sea for the Israelites and responded to the supplications of the faithful. A God like that was already caricatured as the amateur sideshow act that only young girls and scarecrows believed in. A more impersonal set of concepts, bordering on the scientific language that would anticipate twentieth-century physics, was marshalled to give some meaning to this supernatural source of all being, who gave life to all creation, like some divine energy, power or force.

Today, more than a century later, any number of terms are used to hint at divinity in creation or some mysterious essence of life, without naming it theologically and exclusively. It is not God but the essence of God which is sought. The notion of a biblically inspired transcendent personality who gave us life and to whom we forge a relationship through penitent prayer and servitude has been abandoned by those who prefer the quasi-scientific alchemical search for the key to life, represented, for example, in the five elements — fire, air, water, earth and quintessence or etheric — which if fully understood may be harnessed and used for one's benefit. The hero God has not faded entirely from view. He remains a perennial ideal, but the aim is not to discern his footprints in history nor to foster loyalty to the heroes of our time. It is to look inward and to discover and awaken the seeds of the hero in oneself.

As if writing a new theology, which after all is merely a description of the ways in which we understand faith, contemporary writers are attempting to hone a distinctive language in which to encapsulate as precisely as possible the process of this spiritual awareness. Often it is descriptive of the experience of the numinous, while at other times it is a step by step series of exercises designed to bring the individual as close as possible to realising union with this supposed divine energy.

Entelechy is the philosophical term that New Age guru Jean Houston uses to encapsulate the process of uncovering the full power of the self.[12] A dictionary definition of the Greek word describes it as nothing more than 'the supposed essential nature or guiding principle of a living thing', but in Jean Houston's vocabulary entelechy has become 'the divine purpose that drives us toward realizing our essential self, that gives us our higher destiny ...'.[13] Discovering, awakening, and using entelechy as a form of self-empowerment is what she has lectured on, written about and workshopped for a good deal of her professional life. Houston believes that to be without an awareness of this potential greatness, which lies hidden, is to 'feel horribly incomplete'.[14] It is to be part of the mediocre mob, who it would seem are fated always to be doing their best, as the joke goes, but in reality are unconscious losers.

Jean Houston was an enthusiastic student and friend of Joseph Campbell, and she relates a conversation with him, in which she asked if he had ever experienced 'Essence'. He answered that as a young man, while running a race, he had entered a state of perfection, which was the same thing. Runner, running and the run became one. Jean Houston answered with an account of her own, in which as a young fencer she was declared the winner in a round against the city's leading fencers, much older and more experienced than she was.[15] Reading this passage, one gets a vivid picture of the new believer as athlete. Yet there is more here than the Olympic ethic of personal best turned spiritual or the simple rush of endorphins allowing one to transcend physical limitations. For Jean Houston, as undoubtedly for her mentor, Joseph Campbell, there is the ever-present opportunity for everyone to tap into the divine power, this essence, and become nothing less than heroic, brilliant and divine: 'I firmly believe that all human beings have access to an alternative or archetypal energy system that allows vital energy to mutate into extraordinary capacities and powers.'[16]

This language borrows the imagery of the alchemist's craft, which outwardly was meant to mutate simple base matter into gold while inwardly unlocking the secret of inner transformation and creativity. One might class Jean Houston as a latter-day alchemist, but without the legendary penchant for secrecy or affectation to a lost medieval cult of wisdom. Blessed with a thoroughly extrovert personality and an all-American egalitarianism, Jean Houston shares her insights with masses of ordinary people as well as the rich and famous, most notably

Hillary Clinton. Handsomely paid for the psycho-spiritual exercises she has designed over the years to enhance a person's performance and wellbeing, Jean Houston is a popular philosopher turned mentor to millions. Like the alchemists of old, Houston has managed to both provide the esoteric goal of inner transformation and realise the exoteric goal of producing gold.

If it sounds like Jean Houston is just another hawker of psycho-spiritual goods in the huge marketplace of self-help, at one level that is so, but her importance for the world of faith is her eclectic use of religious and spiritual myths and stories, rituals and exercises, poetry and metaphysical speculations, which operate outside the clinical and ecclesiastical setting. There may not be a heaven to which believers in the biblical God are promised a place when they die, but in Jean Houston's universe, heaven is more like a hall of fame, where Helen Keller, Emily Dickinson and Thomas Jefferson take their place alongside the Buddha, Christ and White Buffalo Woman — oh, yes, and Luke Skywalker from *Star Wars*, Dr Spock from *Star Trek* and Dorothy from *The Wizard of Oz*. They and countless others, who have experienced the 'essence' that goes by a hundred names, and have attained to great things, are the spiritual heroes of all time.

To be sure, the numerous references to Hollywood movies and TV culture which appear in her works and workshops irritate those who prefer their spiritual teachings to be served in exclusively 'serious' terms, or with reference to indisputably sacred literature. The allusions to the make-believe world of entertainment (in which she grew up with her Hollywood scriptwriter father) might suggest that Houston's spiritual hall of fame somewhat resembles Disney World, but Houston would not be embarrassed by that. The world's most popular theme park gives the illusion that dreams are true, which in itself is a cognitive quality of faith. One might go so far as seeing the annual American ritual of watching *The Wizard of Oz* on television around Thanksgiving as a national religious observance. In any case, the perpetual screening of the 1939 cinematic version of Frank Baum's original story, the book's translation into all the major languages and its continuous publication, including its sequels, indicate that it still has the power to inspire young and old alike, reminding them of the time-honoured virtues of courage, honesty, fidelity, perseverance, humility and love. More simply it reinforces the perennial values of friendship, family and believing in oneself. A young girl's adventurous pursuit of a wizard, which becomes a young heroine's self-discovery, is not only something of a feminist reclamation of the divine spirit which she learns always belonged to her, but it is also a frank disempowerment of the old man wizard, who, it turns out, is only as good as the illusion he manages to create behind the curtain. It is not surprising that *The Wizard of Oz* is Jean Houston's favourite redemptive story.

Yet redemption, in the sense of being delivered from sin and its consequences, through an offering, a ransom, a prayer or the atoning death of Christ, is not the meaning of this saving tale for Jean Houston. What then is one to be saved from if not sin, evil or harm? The answer is in all her works, but most succinctly in a little book entitled *A Passion for the Possible: A Guide to Realizing Your True Potential.*[17] In it, Jean Houston encapsulates the whole project of the modern human potential movement, initiated in the 1970s, which aims to identify and conquer the conditions of personal failure. Taking as given that this is a spiritual condition rather than a problem of will or discipline alone, she treats the failure to achieve what is possible by applying the power of the imagination. Taking her readers on a journey through what is called 'the Mythic Realm', they encounter the gods, the heroes and the models of mastery from the world's religious traditions and from all walks of life. On this guided tour one is just as likely to meet the Egyptian goddess Isis or the Chinese incarnation of the Buddha's compassion, Qwan Yin, as a stonemason or a Japanese Samurai warrior. The point of this mythic adventure is not to get to know the exotic characters of the world's religions, but to claim their qualities as one's own, by first accepting that these beings are all manifestations of 'the Self', and second by calling them up when one is in need of them.

As skilfully as the Pied Piper, Houston leads her readers along a path which culminates in their imaginary union with 'the God Self'.

At a level deeper than the realm of myth lies the 'Realm of the Spirit', where she takes her readers and workshop attendees on a collective descent into the 'Mind of God', the 'State of Grace', the encounter with the perfected creation.[18] Like some latter-day Meister Eckhart, with the addition of an all-American penchant for sharing the faith, Houston is convinced that the divine–human partnership is the essence of who we are, and as such should be entered into vigorously and openly, as if by right, not by grace. Quoting Eckhart's dictum, 'If I am to know God directly, I must become completely God and God I, so that this God and this I become one I,' Houston is on the well-trodden, if not firm, ground of Christian mysticism, when she claims that we can all take a 'God's eye view' of the world.[19] (This is a theme that resurfaces even more radically in the work of Neale Donald Walsch, examined in Chapter 8.) Indeed there is no contemporary New Age teacher who more forcefully and convincingly argues that every individual has a seed of greatness, which is the divine in the human, and that it can be breathed into life, like embers into a flame, than Houston. In her vocabulary, when the individual contacts the entelechy, which is 'the cosmic persona turned to human purpose and possibility,' then it's all systems go.[20] There is nothing you cannot do.

There is a fair degree of hyperbole, inevitably, in the claim that we can tap into the source of all being. How could it not offer us the all-knowing and all-powerful qualities that have traditionally been associated with the God of Creation or the pantheon of Hellenistic gods? As Houston puts it, when people realise the potential of entelechy 'their names become scriptural!'.[21] What could this mean other than that they all become as gods? In this, the imprint of Joseph Campbell and even Thomas Carlyle is visible. Discovering the secret of divinity in human form was the reason they dedicated themselves to plumbing the depths of the world's religions. Becoming the hero and reaping the fruit of that invincible power would be the practical result. Neither of these writers, a hundred years apart, was particularly interested in the sorry and messy histories in which the religious traditions arose and in which their myths were usually couched. It is there — whether in the Indian epic, the Mahabaratha, or the many books of the Bible — we find the human foibles and historical accidents which remind readers that the folly of hubris and all the other human vices come at a cost. That cost usually brings with it another noble urge, perhaps less heroic but no less important. It is the communal desire to establish a system of law and order that interprets the dictums and administers the punishments that bring unbridled heroes to heel.

It is still possible to plumb the Bible and other religious texts for the archetypal hero. Yet even in the story of David, Israel's greatest hero, the youthful valour that led to kingship would later fade into decadence and disappointment. Although his fall from grace is luridly overplayed in some contemporary treatments, like the Hollywood movie *King David*, featuring the young Richard Gere, and Jonathan Kirsch's book *King David*, the motif is consistent enough in the Bible to suggest a powerful message. Human weakness will threaten to undo even the great ones. Consider the denouement that met Israel's first hero, Moses. Scripture has it that he not only valiantly defeated the Egyptians, but in humility and awe took the shoes from his feet and stood before the Lord, vowing to undertake a mission he never dreamed he could accomplish. But the story does not end there. God's commission turned out to be a difficult one for the Israelites to accept. While Moses is on Mount Sinai, his people are in disarray, and with a shameful readiness they turn away from their leader to delight in the golden calf. Sorely angered and disappointed, Moses acts with renewed resolve to impose upon them the burden of the law, which would give society as a whole the means to attain greatness, even as it would judge the mighty and bring low the kings and the heroes. The once heroic Moses would himself die in an obscure place and never enter the Promised Land.

One cannot help thinking that the utilitarian philosopher and social architect John Stuart Mill would have felt vindicated by this and the other unheroic parts of the Bible, precisely because they demonstrate that to the early Israelites who wrote down these stories and preserved them for posterity, it was more important to highlight the foundations of moral and legal justice in the fledgling Jewish society than to provide triumphant accounts of great men, who, it should be remembered, are never so great that they deserve to be worshipped. Carlyle, on the contrary, along with like-minded contemporary writers, would have preferred to read the glittering accounts of the youthful and brilliant Moses and David, whose acts of bravery and courage were a testament to the eternal and divine call to 'Great Men'. The rest, they would say, is merely history.

2. REWRITING THE BIBLE

Jesus was a Man

There is no man whose life has been a greater battleground between the forces of history and the call to faith than Jesus of Nazareth. From the moment his life was recorded, it was subject to contention, and much of it would divide along the fault line of history on the one side and faith on the other. Two thousand years later, there is little sign of that rift healing, and it could be argued that it has never been deeper, and with more ironic consequences.

Robert Funk is the founder and director of the Jesus Seminar, the world's most influential team of scholars working on the New Testament. After twenty years of closely analysing the Gospels to find the historically authentic sayings of Jesus, as distinct from those 'put in to his mouth' by his followers, Funk has admitted that faith in Jesus needs to be revitalised. This might come as a surprise to those who see the efforts of New Testament scholars as serving the interests of the academy alone, with hardly a thought cast in the direction of the community of the faithful. They would be right in thinking that biblical scholarship has delivered a significant blow to Christian faith, in that it has delved into the historical realities of Jesus' life, as far as it can be known, and come up with conclusions that have significantly undermined the foundational belief of the Church: that the Bible is revealed, wholly and utterly, by God, and that every word of it is true.

Robert Funk would be the first to admit that he is a key culprit in the twentieth-century academic dismantling of traditional Christian faith. He sees the work of the Jesus Seminar as the logical culmination of a grand tradition that was started a century and a half earlier by the German scholar David Friedrich Strauss, whose *Life of Jesus* (1838) would set the ball rolling in what would become identified as a largely Protestant enterprise of subjecting biblical texts to a close historical and literary analysis. Catholics were never as reliant on the Bible for popular faith, having opposed both its translation from the Latin Vulgate and its widespread distribution in the vernacular languages. Indeed, with the rise of critical scholarship of the Bible, especially the work of the Lutheran scholar Julius Wellhausen (1844–1918), who first established that the Bible was a collection of accounts by different authors writing in different periods, it looked as if the Roman Catholic predictions of religious mayhem resulting from putting the Bible into the hands of the people had an even more diabolical consequence than the ecclesiastical and theological reforms of the Protestant Reformation. Belief itself would be eradicated!

Fuelled by the philosophical and political rationalism of the Enlightenment, Protestants would merge their newly found taste for scientific analysis with their careful reading of the Bible and produce sceptical interpretations of its miraculous narratives that would positively shatter the central tenets of Christianity. In study after study, scholars would deny or disprove some of the fundamentals of the faith. The following were among their conclusions: the Gospel texts were ambiguous on whether Jesus believed himself to be the Messiah; they were inconsistent on whether he was born of a virgin; they were not at all clear as to the meaning of the Hebrew expressions 'the son of God' and 'son of man'; and the plain meaning of certain passages was contradictory to the notion that Jesus himself was God. A convention adopted by scholars was to attribute these Christological beliefs in Jesus as the saving messiah to his band of disciples and the later Church. It was assumed that in their zeal to make converts and to shore up their own disappointment at Jesus' tragic death, they were responsible for promoting a raft of optimistic beliefs, such as Jesus Christ's atoning death, his bodily resurrection and his triumphant return to usher in the millennium, the Day of Judgment and the Kingdom of Heaven. Invariably, this meant that the study of the Gospels and the Pauline letters became a window onto the early Church, affording barely a glimpse of Jesus in the background.

Doubting the literal truth of the Gospels has a long history. Heresies, like those of the Marcionites, the Gnostics and the Cathars erupted in the early and medieval periods, but they were largely put down or had few followers who dwindled away. In the early modern period, however, they were not always confined to the margins. The influential German biblical scholar Bruno Bauer (1809–82) expressed the extremely radical opinion that Jesus never existed, but was an imaginary combination of the Roman philosopher Seneca and the first-century Alexandrine Jewish philosopher Philo. Most scholars couched their considered doubts about the doctrinal truths of Christianity in more sensitive terms,[1] and it would be some time before New Testament scholarship would arrive at a wholly negative conclusion about the verities of the received tradition. But two major trends would inadvertently help to bring it on. The first was a keen focus on the history of Jesus' rise and ministry in so far as that could be discerned from the available sources. This involved a closer look at the Jewish tradition and milieu in late antiquity, as well as a consideration of the non-canonical Gnostic Gospels found in 1945 and the Dead Sea Scrolls found in 1947. The second trend was entirely opposed to this focus. By co-opting existential philosophy it would ditch history and go with the poetic flow and meaning of Jesus' life and teaching, while at the same time rejecting the value of supernatural claims of the tradition. Both perspectives would dispense with some significant and central claims of the Christian Church.

Already in the mid nineteenth century, two German scholars, August Friedrich Gfrorer and Richard von der Alm (a pseudonym for

Friedrich Wilhelm Ghillany) had plumbed the messianic ideas recorded in Jewish writings in the period immediately before and after Jesus. They sought to answer the question of whether Jesus had indeed become a unique suffering and saving messiah, or whether tradition recorded his life that way because it was consistent with the beliefs that already prevailed within Judaism, and in which he himself may have believed. Gfrorer demonstrated that Jesus' beliefs mirrored messianic ideas in the writings of the rabbis, whereas von der Alm argued that Jesus' ethical teachings resembled those of Rabbi Hillel the Elder (30BCE–20CE) and others recorded in the early rabbinic sources. Von der Alm was also the first to discuss the importance of the Jewish belief in the 'Messiah, the son of Joseph' and in the 'suffering messiah', which preceded the appearance of Jesus. The discovery that these ideas were alive in Jewish thought at the time of Jesus clearly weakened the claim that Jesus represented a unique and unprecedented development. It still left open, however, the possibility that he was the fulfilment of Jewish hopes, a fundamental Christian belief.

Gfrorer and von der Alm were not Jewish, as far as can be ascertained, but they sensed that the life of a first-century Jew in Roman Palestine could be illuminated by a closer examination of the Jewish beliefs that circulated within and about him. Although that assumption would be regularly challenged by those who believed that Jesus represented a right-angle turn or break with Judaism at the time, realising the importance of Jesus' Jewish roots was nonetheless an idea whose time had come, prompted by a slow but sure awakening to the rising tide of anti-Semitism in Europe. The end of the nineteenth and the early twentieth centuries saw bitter pogroms and some infamous anti-Semitic show trials against Jews in Eastern and Western Europe, based on the 'blood libel', the originally medieval Christian myth that Jews required the blood of Christian children to make the Passover *matzos*, or unleavened bread.[2] Less than fifty years later, after World War II, an entire generation of Europeans would come face to face with their complicity, whether passive or active, in the Holocaust, the murder of millions of Jewish civilians simply because they were Jewish. In scholarly circles the pursuit of anti-Jewish attitudes had been no less significant. Gerhard Kittel, whose *Theological Dictionary of the New Testament* has been a standard source for fifty years, was a regular contributor to one of the official Nazi publications on the 'Jewish question' in Germany.[3] It stands to reason that a profound desire to come to grips with anti-Judaism and the role of the Church in promoting it was propelled by the sheer force of historical circumstances, which after the war was reduced to the devastating realisation that as Jesus was Jewish, born of Jewish parents, he too would have ended in Auschwitz.

This realisation would have almost as much significance to Jews as to Christians, in that it revealed how far the Church had drifted from its founder. Indeed, two Jewish scholars would have a very important role in helping Christians as well as Jews understand the Jewish nature of Jesus: Joseph Klausner and Geza Vermes.

Working at the turn of the last century, Joseph Klausner, born in 1874, was a Russian Jewish biblical scholar and historian who wrote the first full-length analysis of Jesus' life in Hebrew. He was among the first to take up a professorship at the fledgling Hebrew University in Jerusalem, in 1918, just after the Balfour Declaration of 1917 had given legal sanction to a Jewish national home under British protection. Klausner's *Jesus of Nazareth* evinced such familiarity with the relevant Jewish texts as well as the texture of life and national aspirations of the Jewish people that for the first time the authentic Jewish milieu in which Jesus lived and in which his ideas were formed seemed to have been palpably entered into and brought to bear on an assessment of his life and death. Klausner's portrait of Jesus was nuanced and sensitive, and placed him squarely within the Jewish messianic hopes that had already rocked the Jewish people two hundred years before Jesus was born, and would do so after him in the final revolt against Rome in AD 132–135 led by another inspirational leader who was believed by many to be the Messiah, Simon bar Kochba. Indeed, in Klausner's own time the Zionist movement had already gathered force, and messianic strivings were finding expression again. It seemed that the ancient context of Jesus' rise was virtually recurring, and Klausner's timely study of Jesus Christ (and his previous study, *The Messianic Idea in Israel*) would be cited and often deferred to by some of the most eminent Jesus scholars writing in the later part of the twentieth century, such as C.H. Dodd, W.D. Davies and E.P. Sanders.

Sixty years after Klausner, another Jewish scholar, with the unusual distinction of having been a member of a Catholic order for about twenty years, from the late 1930s to the 1960s, before he returned to Judaism, would weigh in with a series of studies on the Jewish Messiah named Jesus. It is hard to overestimate the impact of *Jesus the Jew* when it was published in 1973 because its author, Geza Vermes, was much more than a run-of-the-mill New Testament scholar, ploughing the same few texts for heretofore hidden gems of information. He was already world-renowned for being the first and most respected translator and interpreter of the complete Dead Sea Scrolls. This remarkable collection of texts, discovered between 1947 and 1952, not only contained the complete Hebrew Bible with some commentaries, but extra-canonical biblical writings, as well as writings emanating from a Jewish sect, which Vermes identified (with most scholars) as the Essenes, a largely separatist, messianic and apocalyptic group that existed from about 150 years before Christ until the Roman destruction of Jerusalem in AD 70. Until the discovery of the Dead Sea Scrolls no significant Jewish writing from Jesus' time was extant. At ten-year intervals, Vermes wrote four major books on Jesus, and to each of them he brought the full force of his knowledge of the Hebrew Bible, the New Testament, the rabbinic tradition and the Dead Sea Scrolls. In his view Jesus was a first-century 'charismatic healer, exorcist and champion of the Kingdom of God', who could only be clearly understood as a figure emerging within the swirling cultural and political realities that made Roman Palestine a tinderbox, ready to catch fire.

Not without irony did Vermes title his fourth and most recent work *The Changing Faces of Jesus,* an examination of the varying portraits of Jesus found in the Gospels, Acts of the Apostles and the Letters of Paul. The desire to see the metaphorical face of Jesus has been irresistible from ancient times to the present, and it invariably takes on the features of those seeking him. Nowhere is this more evident than in the long tradition of religious art in which the depiction of Jesus is often an exercise in vanity as much as piety. The latest twist in the pursuit of Jesus' face was the front-page article featuring an approximation of his likeness, based on measurements of an ancient skull from the first century discovered in the West Bank. A computer-regenerated face revealed Jesus resembling a Palestinian.

The political has never been far from the imagined Jesus, and thus it has been since the first modern history of his life. When the nineteenth-century French orientalist and philologist Ernest Renan was sent by Napoleon III to Phoenicia and Syria on an archaeological mission, the rugged realities of the ancient Near East blended with his already considerable doubt about the Christian mysteries. He was inspired to write *La Vie de Jésus* [The Life of Jesus], (1863), which imagined the Galilean preacher in highly romantic, genial and entirely non-miraculous terms. It was a runaway best seller, but it lost him his professorship at the Collège de France, and he decided to remain an independent scholar not confined by the theological politics of the university.

The simple truth was that Renan and many of his readers were not in need of a *supernatural* Jesus to believe in as the pinnacle of morality and model to the world: 'In him was condensed all that is good and elevated in our nature ... all the ages will proclaim that among the sons of men there is none born who is greater than Jesus.'[4]

Motivated by similar sentiments but a very different understanding of how Jesus saw himself, the Lutheran pastor and New Testament scholar Albert Schweitzer (1875–1965) interpreted the urgency of Jesus' message as evidence of his apocalyptic belief in the imminent arrival of the Kingdom of Heaven and his own role as God's anointed, his Messiah. But Schweitzer made no bones about the fact that Jesus had committed an error of judgment, and knew it when the Kingdom did not arrive. Jesus then reimagined his role to be a suffering Messiah, who would die so that his people would not have to endure the tribulations preceding the impending End of Days. Not surprisingly, the idea that God knew Jesus was in error but did not tell him was too much for some people to accept. Fortunately for

Schweitzer, less than three years after he published his ground-breaking work in 1906 (which was translated as *The Quest for the Historical Jesus* in 1910), he earned his medical degree and went to work in deepest Africa, far from the fallout of his theological daring. Yet with this book, Schweitzer blazed a trail for an illustrious parade of questers who have attempted to discern the tracks of Jesus' life in the spare clues left in the sources.

The desire to capture the true Jesus has not abated, and in the present day John Dominic Crossan portrays him as a proto-hippy, a Jewish peasant with an egalitarian outlook, who battled for social justice in class-riven imperial Palestine, groaning under oppressive Roman rule. Theologically, this translated into an unmediated relationship to God and a 'brokerless' heaven.

> Miracle and parable, healing and eating were calculated to force individuals into unmediated physical and spiritual contact with God and unmediated physical and spiritual contact with one another. He announced, in other words, the brokerless kingdom of God.[5]

In Crossan's treatment, which incidentally signals the relatively recent involvement of Roman Catholic scholars in the quest for the historical Jesus, the Galilean preacher is not driven by mystical or apocalyptic convictions, but by the teachings of the prophets who hold social and moral righteousness above all commandments, and who believe their fulfilment earns one a place alongside the righteous of the past, who are resurrected in 'the world to come'. Hence, Jesus' own resurrection as a 'righteous one'. Crossan's interpretation, as with all the others, betrays a simple truth: that the redemptive meaning of Jesus' life always takes on the values of those who subject it to critical scrutiny.

This observation could be construed as cynical were it not for the fact that it is entirely consistent with the purpose of Jesus' existence, which, after all, is to inspire faith. Nowhere was this more strikingly evident in the twentieth century than in the biblical scholarship of Rudolf Bultmann (1884–1976). An evangelical Lutheran pastor,

Bultmann's interest was deeply theological, but committed to rescuing the significance of the Christian Messiah from what he presumed was its outmoded supernatural framework and the barely knowable historical details of an ancient Jewish society. Bultmann dispensed with heaven and hell, miracles and resurrection, punishment for sin and vicarious redemption through the death of God's son. All these properly belonged to the world-view of antiquity where mythology rather than scientific knowledge reigned. The modern world was no longer convinced by such beliefs, and Bultmann argued instead for an existentialist understanding of Jesus, in which his love and self-sacrifice would continue to inform human society as if it were an ever-present event, never finished, and in a sense always being fulfilled in the Christian's encounter with God. The crucial person in this inquiry was the Christ of faith — in fact, the crucified and resurrected Christ — not the Jesus of history, whom Bultmann argued was largely unknowable by the standard methods of historical analysis.

It would not be hard to characterise Bultmann as a heretic of sorts, since he appeared to sweep aside the central creedal statements of Christianity as mere mythology. The same could be said about Schweitzer, who implied Jesus had developed his beliefs in response to his own failure. Neither, however, could be said to have led unchristian lives. Bultmann developed a far-reaching and deeply moral Christian theology, while Schweitzer spent more than thirty years living according to the principles of Jesus' life, serving the sick and the poor in equatorial Africa, and urging upon his generation a reverence for life and a rejection of scepticism.[6]

The achievements of these exemplary scholars dispelled some of the fears of apostasy resulting from biblical scholarship. And yet something had certainly changed, which scholars like Robert Funk, the founder of the Jesus Seminar, were well aware of, even if the great mass of ordinary people was slow to react. It was as if the horse had disengaged from the cart and had bolted, but the rider was still sitting in the cab. Bultmann and the legion of scholars and seminarians who were immersed in the critical analysis of biblical texts were nonetheless obliged to carry on with their Christian faith and teaching in divinity schools as if nothing major had happened. In turn, the typical graduate assuming a ministerial post would undergo a strange form of split personality, in which he suspended all that he learned in the classroom in order to keep preaching the creedal truths of Christianity. Something had to give, and according to Funk, it finally has. The gap between the truths uncovered in the academy and those preached in church has now grown too large to bridge by mere mental acrobatics, and the result is fewer graduates heading for the pulpit.

All is not lost, however, and Robert Funk and his fellow travellers at the Westar Institute (the home of the Jesus Seminar) believe they can rescue Jesus from obscurity simply by allowing him to speak in his *own* words. Faith in the man from Galilee is still possible, argues Funk, but it should no longer be reliant on the Gospel and Pauline texts, which he believes, along with most New Testament scholars, were constructed by a first-century community with its own institutional agenda. Like Bultmann before him, Funk's version of Christian faith does not rest on a Christ figure whose saving message is embedded in a belief system and world-view that is, in a word, 'incredible'. The divinity of Jesus, his virgin birth, the blood atonement, the bodily resurrection and the second coming are all, in Funk's view, old dogmas that are neither believable nor interesting to discuss.[7]

Whether the supernatural aspects of Jesus' life are too incredible to be believed is a question that individuals can answer only for themselves, but it is an undeniable fact that interest in the sayings of Jesus, denuded of their supernatural narrative context, continues unabated in the modern world. The importance of Jesus' parables was significantly boosted by the finding at Nag Hammadi in 1945 of a library of documents identified with a Gnostic (and therefore heretical) community in Egypt, including the fourth-century Gospel of Thomas. It is a rather spare document, which contains a list of Jesus' sayings, many of them common to the parables already known in the New Testament. Scholars have long argued that the Gospel parables derived from a single document of Jesus' collected sayings, which may indeed be an early version of the Gospel of Thomas. In any case, to the contemporary reader, such a collection of sayings has the beauty of being available with no strings attached, in the same way that the Book of Proverbs has become one of the most cited texts in English literature. The power of Jesus' sayings is measured in one's own response to them, and it is this wisdom tradition that Funk suggests might form the basis of a 'new' New Testament. The following saying from the Gospel of Thomas, for example, is also found in the Gospels and in Paul's letter to the Thessalonians:

> So I tell you, ask — it will be given to you; seek — you will find; knock — it will be opened for you. Rest assured: everyone who asks receives; everyone who seeks finds; and for the one who knocks it is opened.[8]

Apart from comprising the refrain of one of the most popular gospel hymns, this saying and many others are distinguished by their earthy simplicity, not by their interest in end-of-the-world expectations. According to the Jesus Seminar, none of the authentic sayings of Jesus, like the Proverbs of the Hebrew Bible, show the slightest interest in apocalyptic imaginings.

This would come as a surprise to the many apocalyptic sects that have emerged over the centuries. But for the vast majority of Christians disinclined to hold their lives hostage to a date when the world will end, this is good news. In fact, they did not even need a century and a half of biblical scholarship to arrive at it. Yet no-one could deny the value of that scholarship and the benefits that have accrued to Western civilisation as a direct result of the historical analysis and appreciation of the founding texts of biblical religion. At the very least, it has wrested the authority of interpretation from a coterie of clerics, whose aim was to ensure their continuity as the sole arbiters of truth. Biblical scholarship has handed that authority back to men and women who are free to study and interpret the texts according to all the scholarly principles and tools at their disposal. The benefit of this development to the community of believers, which is thereby liberated from theological ideas that are contradicted by the original Christian sources, cannot be gainsaid. More importantly, it has allowed the real-life situations of ordinary people to speak through their interpretation of the scriptures, and thereby enliven and enrich their meaning. In addition to this essential requirement of a truly living faith, biblical scholarship has opened up the embattled territory between Judaism and Christianity and provided the context where mutual understanding can grow, replacing two millennia of suspicion and ignorance.

As to the singular aim of uncovering the real Jesus, it turns out to be something of an irony. The story of Jesus' life as transmitted in the four canonical Gospels and variously interpreted by hundreds of scholars may turn out to have less appeal to the contemporary generation of new believers than the simple timeless sayings that capture truths about how to be in the world with faith, hope, love and charity. There is an open-ended quality to the sayings that invites response, whereas the 'life of Jesus' presupposes completeness, and requires unqualified acceptance of a divine plan and its attendant miraculous unfolding. Perhaps this quality of universality is why the most popular feature of America's leading website, Beliefnet, is a daily Jesus' saying to subscribers. This is by no means to say that the story of Jesus' life, death and resurrection — that is, the passion narrative — does not have the power to transform lives, only that for the many people who are unwilling to suspend their disbelief, it is too confining and ultimately exclusive. His sayings, on the other hand, are liberating, and they can speak to the present as easily as they can take their place alongside the larger wisdom tradition of the Greeks and the Hebrew Bible (such as Proverbs, Job and the non-canonical Wisdom of Ben Sira), where it is no accident that wisdom is a woman. But before launching into that discussion, there is one more element to the story of the battle for Jesus without which this chapter would not be complete: the Spong phenomenon.

Episcopal Bishop of Newark, New Jersey, John Shelby Spong is the self-appointed spokesman for people who do not go to church, yet in some way still regard themselves as Christian. They are a vast and varied group of people whom Spong calls the 'church alumni', and although it would be impossible to identify a uniform set of shared characteristics, they clamour to hear Spong disseminate his dream of a future Christianity, stripped of its miraculous saviour God and denuded of its exclusivity. In many ways, he is the theologian his friend Robert Funk and others are waiting for. Spong offers a way to believe in Jesus but saves one the trouble of suspending disbelief in miracles. Spong's Jesus is not God, nor did he die a death that vicariously washed humanity of original sin. He was not the son of a virgin and when he died he did not bodily resurrect leaving behind an empty tomb. Jesus was a man whose exemplary life is a doorway to God, in the same way, Spong maintains, that the lives of other great men and women are also doorways to God.

Who is this God then, if the Buddha, Muhammad, Krishna and Moses (not to mention Florence Nightingale, Hildegard of Bingen and Rosa Parks) are all on par with Jesus? The question is wrong it seems. We should ask not 'who' but 'what' is this God. For Spong, God is not the all-knowing personality of the Bible who creates Adam and miraculously begets Jesus. God is the foundation of all existence, what the great American Lutheran theologian Paul Tillich called 'the Ground of Being'. Like Bultmann, Tillich was an existentialist who influenced generations of seminary students from the 1950s onwards. Tillich's most memorable expression for the object of faith was 'ultimate concern', a term that already signalled a move away from theism. Spong, however, rejects the biblical notion of a personal God altogether.[9]

Before a public audience at the Graduate Theological Union, Berkeley, California in 2001, Spong declared an anti-creed, in which he rejected as naïve and objectionable the central dogmatic beliefs of Christianity.[10] It was far and away more radical than anything Tillich or Bultmann would have done, but Bishop Spong is neither a mere churchman nor an academic. He is a popular writer and thinker, more at home in public halls on the international lecture circuit than in university classes or the church pulpit — that is, when he can find a friendly one to preach in! With a long list of challenging publications, like *Why Christianity Must Change or Die* and *Rescuing the Bible from Fundamentalism*, Spong is hoping to provoke nothing less than a full-scale reformation, which he predicts will make Luther's effort look like a 'tea party'.[11]

Whether this reformation will take place in the way that Spong hopes is an open question, but it seems unlikely, if only because the massive dissemination of his ideas through his own publications and like-minded thinkers, such as Robert Funk and to some extent Don Cupitt (who is discussed in Chapter 8), has probably rendered it unnecessary. There is already a considerable accumulation of non-believers in traditional Christianity, indeed with the barest knowledge of its principal texts, who are most available to the message that a lot of the Bible is not true anyway. And when it comes to traditional believers, Spong makes abundantly clear that the Evangelical Christians and other traditional types who fill the pews are not interested in his message any more than he is interested in entering into a shouting match with them. They are bound to go their separate ways, which for Spong is akin to the process of evolution, where some species adapt to new environments and thrive, and others do not and die out. At least that is what he is hoping.

There is a fair amount of assumption and conjecture in Spong's argument for a 'new Christianity', not least the notion that what adapts necessarily survives, while that which remains the same dies out. It begs the question, what is it that survives, if by this new version of Christianity he means a set of ideas that bear little relation to the beliefs propounded by the New Testament? It could be said that what is actually happening in this selective adaptation process is the reverse: Christianity dies out, and what replaces it is something entirely different, like Spongism.

The bishop from New Jersey may be right, that this is just what will eventually win the day with a large body of people, who sees no contradiction in going through the door marked Jesus, while also occasionally going through several other doors marked the Buddha, the Bal Shem Tov, Swami Yogananda, Bahá'u'lláh and so on. It is not that these are all the same, else why would they exist in the first place, but where they lead; that is, the God Presence, as Spong calls it, is not bound or limited by human creeds. 'No fence can be placed around the Being of God,' says Spong,[12] and therefore the doors that lead to this boundless mystery should not be denigrated. Spong anticipates a future of religious co-operation that will be 'breathtaking'.[13]

Breathtaking is certainly the word, but not for the reasons he imagines. If one accepts Spong's formulation as a matter of faith, that individual creeds do not exhaust God, it does not necessarily follow that they will live peaceably alongside one another in a spirit of co-operation and dialogue. Nor does it mean that the creeds themselves (like paths up a mountain) are particularly desirable, pleasant or safe. It is difficult to see the advantage of this view for anyone other than those who are open to the diverse religious creeds because they are the new believers in the non-exclusive form of Christianity, a bit like the Theosophists and Freethinkers were before them. After all, Spong's call to reformation is directed only to the Church, not to the world's religious traditions. So if a great new ecumenical project ensues, as Spong hopes, it may well be irrelevant to the religious communities of the world, which will keep on pursuing their own singular traditions. Even the Baha'i Faith, which emerged in the nineteenth century, purporting to contain all the world's faiths within it, offers its own founder, Bahá'u'lláh, as the Last and Greatest Prophet, necessarily rendering all who came before him — like Abraham, Moses, Jesus, the Buddha, Muhammad, the Bal Shem Tov — and all those who came after him, as his spiritual inferiors. That ranking will not alter with the appearance of this new Christianity.

The hope for religious co-operation, however, is not the central message of Spong's new dispensation. It is a newly devised faith in the very person of Jesus and a revamping of the nature of God. Questions still need to be asked, such as what really is the 'God presence' and how do we know that all creeds lead to it? Furthermore, if Jesus is not God but just a man how does his life become a doorway to the ultimate religious experience?

The God beyond theism is, for Spong, the Life Source, the Mystery, the Holy; that is, a limitless power which is the very essence of life. Given that the man Jesus is the doorway to the God presence, then it is the human qualities which this first-century Galilean demonstrated that are indistinguishable from God. These qualities all come down to one, according to Spong. Jesus is the ultimate embodiment of love for which he freely gave his life. (Spong avoids the word 'sacrifice' because it implies a 'blood-seeking deity'.[14]) For Spong, it is Jesus' 'threatening power of love' that is the revolutionary teaching bequeathed by the Christian tradition to its followers.[15] Everything else virtually melts away, and it is clear that Spong sees himself as living up to this call in the open and warm acceptance he extends to homosexuals in the Church.

So far, the meaning of Jesus' life as a radical call to love is not very different from mainstream Christian thinking, although it is usually assumed that other biblical prescriptions and prohibitions also would apply. But Spong is not so sure. Jesus' own actions occasionally challenged the norms of tradition and gave the impression that the love ethic surpassed all, and that is where the bishop for a new Christianity takes his cue.

Nevertheless, the problem of evil rears its head, even though Spong rejects the notion of original sin. He finds the concept repugnant when applied to a newborn baby, whose sweet innocence would cause even the most conservative Christian to blush with embarrassment. On the other hand, the notion of sinfulness or evil as an essential human trait is not consigned to the dustbin. In a curious reworking of this biblical notion, Spong adopts Carl Jung's formulation of evil as the 'shadow,' perennially cast over the human soul. Spong echoes the Swiss psychologist who counselled that human beings must face their shadow, and embrace and transform it as part of the process toward individual wholeness. But this does not seem very different from the Jewish and Christian traditions, which urge their adherents to face their intrinsic sinfulness, confess their evil ways and recognise that the road to holiness cannot proceed without the full acknowledgment of their own basic and abiding temptation to do evil. Otherwise the holy path would not be necessary at all.

Be that as it may, psychology's language of self-responsibility and personal transformation is important to Spong, as it is for a fairly large swathe of New Age thinkers. It lends the credibility of the clinician to his belief that humanity is on a spiritual evolutionary path, away from a sense of powerlessness and belief in 'a God out there', toward the next stage of development, which Spong believes is marked by personal wholeness and self-giving love. Of course Jesus knew nothing of Jungian psychology, nor could his life, as recounted in the Gospels, be construed as a quest for 'personal wholeness'. He did nevertheless demonstrate self-giving love. Could it be that it was precisely the brokenness of Jesus which was the wellspring of his self-giving love, something that made it all the more precious? One shudders to think — that is too much like traditional theology, which reeks of sacrifice and suffering, incompleteness and hope. Spong prefers a more upbeat approach to conveying the message of love, and puts his faith in psychology's elusive promise to deliver wholeness, which will also automatically turn into goodness.[16] It is a therapeutic model that will be explored further in Chapter 7, but if Spong's formula holds true, any more than the belief he has rejected, it is yet to be proved, and for now must remain a matter of faith.

3. RETURNING TO THE MOTHER
God was a Woman

Women who have been ordained to the priesthood often complain that their role in the Church is usually pastoral, emphasising their skills as counsellors, social workers and teachers, while positions of real power are still largely left to the men. Whether this spells a failure or a fulfilment of women's divinely ordained role is the abiding question that haunts the feminist movement. Are women the same as men or different?

One way to answer that question is to look back in time, when women appeared to have a more important and respected role in religious life. Or did they? To be sure, in the annals of feminism nothing was as uplifting as discovering that the age-old and revered gift of wisdom was to a woman, whose name was Sophia. She had been suppressed, of course, sublimated and hidden in the biblical tradition that once included her proudly as the emanation of God's glory. In the Septuagint, the Greek version of the Hebrew Bible, *Sophia* appears frequently as the Greek word substituted for *Hokhmah*, the Hebrew term for wisdom. So both the Hebrew and the Greek sources personify wisdom as a woman. In one of the books included in the Septuagint, the Wisdom of Solomon, an apocryphal work written in the first century, Sophia appears, among other things, as God's spouse.[1] In another apocryphal work, Jesus Ben Sira, Sophia is depicted as the author's mother and also as his mistress.[2] In the biblical book of Proverbs, Sophia is a bold figure, proclaiming her wisdom in high places and amusing the mighty Creator as his 'daily delight'.[3]

No-one would deny the great value attached to wisdom, but the role of Sophia in these references is ambiguous to say the least. She may be the one who prepares the banquet and calls forth ignorant men to partake of it and walk away in the path of understanding,[4] but she is still dispensing these canapés of wisdom in the traditional female role of mother, wife or mistress. Even if it is found that Sophia as a goddess reflects a Hellenised–Egyptian cultural influence during the period when biblical wisdom literature was being produced in Alexandria around the turn of the first century, there are other sources that point to her presumed synergy with the male of the species. The idea of God having a spouse received support in recent archaeological discoveries in the Negev desert region of Israel, dating to the eighth century. Inscriptions have been unearthed which refer to 'the Lord and his Asherah', the latter being a Canaanite fertility goddess. She in turn may be the offspring of an earlier tradition, the Sumerian goddess of Anat or Astarte, who was venerated as both a goddess and a whore, a sacred prostitute.

Ancient history is a double-edged sword. It is helpful in establishing the importance of women as respected dispensers of wisdom, but it is also cold comfort to the contemporary woman who does not wish to see herself as a fertility goddess, a sacred prostitute or the Lord's plaything. The truth is that in the extremely diverse world of metaphysical ideas swirling around the Middle East of late antiquity, a large degree of selective reading is necessary if the feminist woman wishes to come out as a person respected for her intellect alone.[5] Not even in Gnostic writings, a real favourite with feminist theologians, does Sophia escape her sexual wantonness. Although the Gnostics were a heterodox Christian community that accorded Mary more respect than did the Church, Sophia is an ultimately pitiful creature, who valiantly struggles with the Demiurge in order to bring spiritual awareness to men, but is cast down by her own hubris, and finally saved by Christ. 'Wisdom thou name art woman' was a bit of a failure on her own.

Leaving aside the archaeological tools for the moment, other means of opening up the ancient inheritance of the Bible would yield more promising results for women in the Church. In the late 1800s, in a way that prefigures by almost a century the Jesus Seminar's committee of scholars working on the Gospels, Elizabeth Cady Stanton enlisted the assistance of twenty-three educated women, some of them ministers, to produce commentaries on the Old and New Testaments of the Christian Bible. (One of the contributors was Matilda Joslyn Gage, feminist and the mother-in-law of Frank Baum, the author of *The Wonderful Wizard of Oz*.) In 1895 *The Woman's Bible* was published, with an introduction by Stanton, which left no doubt as to the revolutionary aim of the work and the urgency of its task. It was an era that had already seen successful lobbying for legislative change on behalf of women and children, so why not compel the bishops to modify their creeds? Stanton exhorted her more timid women associates, who were fearful of the public opprobrium they would suffer were they to put their much needed classical scholarship in service of *The Woman's Bible*:

> Come, come, my conservative friend, wipe the dew off your spectacles and see that the world is moving. Whatever your views may be as to the importance of the proposed work, your political and social degradation are but an outgrowth of your status in the Bible.[6]

While the women on Stanton's editorial committee were not all in the strict sense scholars, their straightforward reading of the biblical texts produced some unassailable observations. For example, Stanton's own consideration of the text of Genesis could find no redeeming moral qualities in Isaac's wife, Rebecca, who aided Jacob in defrauding his father and robbing Esau of his birthright and blessing. Stanton concluded her commentary on this passage with a rebuff to the men who both stood in the way of women's emancipation and yet urged them to be more like the women in the Bible. Failing to find any merit among the matriarchs, Stanton declared the proposition absurd: 'The only significance of dwelling on these women and this period of woman's history is to show the absurdity of pointing the women of the nineteenth century to these, as examples of virtue.'[7]

Stanton was inclined to be extreme and at times contradicted what her female colleagues wrote about the matriarchs. In contrast to Stanton, Clara Bewick Colby, for example, found the dignified position of Sarah and Rebekah (Rebecca) a consolation for the captive and menial status of women of her day. Stanton's strident tone was driven by the belief that only revolutionaries, like the political philosopher John Stuart Mill, whom she admired, achieved real change, because they enunciated truths that reason unsheathed. Stanton believed that these truths, once revealed, were self-evident to intelligent women, who were fully capable of revising the theological views that men had devised in service to their own interests. Indeed, women were fully equal to the task of writing commentaries on the Bible that favoured their own interests, of which the opening argument of *The Woman's Bible* is an unabashed example. The sturdiest plank of their platform was taken from the first chapter in Genesis which states that God said, 'Let us make man in our own image, after our likeness', and that 'God made man in his own image, male and female he created them'.[8] With this opening passage, Stanton and her women had the only justification they needed to claim that God was not singular but plural, and in fact was both male and female.

> If language has any meaning, we have here in these texts a plain declaration of the existence of the feminine element in the Godhead, equal in power and glory with the masculine. The Heavenly Mother and Father![9]

Not content to leave it there, Stanton, whose only interest in the Bible was to exploit its hidden potential to elevate the status of women, was quick to point out the implications.

As to woman's subjection, on which both the canon and the civil law delight to dwell, it is important to note that equal dominion is given to women over every living thing, but not one word is said giving man dominion over woman.[10]

The Woman's Bible is a curious and compelling document, but it is also somewhat confusing, due partly to its piecemeal approach to the conflicting messages in the Bible (in which it is abundantly clear that men behaved as if they had legal if not divine sanction to exercise authority over women), and partly to the differences among the women commentators. While Stanton was inclined to stress equality between the sexes, Lillie Devereux Blake was unequivocal about women's superiority, referring to Eve as '... the eternal mother, the first representative of the more valuable and important half of the human race'.[11] The Reverend Phebe Hanaford wrote with reverence and affection for the Old as well as the New Testament, reminding the reader of the truths of its prophetic claims and most especially the centrality of its moral teaching, which continued in the New Testament.[12] Ursula N. Gestefeld, on the other hand, interpreted the first five books of the Bible, the Pentateuch, as an allegory, a narrative that possessed an inner meaning which was mystical and esoteric. Her reading of Genesis, for example, claimed that it symbolised the evolution of the soul through seven stages represented by Adam, Enos, Noah, Abraham, Isaac, Jacob and Joseph.[13] With these and many more perspectives assembled together, *The Woman's Bible* could not convey a consistent message about the value of the sacred texts. Nor could it act as a substitute for the Bible. It became instead a sourcebook of ideas sympathetic to feminism and popular among the new believers of the day, many of whom were deeply influenced by Theosophy and its fellow travellers.

Theosophy, which was popular among the freethinking clubs that flourished at the end of the nineteenth century, was, one might say, on the ground floor of the comparative religion movement.[14] Travel to the colonial nations in the Far East, India, the Pacific and the Levant afforded encounters with a variety of religious traditions and customs, which challenged the presumed hegemony of the Christian Church, and offered untold adventures to the European woman of means.

Possibly the most amazing woman of this type was French-born Alexandra David-Neel (1868–1969). As a young woman in Paris, David-Neel had been an early dabbler in Theosophy; in London she joined the Society for the Supreme Gnosis and moved in occult circles. In Paris, the Musée Guimet, with its impressive collection of Eastern art, was the charged setting in which she read books on the Orient and Buddhism, and cultivated a desire to travel to Asia and learn Sanskrit. She may well have shown signs of her forceful personality as a student, although her claim that she was the first woman to study at the Sorbonne, and had to leave due to the hostility that she encountered there, is hard to verify. She married a French engineer stationed in Tunisia, but spent a very large part of her life travelling, often alone, to remote and exotic destinations such as China, Bhutan, Sikkim, Nepal, Japan, Korea and Tibet (where she had to disguise herself as a man). With a passion for Buddhism, she became an initiate of its Tantric practices, about which she wrote several books.

David-Neel was clearly a woman 'before her time' in more senses than one. Her twenty-eight books and many more articles based on her travels would become very popular many decades on, with hippies in search of Eastern wisdom making the pilgrimage to her home in the south of France when she was almost one hundred. For women yearning to break out of domestic and economic dependency, on the other hand, David-Neel's accounts of her solitary travels and her adventures as a shaman and lama (a reincarnated teacher in Tibetan Buddhism) would form part of a growing fascination with exotic traditions that contained goddesses, female priests and divine queens.

Similar inspiration would be drawn from archaeological discoveries in Egypt, prompting women to claim a glorious and powerful past before the 'dreaded patriarchy' descended upon the female of the species. Helena Blavatsky, the founder of Theosophy, and another adventurer to the East, named her first major work *Isis Unveiled* after the Egyptian goddess, who apparently provided classical antiquity with its most complete female deity — identified with time, beauty, motherhood, sex and nature — and whom Blavatsky hoped could do the same for women of her own time. The trouble with much of this literature, including that written by scholars trained in the languages of the East, was that it romanticised its subject, removing all its unsavoury characteristics and complex history. It also betrayed resentment toward Judaism and Christianity, which was palpable and matched only by its demonstrated ignorance, particularly of Judaism, upon which most of the blame for the Judaeo–Christian tradition was laid. At every turn, the various contributors to *The Woman's Bible*, for example, read the ancient texts with reference to their own circumstances, not to those of antiquity, and found fault with 'the Jews' for every possible permutation of the present predicament of women. Using this ploy they were no better than their own preachers whom they castigated for citing chapter and verse of the Bible as if it were an arsenal of weapons with which to subordinate women.

The fundamental flaw in this approach was simply that it reflected a Christian reading of the Bible, not a Jewish one, the latter by no means being literal but consisting of a vast tradition of rabbinic commentaries from post-biblical times to the present. Indeed, at the time that Elizabeth Cady Stanton was pouring scorn upon the Jews for their barbaric attitudes to women, some forty years had already passed since Judaism's Reform movement had commenced in Germany (which would see the first woman rabbi in 1934) and ten years since its establishment in America on a platform of scientific rationalism and ethics. However, Judaism's reforms meant little or nothing to Stanton, who evidently was aware of the persecution of Jews in the nineteenth century and offered this advice: 'If the Jews of our day had followed … their ancestors and intermarried with other nations there would have been by this time no peculiar people to persecute.'[15]

If only the Jews had disappeared! For someone who was both active against slavery and keen to argue for the equal rights of women, Stanton was not inclined to extend the same consideration to the Jews, whose largest mistake was that they existed at all. Subjecting

Jews and Judaism to ridicule was not, however, the purpose of the editors of *The Woman's Bible*, even if that is one of its consequences. Its real target was the Church.

> If the Bible teaches the equality of Woman, why does the church refuse to ordain women to preach the gospel, to fill the offices of deacons and elders, and to administer the Sacraments, or to admit them as delegates to the Synods, General Assemblies and Conferences of the different denominations?[16]

More than a century later that victory has been won in the Uniting Church of Australia and the United Church of Canada, but only partially won in the Anglican Communion and not at all in the Roman Catholic Church. As for Judaism, its Reform, Liberal and Reconstructionist schools have ordained women since the 1970s, and although Conservative Judaism stopped ordaining women in 1979, in 2001 it elected a woman to the presidency of its roof body, the United Conservative Synagogues in America. Orthodox Judaism, like the Roman Catholic Church and evangelical Anglicanism, does not ordain women; all three communities preserving their traditions against radical gender equality.

Without going into the manifold reasons for the refusal to ordain women, history is witness to the fact that tradition is not as susceptible to 'common sense reason', regardless of how obvious its merits, as Stanton had hoped. Tradition is not only kept in place by powerful men who guard its statutes, but also by women who preserve its customs and who identify themselves and their forebears with its moral, liturgical and communal expressions. This suggests that there is much more at stake than power alone. Stanton knew that her most significant opponents were women, who were not about to relinquish the very fabric of their lives because other women did not appreciate its value, and indeed were openly ridiculing its conventions. The legal side of religious traditions, such as canon law, always has been subject to deliberate revision, whereas when central beliefs are overturned vehement passions are predictably aroused. Imagine the furore caused by Elizabeth Cady Stanton's friend, the feminist Matilda Joslyn Gage, more than a century ago, when she opened a conference on women's rights with a prayer to God, our Mother!

A radical gesture perhaps, but it is one that has some foundation in the biblical tradition and reappears in Catholicism, both ancient and modern. In a touching account of the birth of her three children, Margaret Hebblethwaite, the Catholic writer and former editor of the British Catholic weekly, *The Tablet*, explores the profound nexus between the self-giving love of motherhood and the grace of God.[17] Only at the end of her book does she reveal the theological supports for such an audacious comparison. The biblical prophet Isaiah likens God to a suckling mother who would not forget her child;[18] the Psalmist compares the peace and calm of the soul in God's embrace to the quiet and security of a child at his mother's breast.[19] The New Testament suggests that new Christians are like babies, feeding on the pure spiritual milk of the Lord.[20] In his Confessions, St Augustine cries out to God, '... what am I but a creature suckled on your milk and feeding on yourself, the food that never perishes?'.[21] In the fourteenth century St Julian of Norwich did more than compare Jesus to a mother, she addressed him as such: 'But our true Mother Jesus, he alone bears us for joy and for endless life, blessed may he be ... The mother can give her child to suck of her milk, but our precious Mother Jesus can feed us with himself.'[22]

The nursing mother is a beloved image that has been immortalised by Christian painters throughout the centuries, casting Mary, the mother of Jesus, in a theologically ambiguous role. The Roman Catholic cult of Mary would certainly project her into a divine realm that in practice comes close to deifying her. She is, after all, the mother of God, or as the Greek Orthodox Church recognises her liturgically, the *Theotokos*, the God-bearer. Despite the concerted efforts by some feminist theologians to refashion the doctrine of the Divine Trinity as Mother, Father and Son, and the vain hope that in 1963 the Second Vatican Council of the Catholic Church would declare Mary 'Co-redemptrix' with Christ, there seems little chance that this radical notion will take hold in mainstream Christianity. And it is not only the conservatives who would find it unpalatable. Among some of those who are pushing for reform, the value of the traditional family structure of mother, father and child is not as important as it once was. Apart from the fact that the Catholic nuns and sisters who are chafing for change are far more influenced by the woman-centred culture of their communities than the conventional nuclear family, in society at large the diverse sexual agendas that have developed since the 1960s have significantly changed the way people idealise their relationships. Even the once radical redefinition of the Trinity as Mother, Father, Son has been surpassed.

Fay Weldon, the sardonic social critic of feminism, is convinced that women have pushed so hard against the conventional family arrangements that they finally have what they always wanted — to be alone![23] Having broken out of hearth and home they are now at the office for twelve hours at a stretch, only to bring home a briefcase of paperwork so they can exhibit their legendary perfectionism when they return to work in the morning. She may be right, but one has to wonder how they do it. Traditional religions, let alone marriages, do not encourage raw individualism for a woman, nor do they make allowances for the busy life of a woman as corporate manager. Women in the professional and corporate world are on their own, they are in fear of failing, and they are hungry for encouragement and support. Some women, like the former singer with the Australian band Def FX and now popular witch residing in Los Angeles, Fiona Horne, are finding new strength and conviction in the alternative woman-centred spiritual tradition that has given them not only the all-powerful Great Goddess, but also a raft of recipes for spells promising everything from the right lover to increased financial wealth.[24] For these women it is not sufficient to cite the occasional passage in the Bible where God is imagined with female characteristics, even if they are ferocious ones, as in Hosea where God's anger takes female form: 'I will fall on them, like a bear robbed of her cubs and will tear the flesh around their heart.'[25]

Owing to the 'alternative' image of witchcraft it is often difficult to associate it with people who occupy mainstream professions and sit on corporate boards, which is why the example of Phyllis Curott is so compelling. Curott is a New York City lawyer and a witch, but her climb up the corporate ladder did not come by casting spells on others, although it seems a talisman helped to secure a coveted job! The past president of the oldest and largest international religious organisation in the Wiccan tradition, Covenant of the Goddess, as well as a practising attorney fighting for Wiccan civil liberties, Curott believes she owes her success and her peace of mind to being a witch. She came to the Craft, as the witch's practice is known, after reading books from her father's library on ancient fertility religions, and a chance meeting with a 'white witch' who introduced her to a 'circle'. Trained as a lawyer with a social conscience, Curott was searching for something more in her life than the humanism that her parents passed on to her. She was looking for a sense of enchantment, a silver lining that was not discernible in her legal work for unions or in the edgy backstage scene of the rock bands she was managing. She found it in her dreams and in the moonlight, the spells, the talismans and the cleansing rituals that are part of the witch's Craft.

She would soon discover that she shared many of the popular misconceptions about witchcraft, believing, for example, that it is practised to gain power over others. Although this is part of it, she claims witchcraft is really about accomplishing self-mastery. Not even this is particularly supernatural; there is no emphasis on tricks like materialising in another form and in another place. As it turns out, self-mastery entails possessing qualities that resemble those taught by Buddhism and humanistic psychology, such as healing, wisdom, compassion, freedom and liberation from the outward constraints imposed by society and culture. Magic (sometimes spelled Magick to distinguish it from stage magic), like the begging bowl of Buddhism or the talking cure of psychology, is the means and the method of achieving this personal prowess, and although wands, crystal balls, herbal infusions and specially made costumes worn for nocturnal rites might seem like so many leftover props from a bad horror movie, they are the tool-kit for enacting rituals that women like Phyllis Curott and Fiona Horne believe lead to self-awareness, liberation and empowerment.[26]

Ever since women flooded into universities in the late 1960s, they have expected that education and professional employment would deliver all these personal outcomes. One of a vast number of women who were bright, ambitious and beautiful, Curott soon discovered that she was nonetheless at a disadvantage in the workforce precisely because her attributes elicited a nervous response from men, who understandably felt threatened by the new competition. Men have historically sought to make women feel inferior and incompetent in situations where they believe they have a lot to lose. We have already seen that in the early stages of the feminist movement at the end of the nineteenth century, women activists blamed their narrowly defined social role on the Bible and early Church writings, which not only placed them in an inferior status to men, but also continued to inform the preachers and the common law of their day on women's issues. Yet unlike the writers of *The Woman's Bible*, who reinterpreted texts in the Old and New Testaments to support women's equal status, the modern Wiccan movement in late 1960s California, spearheaded by personalities like Z. Budapest and Starhawk (Miriam Simos), simply threw the Bible overboard, and reconjured the Old Religion in which the Goddess rules and her helpers on earth are high priestesses.

A high priestess herself, Curott says that the discovery of the Goddess was empowering for her and other women in a way that was entirely woman-centred. She also had the benefit of inheriting a well-rehearsed anti-patriarchy critique, which is fundamental to the gospel according to Wicca:

> The roots of women's inequality and the destruction of the earth are to be found in this early religious shift away from the mother Goddess, who was immanent and present in the world, to the father God, who was transcendent and removed.[27]

The violent destruction of the planet and the subordination of women that apparently resulted from replacing the earth Goddess with the heavenly God are central tenets of Wiccan earth-based spirituality. It goes without saying that the Wiccan promise of redemption is to cultivate an earthly as opposed to a heavenly paradise, an idea that we will revisit in the next chapter. Before the restoration of this Eden, however, the power of another idea will have to hold sway in the world, and that is the return of the matriarchal Trinity, which will replace the patriarchal one. The Father, the Son and the Holy Spirit will need to give way to the Mother, the Maiden and the Crone. All the negative aspects of religion also will be washed away by the ascendance of the Goddess, who will destroy the notion of hierarchy, sexual suppression and overbearing notions of righteousness and war. (Forgotten, it seems, is Athena, the Goddess of War.) Authority itself is relegated to the dustbin of male power, which imposed religious edicts, expected obedience and resulted in the domination of everything and everyone. Somehow, the Old (Goddess) Religion escaped all such expressions of power and was entirely without coercion or will. It just existed as a manifestation of nature itself: 'But in the Old Religion, everything in nature and in the desire of humanity emanated from and was a part of the Goddess.'[28]

Apart from declaring that the Goddess of Wicca is the origin of all life on earth, Curott has taken this divine imperative as permission to reclaim her femininity, and so to bring feminist spirituality to new womanly heights: 'A conception of spirituality was taking shape in my consciousness and it had the sensate curves of something feminine, for I had eaten from the Tree of Knowledge and begun to dream of Paradise.'[29]

There are two witches in Frank Baum's story, *The Wonderful Wizard of Oz*. The Wicked Witch of the West looks like a stick figure in black. She is evil and ugly, with a voice like a crow's. She rides a broomstick and does everything to hinder Dorothy's progress. She is the negative portrayal of the witch as imagined by the Christian Church, which persecuted witches and burned them at the stake. In the film version, *The Wizard of Oz*, the wicked witch expires in a pool of smoking liquid. Glinda, the Good Witch of the North, is the embodiment of feminine beauty: her hair is golden, her dress is white and bows out from her small waist, she carries a sparkling wand, and her voice is sing-song like a nightingale's. She possesses the care of the mother, the beauty of the maiden and the wisdom of the crone, and she opens the portal in Dorothy's heart that makes her realise she has had the power all along to set her mind at rest and find her way home. (Perhaps this new-found awareness is signified by the bright red shoes that Glinda gives to Dorothy, in place of the apple of the tree of knowledge.) In the story, Glinda appears after the old man wizard is found to be a useless fake, who can no more save Dorothy than can a sideshow magician turn water into wine. Dorothy is furious when she discovers this, and rails against the old man, indignant that he has fooled her, and hurt that she believed in him. Like the commentators of *The Woman's Bible*, she does not take the deception lying down.

While the doll-like sweetness of Glinda the Good Witch of the North is far from the earth mother persona that evolved during Wiccan's rise in the 1970s, they both idealise the intrinsic qualities of women. For educated professional women, however, either of these expressions of 'woman' is usually considered out of place on the job, where dark suits with square shoulders and knee-length skirts are meant to hide sexual differences, and play down womanly attributes. In defiance of the notion that it's a man's world, women like Phyllis Curott draw near to the Goddess who gives them permission to reassert their uniquely feminine qualities:

> I was also beginning to see that without the Goddess, without an appreciation for those aspects of being which we think of as feminine, without nurturance, compassion, intuition, connectedness, beauty, and the uniquely feminine creative, generative, and destructive powers, it is impossible even to begin to fathom the fullness of sacred meaning.[30]

Newly ordained Anglican women are obliged to hide their difference under cassocks and often choose to wear their hair shorn, allowing little of their sex to disturb the male role they have come to occupy. Yet their femaleness is inescapable, as the tasks they are assigned and the way they undertake them continue to highlight their compassionate and nurturing nature. This is also evident in the way they have rewritten liturgies, to focus on imagery drawn from nature and the journey of life from birth to death. It is likely that the female Anglican priest will eventually reshape her clerical role to reflect the unique characteristics that she brings to it. Indeed, feminist theology finds justification for this by arguing that Jesus' compassion and propensity to forgiveness were actually demonstrated feminine qualities.[31] The Wiccan priestess, on the other hand, needs no feminised reading of Jesus Christ, nor does she have to subsume her womanliness in an entrenched male tradition, but proudly accentuates the qualities that announce her sexual difference from men. The high priestess even takes advantage of women's customary expertise in the kitchen, as she is relied upon for recipes and concoctions of herbs that are used with spells.

In the end, Goddess religion is a reflection of the way women define their gender. Lesbian Wicca groups abound, as do heterosexual ones, and members of one would not easily cross over into another. The sexual politics of society at large are by no means solved by the return to the Goddess; instead they are merely reflected in the religious cultures they evolve. And there is a mirroring in Wicca that is even more pervasive. Phyllis Curott says that drawing near to the Goddess she would find 'the ultimate magic mirror, the revealer of truth and the truth itself'.[32] But when one looks into the mirror what does it reveal, but oneself? This is what the Wiccan tradition has done for women, it has put them back into the picture. It is a mirror, however, that only they are looking into, so the question must be asked whether the metaphor is anything more than a case of runaway vanity, inverting the moral of Narcissus and holding it up as a model for women. Hubris is its own worst punishment. If the Goddess in the mirror is an endless well of power to women, and exists by virtue of her unquestioned identity with nature itself, then what or whom can limit her scope or censure her excesses? After all, there is no arguing with nature, it simply is!

This is convenient, because women in the Wiccan movement spend little time worrying about philosophical argument or systematic theology. They are more concerned with experiencing the divine reality and embroidering concepts from a very broad range of traditional religions onto the fabric of this recently-invented and eclectic spirituality. Patriarchal religion, it seems, is too much head and not enough body, a religion of too many words, that ends up repressing the sexual dimension of men and demonising women. As for excess, that too is not likely to be considered a problem, since women in Wicca (and feminist paganism in general) are on a campaign to redress the imbalance that it would take two thousand years to put right. Recitation of the violent deeds done to women and to witches over the centuries ensures that a certain moral imperative gives women confidence to practise the magic that can seem an audacious use of power, such as the binding ritual that is meant to psychologically or otherwise restrain someone who intends to do one harm. For all the focus on the Wiccan road to self-mastery, there are rituals one learns along the way that are intended to exert control over other people.

In one of the best known childhood refrains, the wicked queen in the fairytale *Snow White* looks into her enchanted mirror and asks, 'Mirror, mirror on the wall, who is the fairest of them all?' She beams with delight as the mirror answers that she is the fairest of them all. But as the queen's nemesis, Snow White, gains ascendency and the young girl's goodness becomes legendary, the mirror answers the queen's entreaty by cracking violently. Her spirit had become ugly enough to crack the proverbial mirror. In fairytales where mirrors speak and a young girl sleeps with dwarfs there is an equally unlikely moral economy that swiftly delivers punishment when human avarice and pride get out of hand. The question is whether the Goddess in the mirror of the Wiccan movement has the power to answer back to women who overstep their claim to superiority. If the Goddess in the mirror is merely reflecting women's vanity back to themselves, don't count on it.

Although one cannot speak categorically about the Wiccan movement because of the great variety one finds within its non-centralised structure, there is an uncomfortable similarity between the male-centred misogynous theology that developed in the Church and the female-centred spirituality of the Wiccan movement. When men were so convinced of their superiority to women that they claimed

Christ's attributes for themselves exclusively, they were not only socially irresponsible, but they were wrong about the human qualities that men and women share alike. The Wiccan movement has learned from the Church's mistakes and has repeated them exactly, as the saying goes. It triumphantly assumes that all the loving and compassionate qualities idealised in the Goddess are naturally found in women, and not in men, except for Jesus, who Wiccans claim was not an ordinary man by virtue of the fact that he was more like a woman. Women are morally superior to men, a situation which, in the Wiccan view of history, is buttressed by the priority of the Old Religion to the patriarchal religion of the Bible. All that has changed, it seems, is that one set of unlikely claims about men has been replaced by another set of unlikely claims about women. It is a view, incidentally, that owes much to the romanticising of Goddess religion by Joseph Campbell. Comparing it to the story of creation in Genesis and 'the manipulated systems of the West,' Campbell rhapsodises that Goddess religion was 'that primordial attempt on humanity's part to understand and live in harmony with the beauty and wonder of Creation.' Today such unabashed claims are being reassessed by scholars of antiquity and found to be convenient inventions unsupported by the archaeological and historical record, even if they did address the need, as Campbell put it, 'for a general transformation on consciousness.'[33]

Consider only two examples drawn from the past and the present that give pause to the unbridled optimism about the exclusive and natural qualities that women have given to the world and with which they hope to imbue their new-found spirituality. The first example is drawn from the unlikely setting of Puritan America, which has long supplied the modern world with stereotyped images of sexually repressed men who persecuted and tortured to death the women of Salem, Massachusetts, in the belief that they were malevolent witches. In a recent study by Richard Godbeer,[34] a most surprising picture emerges of Puritan religion. In their sermons to the faithful, ministers freely imagined the true believer's relationship to Jesus in highly sensual language, taking on the role of bride to the groom, Christ, and in rapturous praise describing kissing his lips ('not for a single kisse, but for kisse upon kisse'), being impregnated by his love, and falling in a swoon of faith. Men as well as women engaged in this orgasmic imagery, where church services were likened to a marriage bed. At the very least, this preaching style of Bible-believing Christians, which emphasises the love of Christ as a groom for his bride, demonstrates that men were every bit as capable of expressing the affectionate and sensual side of human nature in their theology as the Wiccan movement suggests is their unique feminine contribution to contemporary spirituality.

The second example of religious and ideological expression that disturbs the claim to the uniquely feminine characteristics of compassion, love, forgiveness and tolerance is found in another recent study, this time of contemporary women who elect to be members of violent racist movements. *Inside Organized Racism,*[35] Kathleen Blee's second major study of women in the hate movement, including groups such as the Ku Klux Klan, skinhead gangs, neo-Nazi cells and Christian Identity (white supremacist) sects, challenges many of the preconceptions that feed feminist rhetoric about the innate qualities of women. Contrary to widely held assumptions, women in these groups do not primarily join as wives and girlfriends, following their violent men into their causes, but sign up voluntarily as individuals. Nor are they primarily poor or uneducated. Most are educated and were not raised in abusive families. They hold their racist and anti-Semitic views while living in the mainstream, holding down jobs and managing family life.

Today, one of the leading distributors of hate propaganda in Australia is a woman, Olga Scully. Defending herself in the Federal Court over charges of breaching the Racial Discrimination Act, Scully's litany of allegations against Jews rivalled the Nazi propaganda of Joseph Goebbels for its vile and outlandish claims. One does not need to look far for other examples of women taking the lead in political and religious movements in which they are driven by a singular and one-eyed pursuit of power with the aim of dominating 'lesser' groups. Surely this phenomenon belies the claim that women are naturally disinclined to the intolerant and abusive excesses of which patriarchal societies are guilty. Rather, it shows that given a chance, women will jump in with both feet to demonise and persecute others, and take up where men, for want of interest, have left off.

It may be that the only thing which distinguishes men and women in respect to their abuse of power is their unequal access to it, which until very recently has favoured men. That record may change in the contemporary world when women assume an exclusive status based on a renewed notion of divine right, symbolised by the neologism, 'womon', a preferred term for the female sex, denuded of all trace of 'man'.[36] It is ironic in any case that the women's liberation movement, which for the great majority of its beneficiaries meant the equal treatment of women and men, and for its feminist theologians meant both sexes were created in the image of the one God, has given rise to a spiritual movement that vigorously reasserts the uniqueness of the female sex under the aegis of her very own Goddess. It seems the battle of the sexes is fated to sally forth into the future.

4. RESTORING THE EARTH
The Earth is a Bible

If we all believe what we want to believe, as Fay Weldon succinctly points out in her critique of the therapeutic culture, *Godless in Eden*,[1] it is also true that some people prefer more precision than others. It is the difference among people that makes some of them literal readers and followers of a text and makes others open-ended interpreters of the ideas contained in it. Perhaps it is a matter of taste, but all the same a chasm between the two preferences opens up when changing cultural trends throw accepted norms into confusion. Some people will head straight for the Bible (or some other authoritative text) to get a clear ruling — for example, to Leviticus where homosexuality is prohibited: 'You shall not lie with a male as with a woman. It is an abomination.'[2] In matters of women's place in society, Paul, in the New Testament offers this: 'I permit no woman to teach or have authority over men. She is to keep silent.'[3] This approach works wonders if you are happy to use your religious belief as a refuge from the big bad world — and if you are not too fussed about losing a few friends along the way. You would not want them anyway.

There are other ways to use the Bible, and one thing is certain, the great collection of ancient works written by the Hebrews and the early Christians is nothing if not flexible. When it comes to finding support for both homosexuality and women's equality, passages have been cited as suggestive. In gay circles, the love between David and Jonathan, for example, is taken to be more than a platonic relationship, while feminist readings of the act of creation in Genesis and of Jesus' friendship with women, have been touted as conclusive proof that women are equal to men. This is a tremendously reassuring outcome if the Bible is the necessary and final arbiter of your moral universe.

Today, however, there is a new generation of people who are convinced that the most pressing moral and social issue before the human race is not addressed by the Bible. In fact, they believe that the environmental destruction of our planet was caused by biblical religion. The environmental crisis, which is the usual way of referring to the present state of the natural world, is not a mere unhappy consequence of Western civilisation's pursuit of the good life, nor indeed of the sub-Saharan African people's preference for following goat herds around the continent as they chewed up all the available vegetation and turned once verdant lands into one of the world's largest deserts. No, the received opinion is that it has been perpetrated by the West's belief in the biblical mandate to have 'dominion over the earth'.[4] Never mind that scholars have begged to differ with this translation and point out that the Hebrew expression implied stewardship of the earth. Even less noteworthy to the critics is the fact that an industrialised approach to farming on a mass scale is a relative latecomer to the peoples of the Bible, and it could be said really got underway as biblical religion declined. Nor is it readily acknowledged that environmental degradation is not the unique privilege of the Christian West. It quite happily proceeded apace in Communist China, in the former Soviet Union, and in parts of Africa and Asia, which needed no such dictum from the creation story in Genesis. These are piffling academic details for environmentalists who place all responsibility for the exploitation of earth's bounty on the affluent societies of the First World. For them, the final arbiter of the truth of radical environmentalism is the earth itself.

Believing in the earth is now one of the most widespread spiritual movements in the post Baby Boomer West. For a generation that had the least exposure to the Bible since it was committed to print, the earth has the distinct advantage of being unencumbered with language and texts or traditions. It also has a vague and imprecise set of values which anyone, with any sort of personal moral taste, can freely subscribe to. It is literally outside of oneself, and is something of an antidote to the anthropocentricism that has characterised so much of Western culture, and reached new heights during the 'Me Decade' of the 1970s and ended up lasting thirty years. The earth has the beauty of being a tangible object of care, mutely awaiting our ministrations, but unable to pass judgment upon our failures — except perhaps by becoming uninhabitable. When the earth 'dies' to us, as once freshwater lakes turn into poison wells or sand pans, the message is incontrovertible — the earth 'hurts'. Or so we think. In any case, believing in the earth comes at a time when some people are willing to turn their gaze away from a total preoccupation with the self, which they feel they have more or less figured out how to keep happy — with regular visits to the therapist, the retreat, the yoga class, the gym and the life coach. The time has come to turn toward the silent partner who has been there for us all along.

The earth has priority to humankind. Whether you are a Bible-believing Christian, in which case Genesis clearly states that God created the earth and all of nature before creating humans, or a hard-headed palaeontologist, the earth was established before we came along. And by the time humans arrived on the scene, the earth was more than a hot rock hurtling through space; it was clothed in a dazzling array of plants and animals that throbbed with life. It was awesome, and humans could not but be impressed by the splendid diversity around them, as grand as a mountain range and as tiny and delicate as a butterfly's wing; as beautiful as a life-giving stream and as ugly as a treacherous tidal wave. The earth would be eminently knowable and yet with an almost mysterious power and momentum. No wonder preliterate societies regularly imbued the earth with a personality all its own and treated it with the reverence of a god to whom one offers sacrifices and begs indulgence.

In the West, however, the biblical tradition made one thing perfectly clear: God was God, and the earth was His creation. The earth was not God any more than humankind was God. Neither was the earth a gift to humans, freely bestowed to do with whatever they wished. On the contrary, the earth and animal life were given to humans with a set of accompanying obligations and a duty of care; hence it was not a gift. When humans' divine obligation to conduct relations properly amongst themselves was broken, a flood was sent that consumed the earth. When humans were restored to the earth, their relationship to it implied limited use, as can be seen in the laws in Deuteronomy that restrict what can be eaten,[5] and in the prohibition of sexual intercourse with animals. It also implied responsibility, as in the law obliging one to give a Sabbath to the land, 'a year of solemn rest for the land' every seventh year.[6]

Jump to the present, and it is easy to see that the guiding principles of limited use and responsibility are not observed well enough. One of the biggest problems facing the world is that environmental degradation is serious and growing. Most assuredly, it is not confined to the most advanced or affluent countries. Brazil, for example, 'rains' soap, and China has so much air and water pollution that its much lauded green tea has been recently reported to contain extremely high levels of lead. Although affluent countries have spent money on emission controls, industrial safety measures and water purifying systems, a series of environmental disasters sent a clear message in the 1970s and 1980s that our natural world was vulnerable. Such infamous cases as the industrial pollution of Love Canal by Hooker Chemical in upstate New York, the massive oil spill by the tanker *Exxon Valdez* off the coast of the Alaskan peninsula, the horrific fallout of the Chernobyl nuclear reactor in Ukraine and the devastating Union Carbide gas leak and explosion in Bhopal, India have joined a litany of other assaults on the natural environment, and reinforce the view that the human race has reneged on its responsibilities to the earth.

To speak of responsibilities to the earth is already to grant the planet a quality of life akin to an organism, a being, with which one has a relationship. In contrast, one does not have a relationship with an inanimate object however much one may value it. A painting, for example, may have great value and provide much satisfaction, but burn it or cut it to pieces and the only thing that is gone is the space it occupied. Its imprint on one's brain remains, perhaps aided through reproductions in books, which underlines the fact that the 'relationship' one has with a painting is a fantasy, an array of mental associations. The same cannot be said for the removal of a forest, the drying up of a lake or the washing away of an escarpment. Whole complex ecologies of living organisms will have gone and the climate and atmosphere will have changed, regardless of whether one nostalgically remembers them by looking at old photographs of long gone forests or composing odes to extinct animals. The relationship one has to the environment is not merely imagined, it is empirically real, whether one is fully aware of it or not. The trouble is that many people are not aware of it.

Making people conscious of their physical relationship to the environment has been the primary aim of influential scientists like James P. Lovelock and David Suzuki. This is where imagination comes in, and it has a decidedly spiritual cast. English-born Lovelock was originally a medical researcher who invented a unique machine that detected the hole in the ozone layer above Antarctica. He became fascinated by the way in which the levels of the earth's oxygen, its temperature and the salinity of the sea had remained relatively stable over millions of years. He concluded that the elements of the natural world worked together in a symbiotic process like that of a human body, which functions at a high degree as a combination of finely attuned interdependent parts. Frustrated by his fellow scientists' tendency to think of nature as merely an object of study, and keen to engender a sense of reverence and care for the earth, he bestowed the name Gaia upon the planet, after the primordial creative force in Greek mythology, the 'deep breasted' earth, immortalised by Homer:

Mother Earth
The Mother of us all
The oldest of all,
Hard, splendid as rock
Whatever there is that is of the land
It is she who nourishes it
It is the Earth that I sing.[7]

Lovelock was aware that he was using a metaphorical device to arouse a sense of personal relationship to the earth. It turned out to be a stroke of genius because that is exactly what a great many people in the environmental movement needed: a divine sanction for their love of the earth, giving it an undeniable moral status. But Lovelock's solution, which attributed neither consciousness nor purpose to the earth, was taken up as more than a divine endorsement by the environmental movement. The earth assumed the personality and personhood of Gaia herself, the pre-Christian Greek Goddess who required devoted action and sacrifice from her earthlings. Today environmental organisations bearing her name are devoted to activism, echoing the vitality of Gaia, from whom all life comes forth. Indeed, one could easily rename this branch of the environmental movement, 'Gaiaism', where faith in Gaia and the practice of ensuring her survival for one's children and one's children's children unto eternity is the central focus and organising idea of its devotees.

Every faith movement needs its theologians, and there has been no shortage of them drawn from the disgruntled ranks of the Church, reflecting as much the desire to save the earth as to reinvent a spiritual universe that is close to the Christian sensibility of the medieval mystics, like Hildegard of Bingen and Francis of Assisi. Clerical refugees Matthew Fox and Thomas Berry led the way in America, while Paul Collins has been trumpeting the cause in Australia by means of his 1995 television documentary and book, *The Good Earth*. Their efforts are valuable largely in providing an opening to environmentalism through the back door of the Church. It is too early to judge whether they will be successful in broadening Christianity's social conscience to include non-human life systems, but the 17 January 2001 address of Pope John Paul II, calling for the ecological conversion of the Church, comes close: 'It is immediately evident that humanity has disappointed divine expectations ... humiliating the earth, our home. It is necessary, therefore, to stimulate and sustain ecological conversion.'[8] It is scientists like Lovelock, who are the movement's most authentic spiritual innovators. Having risen through the ranks of their profession, and, after laying claim to nature as their stomping ground and object of study, they redefined their relationship as nature's friend. Making the leap from the objective observer of nature to its subjective partner is not easy for the scientist, and some, it could be argued, have fallen down the crevice of credibility. There even seems to be a move to the acceptance of psychic abilities and the paranormal, which is the case with the self-confessed promoter of 'really popular science', Rupert Sheldrake.[9] The English biologist cum advocate of 'morphic resonance', the theory that ideas can leap from organism to organism without any communication between them, has made Sheldrake a target for scientific opprobrium and exposés by professional sceptics.

Another scientist who has attracted criticism from some of his colleagues is the person who probably best suits the role of popular 'ecologian', the Canadian environmentalist David Suzuki. Through his books and television documentaries, as well as a non-profit foundation, Suzuki has lent his name and scientific credentials to addressing not only the practical challenges of environmental sustainability but also the change of heart that is required of everyone if we are to relate to the planet in a new way. Suzuki draws on his experience with Canada's indigenous people, the First Nations and the Inuit, who live off the land in ways that he argues are not only sustainable but wrapped in a shroud of spiritual reverence. He argues that they have achieved a state of 'sacred balance' with the environment, and he hopes that the developed world will do so as well.

In an almost poetic vein, expertly intermingling natural science, human biology and a sense of the sacred, Suzuki invokes the four elements — air, water, fire (energy) and earth — and shows how they are the essential building blocks of human life, and therefore should attract our highest sense of gratitude. If the creation story of Genesis has imbued humanity with a profound sense of wonder at its own miraculous existence, then our intimate relationship to the earth, as recounted by modern eco-prophets, has the power to call forth every bit as much awe and wonder. In his book *Sacred Balance*, Suzuki considers air:

> Every breath is a sacrament, an affirmation of our connection
> with all other living things, a renewal of our link with our

ancestors and a contribution to generations yet to come. Our breath is part of life's breath, the ocean of air that envelopes the Earth. Unique in the solar system, air is both the creator and creation itself.[10]

Passages like this are prayers for the devotee of Gaiaism, and are the connective tissue between the individual and the seemingly abstract yet natural elements that surround us and are constitutive of our being. In another passage reflecting on the multivalent associations of earth (soil, dirt, ground, land), Suzuki turns to the traditions of the Dakota, one of the major tribes of indigenous Americans, to find a simple truth about humanity that is written into nature:

Dakota children understand that we are of the soil and the soil of us, that we love the birds and beasts that grew with us on the soil. A bond exists between all things because they all drink the same water and breathe the same air.[11]

What the Dakota children experience is something urban dwellers can only imagine, which is why Gaiaism encourages the 'greening' of one's personal existence. This may mean subsistence living in a country commune, garden farming or simply refashioning one's suburban back yard into an oasis for frogs, as John Croft and Vivienne Elanta, the couple who heads the Gaia Foundation in Western Australia, have done. Believing in the earth is not enough. It requires practice, which helps to expand the notion of self to include nature, and thus regard all harm to nature as painful to oneself. Another name for this is eco-psychology, a mind-set that our ancestors would have probably cultivated as a matter of course, living so much closer to nature than do the inhabitants of the developed and urbanised world today.

Scientists like Suzuki and his like-minded, much quoted friend, nuclear physicist and author of *The Tao of Physics*, Fritjof Capra, freely borrow from a range of poetic and indigenous sources in support of their scientific insights to serve the interests of Gaiaism. They continue to make an impact as individuals, comparable perhaps to the prophets of the Old Testament who warned their generation against the consequences of immorality and greed.

In reality, these 'lone voices' have not been the only ones working to restore our relationship to the earth. For the past thirty years, there have been whole groups of people who have attempted to reawaken reverence for the earth through a revival of paganism. Although the emergence of Wicca in the modern West was very much fuelled by the women's liberation movement in the 1960s, its current popularity, along with other earth-based spiritualities, like shamanic vision quests, owes more to the burgeoning environmental movement. Indeed, if paganism has a social conscience it is manifestly a 'green' one, and is expressed most pointedly through anti-nuclear activism. In the United Kingdom, Pagans Against Nukes (PAN) represents a network of pagan groups, whose purpose is summarised in this advertisement in its magazine, *Pipes of Pan*:

> Pagans Against Nukes (PAN) is an activist organisation dedicated to the banishment of nuclear technology from our Earth, and the re-establishment of a culture that lives in harmony with Her. We seek to co-ordinate all Pagans, of whatever land and tradition, in political and magical work to achieve this end, that the Earth be Green Anew.[12]

The activism without which one could scarcely speak of an environmental movement gains many of its willing participants from the ranks of paganism. Wicca's emphasis on practical applications and material outcomes, which we have seen in the previous chapter usefully deployed for women's personal aspirations, also has its advantages when it comes to caring for Mother Earth. As the leading American witch, Starhawk, observed: 'Meditation on the balance of nature might be considered a spiritual act in Witchcraft, but not as much as cleaning up garbage left at a campsite or marching to protest an unsafe nuclear plant.'[13]

If the environmental movement benefits from sympathetic pagans, their methods may not always follow such conventions as clearing campsites of rubbish. The Dragon Environmental Group, based in Essex, England, combines environmental work with eco-magic, and regularly undertakes rituals and casts spells to oppose projects such as the construction of new roads. Staging these rituals publicly has raised awareness of issues in the most dramatic fashion in the public mind. Wicca and other pagan groups have enhanced their image and social standing in the eyes of people who have never prayed to the Goddess, but who care about the planet.

As the anti-nuclear pagan activists indicate, believing in the earth is not just aroused by a desire to shower love on an irresistibly beautiful and gracious mother. It is also driven by its opposite, a conviction that the planet is in grave danger of massive environmental devastation and death. Nothing has so raised the temperature in this thinking as the greenhouse effect. In a nutshell, the earth is warming. Professor Stephen Schneider of Stanford University, the climatologist reputedly expert in this field, says the evidence is conclusive that over the past century the earth's climate has heated up half a degree Celsius. That does not seem like much, but he claims that together with melting glaciers and sea levels rising 10–20 centimetres, there is a lot to worry about. The trouble is that no-one is agreed on what to worry about, since it is not at all clear whether the warming has a human cause or is simply a perverse act of nature.[14]

While the debate rages, one entity that is charged with delivering a consensus on the cause of global warming, the Intergovernmental Panel on Climate Change (which was set up by the World Meteorological Organisation and the United Nations Environment Program), has examined 20 000 research papers on weather and climate and concluded that there is no-one to blame for the rising heat but ourselves. It is almost as if the licks of hellfire burning our heels threaten to consume us if we do not repent our evil ways. But we have heard this before.

In 1992 the world's largest ever gathering of heads of state was held in Rio de Janeiro to discuss the future of the global environment. A few months later, a document was released called the 'World Scientists' Warning to Humanity', which was signed by more than

1600 scientists, half of them Nobel Prize winners. The urgency of the warning, the dire predictions and the threat of annihilation lend an undeniably apocalyptic tone to the document that seems even more pronounced with the hindsight of ten years:

> Human beings and the natural world are on a collision course ...
> Many of our current practices put at serious risk the future for
> human society ... and may so alter the world that it will be
> unable to sustain life in the manner that we know. Fundamental
> changes are urgent ... Not more than one or a few years remain
> before the chance to avert the threats we now confront will be
> lost and the prospects for humanity irrevocably diminished.[15]

It may seem unfair to the environmental movement to compare global warming to the punishment of hellfire, and thereby imply it is an imagined not a real threat. But it is not hysteria that gives rise to an apocalyptic outlook, it is a deeply felt moral conviction that justice has not been done. Apocalyptic beliefs have historically been fuelled by the conviction that the powers that be are so evil in the eyes of God that nothing will save them, and the imminent Last Judgment will decree that they deservedly crash down in a heap of fire and brimstone. Today, however, only the most die-hard biblical literalists view the affairs of the day from such a confident moral high ground. The rest of us have little faith that our political, religious and financial leaders who have committed the most egregious breaches of personal and public honesty and integrity will get their eternal comeuppance. Even if they do, most of them will fool the rest of us in the meantime by making hay while they can. The machinations of politics and the permutations of personal morality seem so far beyond the pale of chastening moral judgment that all conviction is lost in a haze of slick media performance and forgotten public inquiries.

What remains for us to believe in? The planet lures us with its power and its fragility, as both our source of life and our final resting place. Mute and vulnerable, it has given generously over millions of years, and now invites us to repay our debt. Yet the planet makes no promises and turns no-one away. Meanwhile, the new believers in the earth hope for renewal, which requires as much rational dedication as it does faith in the power of this complex and still mysterious organism to regenerate itself and survive our industrial assaults on its being. But it's not a sure thing. The truth is, we are not a necessary part of the natural order. As all ecologists know, if humankind was eliminated from the face of the earth there would be some losses, like domesticated animals and fertile farms, but a great deal gained, like cleaner water, clearer air, no more rubbish dumps and perhaps no more global warming. The reverse, however, does not hold. We cannot live without the earth. It may deliver its own apocalypse to an unprepared and unsuspecting population, but chances are they would be largely guilty and perhaps deserving of annihilation. That is the spectre that hangs before humanity — all 6 billion of us ... and only 4 billion more to go before the experts say that the earth simply will cease to support our demands. In this way, believing in the earth has all the elements of a full-blown religion, with its idyllic Eden, its fatal hell, and its ethical program of life that calls for some of the highest human virtues, such as diligent study, sacrifice, patience, love, humility and simplicity in service to ends that are not overwhelmingly focused on the self. Perhaps it is not far-fetched after all to be having apocalyptic dreams. The ultimate question, however, is not, 'Will we be saved?', but, 'Will we save our planet?'

Unfortunately, the apocalyptic outlook is also conducive to precipitous and destructive behaviour, which the radical new believers are more than equal to. Industrial sabotage and eco-terrorism are extreme measures for an extreme faith and organisations like the Animal Liberation Front (ALF), the Earth Liberation Front (ELF) and Earth First! make it their sacred duty to engage in 'direct action'. 'Monkeywrenching' is the euphemistic term the ELF uses for acts of sabotage and property destruction against entities that it believes are damaging the natural environment. These 'dark green' organisations have all come to the attention of the FBI in the United States for their activities, for which they often are happy to claim responsibility.

In the case of ALF and ELF, these amount to 600 criminal acts in the US since 1996, resulting in US$43 million damage, according to FBI estimates. There are now 1669 special agents working for the FBI's domestic counter-terrorism programs.[16]

It would be a one-sided inheritance if the apocalyptic outlook contained in the Book of Revelation were the Bible's only relevance to the environmental issue. As it turns out, the Psalms, in particular, as well as the Proverbs and the Prophets convey a lively appreciation of the earth as a living being, something one would never know if one relied on the anti-biblical eco-rhetoric emerging from pagan and other sources. To remedy this oversight, a remarkable multi-volume effort called *The Earth Bible*, co-ordinated by the gifted Australian theologian Norman Habel, and involving an international array of scholars, brings into focus the rich stream of earth consciousness that is eloquently given voice in the scriptures. Without delving into the various special interests of the contributing scholars, whose arguments often do not stray out of academe, one can simply take the hint from this project and search the Psalms oneself and find there many examples of the earth consciousness that is so highly valued today. For example, God's love, as expressed in Psalm 36, is for all creation equally:

> *Thy steadfast love, O Lord, extends to the heavens*
> *Thy faithfulness to the clouds*
> *Thy righteousness is like the mountains of God*
> *Thy judgments are like the great deep;*
> *Man and beast thou savest, O Lord.*[17]

Psalm 65 pays homage to the breadth of God's creation, and here the earth assumes a joyous demeanour:

> *The pastures of the wilderness drip,*
> *The hills gird themselves with joy,*
> *The meadows clothe themselves with flocks,*
> *The valleys deck themselves with grain*
> *They shout and sing together for joy.*[18]

The intimate relationship between God and the earth is so fundamental that most of Psalm 148 imagines in detail how every part of creation joyously praises God for giving it life. But there is a moral dimension to this earthly reverie, and numerous passages in the Psalms make abundantly clear that God controls creation according to an 'economy of righteousness', where the meek and righteous will inherit the earth and prosper on the land,[19] whereas the wicked will be cast out,[20] perhaps echoing the first expulsion of the sinful pair from Eden. Also recalling Genesis, Psalm 71 alludes to man's origins in the earth itself, from which he first arises, then returns at death, and wherefrom the righteous might hope to rise again:

> *Thou who hast made me see many sore troubles*
> *Wilt revive me again;*
> *From the depths of the earth*
> *Thou wilt bring me up again*
> *Thou wilt increase my honour*
> *And comfort me again.*[21]

Earthly allusions to God as 'My Rock' and to his 'Holy Mountain' are pervasive, but Psalm 99 also reminds the reader that when Moses, Aaron and Samuel called on God's name, 'He spoke to them in the pillar of cloud.'[22] This is not the only way, however, one can receive instruction from the Lord. At least two scholars contributing to *The Earth Bible* remember that when Job tries to make sense of his travails, he looks to creation:

> *But ask the beasts and they will teach you*
> *The birds of the air and they will tell you*
> *Or the plants of the earth, and they will teach you*
> *And the fish of the sea will declare to you.*
> *Who among all those does not know that the hand of the*
>   *Lord has done this?*[23]

In this and numerous other passages of the Bible, the imagination readily animates the earth, yet always with reference to God. The reader, who frequently is singing such passages in hymns of praise, recognises the earth not as a mute object of exploitation, but as a living, joyous part of creation, all of which owes its being to God. There is no message here of man's domination of the earth, or the planet as plaything of man, but the reverse — the earth which owes its life to God is a primordial partner in creation, and from it humankind was fashioned. The earth in all its glory is an awe-inspiring vision. It humbles humanity, and like all of creation makes it thankful.

A similar gratitude for creation is often found in indigenous traditions. Theologian Norman Habel, who hails from the Lutheran Church, has long understood the potential that lies in identifying affinities between ideas and concepts from seemingly different traditions. He has worked in the borderland area of Rainbow Spirituality, a unique Australian initiative of the Aboriginal elder George Rosendale and other Rainbow Serpent elders. They have merged their indigenous beliefs with Christianity and produced a theology that maintains their connection to the land and its stories, especially those of the Rainbow Serpent, the Creator Spirit, while delivering a saviour God who teaches the Sermon on the Mount and offers redemption to all. In recognising the importance of land for Aboriginal Australians, Habel has renewed his own interest in the presence of the land and nature in the Bible, and opened our eyes to the messages it contains for us in the twenty-first century. What is abundantly clear is that we have been blind to the 'earth Bible', because of our preoccupations born of a different time and place. Our new and urgent concerns emerging out of this time and place are enabling us to see it again.

This chapter began by drawing the distinction between those who expect clear prescriptions in their religious traditions and those who draw out manifold meanings in a text to serve new and burgeoning concerns in society. Both preferences can be seen operating in contemporary approaches to the Bible, but the second approach, which takes as given a fresh reading of the texts, has been essential in buttressing the new believers in the earth. But the question must be asked: are they the same as the pagans who see in every rock and every stream a spirit to be venerated? Has this simply subverted the project of monotheism into its precursor, pantheism, and turned a whole generation of would-be Christians and Jews into an ambiguous and uncertain mix of literate primitives?

It is possible that this could be the result. But it would not be the first time that unlikely and even contradictory notions were allowed to flourish within these two great Western traditions. Here is an example from one of the most beloved saints in the Christian calendar, Francis of Assisi. His 'Canticle of Brother Sun' begins with a panegyric to God as the most high, yet continues by praising the four elements as if they were beings. Reading this poem one would be forgiven for thinking it was written by a native American.

Most high, omnipotent, good Lord
To you alone belong praise and glory
Honour and blessing
No man is worthy to breathe your name.
Be praised, my Lord, for all your creatures.
In the first place for the blessed Brother Sun
Who gives us the day and enlightens us through you
He is beautiful and radiant with his great splendour,
Giving witness of you, most Omnipotent One.
Be praised, my Lord, for Brother Wind
And the airy skies, so cloudy and serene;
For every weather, be praised, for it is life-giving.
Be praised, my Lord, for Sister Water
So necessary yet so humble, precious and chaste.
Be praised, my Lord, for Brother Fire,
Who lights up the night,
He is beautiful and carefree, robust and fierce.
Be praised, my Lord, for our sister, Mother Earth,
Who nourishes and watches us
While bringing forth abundant fruits

With coloured flowers and herbs.
Praise and bless the Lord. Render him thanks.
Serve him with great humility. Amen.[24]

The Jewish tradition is no stranger to personifying the elements, and as we have seen there is precedent for it in the Bible itself. But in so far as the natural elements were God's creation and owed their existence to their Creator, they could not be made into objects of veneration. At the least, it was illogical to do so, as they are only partial emanations of God; at the worst they might be set up as rival gods. This is the reason for the second commandment, elaborated in Deuteronomy, which prohibits the making of a graven image:

> ... of any figure, the likeness of male or female, the likeness of any beast that is on the earth, the likeness of any winged bird that flies in the air, the likeness of anything that creeps on the ground, the likeness of any fish that is in the water under the earth.[25]

A warning follows not to worship the sun, the moon or the stars, but that did not prevent poets from imagining the movements of the celestial bodies as part of the wondrous creation that God had put in place. The eleventh-century Spanish Jewish poet and philosopher, Solomon ibn Gabirol, wrote a religious poem of great influence, 'The Royal Crown', in which he did just that. This is but a short excerpt from a lengthy treatise in verse on the solar system, that combines neo-platonic astronomy and Jewish piety:

Thy grandeur who shall tell? Thou didst confine
Fire's sphere within a sphere, the firmament
Wherein the Moon snuffs in some solar scent
Of radiance, and part from her doth shine;
She beats her bounds in nine-and-twenty days
Full orbit, in her ways
Mysterious, be her secrets deep or slight,

In mass to Earth's as one to thirty-nine
As each month new events she doth excite
In this our world, benignant or malign
Always her own Creator's will she heeds,
That she may show to all mankind his mighty deeds.[26]

The purpose of ibn Gabirol's poem, however, is not to recount the wonders of the solar system, but to compare them to a litany of the puny achievements of man, who is racked by vanity, guilt and shame:

For Thou art One, Thou livest nonpareil
In might, enduring, wise, and great, and God:
And I dust of the earth, a very worm, a clod.[27]

Humanity's identification with the earth is here just as it was in Genesis, where Adam was made from the dust, and received his name from the Hebrew word for it. Yet this complete identification with the earth and creation, which today is so strenuously sought as a reminder of our earthbound nature and fate, has rarely been adequate to human striving. Humanity, more often than not, has attempted to reunite with the Creator, the source of all life, in the hope that some higher form of knowledge and existence awaits it there. It is between these two spheres, this-worldly and other-worldly, that the human spirit has been travelling ever since it was first breathed into existence.

5. REFORMING BUDDHISM
The Buddha is Western

The gleaming Mercedes Benz and Saab cars in the parking lot at Spirit Rock Meditation Center are a long way from the freight-train boxcars and flatbed trucks that were the regular mode of transport in Jack Kerouac's 'dharma bum' existence. In those early days of Buddhism in America, the essence of the enlightened life for a young man who did not want to be a celibate monk was to reject material consumerism and live on the edge of mainstream society. Yet for Kerouac, as with his sometime friend and Buddhist co-conspirator of the Beat Generation, Allen Ginsberg, renunciation of the American Dream was the outward sign of an inner detachment that had already taken place, and was the engine of his poetry:

> *Insincere and sad*
> *The world's a farce*
> *To stand and sneer at . . .*[1]

. . . In America only the
Silent Buddhahood may be possible . . .
The clinging here is so intense and widespread
(democracy) the populace is literally unteachable
and sees life not as sorrow.[2]

Forty years on, Buddhism in the West is not the refuge of a disgruntled counterculture that prefers to see life as sorrow, but increasingly the choice of high-earning mainstream professionals who are searching for the spiritual and moral support that their busy lives demand. Nowhere is this more evident than at Spirit Rock in Woodacre, California, where the simple rural setting gives no clue as to the ambitious program which this eclectic Buddhist centre offers each week to the spiritual seeker. Set in a gentle valley, about forty-five minutes north of San Francisco, its simple, ecologically sensitive buildings host thousands of people over the course of a year, who more often than not would be hoping for some instruction from another Jack, the founder and former Buddhist monk, now family man and popular author, Jack Kornfield. Maybe they will strike lucky, but one of the hallmarks of good teachers in America is that they are often somewhere else, bringing their distinctive gifts to groups of seekers who have read their bestseller books. The day I visit, clutching Kornfield's *After Ecstasy, the Laundry,* he is away. But Australian instructor Sally Clough, one of the impressive staff of teachers at Spirit Rock, greets me, and explains the philosophy of this quintessentially Western version of Buddhism.

Spirit Rock is not a monastery and does not promote an exclusive Buddhist path, but acts like a resource for spiritual seekers from all walks of life. Activities to enhance parenting, meditation retreats for teens and courses for psychotherapists were among the offerings during my visit. And although the Vipassana meditation of Theravada Buddhism is Jack Kornfield's specialty and is the foundation of Spirit Rock, it is not the only spiritual tradition one will encounter at the centre. Jewish mysticism or Kabbalah, Yoga, Sufi dance and Native American practices are just as likely to appear in the courses. Indeed, one of Kornfield's books, *Soulfood*, written with Christina Feldman, is a collection of inspirational stories drawn from a wide range of traditions. Because most people coming to Spirit Rock are well educated, they are self-directed, choosing to attend courses or retreats to deepen their spiritual practice or to deal with particular issues that are facing them either personally or professionally.

The personal and the professional are often one and the same, as psychologist, popular author and staff member Sylvia Boorstein pointed out in her day retreat for psychotherapists. She is also a humorist, and spent a good deal of the time telling stories from 'the other side of the couch'. Like the Dalai Lama's penchant for not taking himself too seriously, Sylvia's approach is based on the belief that true wisdom often has a funny side. There is precedent for this in the tradition's beloved image of the potbellied, laughing Buddha, as well as in the stories and jokes of Boorstein's native Judaism. The bitter truths of reality are paradoxically more easily dispelled by humour than by tears, says Boorstein. It was apparent that the assembled therapists at her retreat thought so too.

Amid the swaying golden grass, a more serene image of the Buddha sits, dwarfed by the sweep of the valley at Spirit Rock. The stone statue's modest size and quiet elegance signals that here the Buddha is not a towering, miraculous personality to be worshipped, but is remembered as a humble man and an enlightened teacher, who was consulted for spiritual guidance. Tradition records his encounters with disciples as if he were the archetypal problem solver who always had ways and means to help the individual come to a mindful state, regardless of where he was on his spiritual path. This is the Buddhist principle of 'skill in means', which refers to the way the Buddha adapted the method of teaching to the aptitude of the particular student or audience that he was addressing. It is the model that is employed at Spirit Rock, where the teachers' credentials reveal an array of training methods found in Theravada, Zen, Tibetan and Dzogchen Buddhist traditions as well as Advaita of the Hindu Vedanta tradition. In addition several of the teachers are trained psychotherapists, who have consciously blended the beneficial effects of silent meditation with the talking cure of classical psychoanalysis. This is an area of cross-fertilisation in which the centre has been a key player, and Kornfield has written about it extensively:

> The best of modern therapy is much like a process of shared meditation, where therapist and client sit together, learning to pay close attention to those aspects and dimensions of the self that the client may be unable to touch on his or her own.[3]

Spirit Rock can afford to be heterodox in its approach to Buddhism because it is not bound by the monastic vows and sectarian rivalries which emerged in the centuries after the Buddha's death, 2500 years ago. Instead, it is uniquely focused on developing a lay community of householders where Buddhist ideals of mindfulness and an awakened heart are practised in the midst of everyday life. At Spirit Rock, the Sangha, which is the third of Buddhism's three 'refuges', the other two being the Buddha and the Dharma, is interpreted as 'community' rather than monastery. This domestication, as it were, of the Sangha is consistent with the overall aim of the centre: to bring Buddhist attitudes and practice into the mainstream. Its emphasis on practical application makes the most of the natural utilitarianism which is at the very heart of Buddhism, and reflects the choice of Jack Kornfield and other well-known exponents of contemporary Buddhism, like Stephen Batchelor, who were once serious followers of the tradition's monastic expression, but have since married and become prolific authors and itinerant teachers of the Buddhist path as a method of gaining personal spiritual wellbeing.

The teachers at Spirit Rock, like all non-monastic Buddhists, are bound by the first five precepts of non-harming — refraining from killing, stealing, sexual misconduct, lying and using intoxicants — and are expected to actively express compassion in a socially useful way. As instructors, they must also abide by a code of ethical conduct. There is no obligation, however, for either teacher or student to take on the larger religious tradition of Buddhism. It is an approach which the Dalai Lama himself has stressed in his books and talks to Western audiences, and has been promoted by Stephen Batchelor in his popular book *Buddhism Without Beliefs*. After studying Jungian psychoanalysis in Zurich, Switzerland, while still a monk, and then travelling to Korea to study Zen meditation, where he met his future wife, Martine, who was a Zen Buddhist nun, Batchelor decided to give away the monastic life and concentrate on bringing Buddhist principles into the community at large.

Batchelor's approach to Buddhism is quintessentially Western, not because he has added specifically Western ideas to an old teaching, but because he has removed the legend and lore that have grown up around the Buddha's simple teaching of awakening. From the confidence of a rational perspective, born of the European Enlightenment, which separates religious history from its founding myths, Batchelor maintains that Siddartha Gautama — the Buddha — was not a mystic, nor was he inclined to esoteric revelations. He was a practical man, who devised a basic set of ethical principles and a straightforward practice leading to psychological awakening. It is in the centuries after his death with the rise of the Mahayana and Vajrayana (Tibetan) traditions that the Buddha is virtually deified as a miraculous intercessor. In refusing to endorse the supernatural beliefs around the Buddha, and refraining from an insistence that belief in reincarnation is necessary, Batchelor's presentation of the Buddhist life may indeed be more faithful to the Indian prince's original intention.

Like the eminently practical orientation of Spirit Rock, *Buddhism Without Beliefs* has appealed to Westerners, whose main attraction to the faith is precisely its rational and utilitarian character, its self-help focus that amounts to a recipe for self-therapy, and the absence of a belief in divine beings. On the other hand, it has proved useful to those who would rather hang onto the mystical leanings and cultural identities of their inherited faith, such as Judaism or Christianity, while accepting selected Buddhist concepts and practices, like meditation, mindfulness and the eightfold path. The resulting hybrid, whose followers are sometimes referred to as 'Jubus' in the case of Jews who combine Buddhist practice with their own tradition, is a subject taken up in the next chapter. It is enough to mention here that the influence of Buddhism has begun a quiet revolution in Judaism and also in Christianity.

Not that a piecemeal approach to Buddhism, with its inevitable inconsistencies, satisfies everyone. In contrast, not to say in rivalry, the San Francisco Zen Center, which has near-iconic status amongst Western Zen Buddhists, is a fully fledged urban community. But like all communities its reputation and its success owe a great deal to its leadership. The Zen Center was fortunate in its wise, whimsical and much-quoted founder, Shunryu Suzuki Roshi (1904–71), whose book *Zen Mind, Beginner's Mind* is still the most widely read Zen book in the West.

> We must have beginner's mind, free from possessing anything, a mind that knows everything is in flowing change. Nothing exists but momentarily in its present form and color. One thing flows into another and cannot be grasped. Before the rain stops we hear a bird.[4]

A traditional Soto Zen priest from Japan with quite humble aspirations, Suzuki Roshi (1904–71) arrived in San Francisco in 1959 and soon attracted a growing number of American students who came to practise sitting meditation and to take his lectures. In two years he opened the San Francisco Zen Center where his philosophy of offering Americans something uniquely tailored to their needs was put into practice.

> Here in America we cannot define Zen Buddhists the same way we do in Japan ... I think you are special people and want some special practice that is not exactly priest's practice and not exactly layman's practice. You are on your way to discovering some appropriate way of life.[5]

Suzuki Roshi was married and his wife imparted her knowledge of traditional Zen art forms to aspiring young women, including Blanche Hartman, who eventually became the first abbess of what is the largest Zen centre in the country.

Abbess Hartman is the warm and friendly married woman with short-cropped silver hair who shares the leadership of the San Francisco Zen Center. Although marriage is typical of Zen priests who head temples in Japan, a woman occupying this role is a rare departure from the traditionally patriarchal Japanese Zen. It is one of the many Western-style improvements that have been implemented in recent years at the centre, following the near breakdown of the community during the notorious period of leadership in the 1980s when Richard Baker was ousted from his role as the centre's abbot amid allegations of serious personal and professional misconduct, and his appointed successor was arrested brandishing a gun that he had taken from the scene of an unsolved crime.[6] Along with the distance of years, Abbess Hartman's sense of humour and wisdom serve her well when reflecting on those times, which, as an 'old hippy', she concedes left more than their share of unhappy legacies. But one legacy that was an indisputable triumph was the elevation of women to equal status with men. It would shake up Zen's legendary misogynous attitude (a hangover of Japanese culture, perhaps, more than of Zen) and turn it into a thriving Western expression of Zen Buddhism, which is very probably more popular in America than it is in Japan itself, where priests are finding it difficult to keep their temples open and even harder to pass on their hereditary mantle to their sons. Not only did a woman assume the role of spiritual leader at the San Francisco Zen Center, but also the traditional hierarchical structure gave way to a horizontal style of shared leadership, democratic boards and a culture of accountability in the day-to-day running of the organisation — changes which Abbess Hartman readily attributes to feminine influence.

It doesn't take long to realise that the San Francisco Zen Center is not an inward-looking community or a haven of the counterculture, but a hive of activity connecting to the community at large. A raft of courses includes a 12-step program for addicts and Buddhist meditation for African–American women, while the centre also supports a social action program that brings food and clothing to the city's homeless. The day I visited, people were filing in with knapsacks, getting ready to embark on a weekend retreat, a welcome escape from their busy lives. Escape is not an option for everyone, and in those cases, Buddhism comes to them. About fourteen inmates at San Quentin Prison, who are in for life, look upon their weekly group meditation with Seido Lee de Barros as a haven of peace and quiet in the midst of their often noisy and violent lives in prison. A Soto Zen Roshi associated with the San Francisco Zen Center's Green Gulch Farm, Seido Lee arrives at the prison every Sunday with two or three student Zen practitioners, and leads the denim-clad group in sitting and walking meditation, followed by a 'sesshin' or discussion, when the participants can ask questions about Buddhist teaching.

When I accompanied Seido Lee, the prisoners spoke to me of the powerful sense of dignified calm they experience during meditation. They spoke of how the Buddhist teaching of non-violence encourages them to confront the serious nature of the acts, including murder, which they have committed. But the most important source of support, it seemed to me, was the Buddhist teaching of detachment, which helped them approach the rest of their lives with some sense of equanimity in a setting that is never going to be happy or free. As one prisoner put it, Buddhist meditation is the most suitable form of spiritual practice for life in prison, where renunciation of all the pleasures of life occurs the moment you enter the place, and endures as long as you are inside. The Buddhist teaching of life's impermanence and inevitable suffering, which detaches the individual from finding gratification in material things, helps this prisoner cope with his circumstances.

What these men do not know is that San Quentin, with its hygiene and electricity, its modern amenities and clean clothes, its doctors on duty and its television sets, is in some ways a palace of dreams compared to the harsh realities that confront one in the heartland of India, where Buddhism was born. Neither would the prisoners know that they are beneficiaries of a largely demythologised expression of Buddhism that one is hard-pressed to find in the East. It is worth a trip to the place of its origins to realise just how much the West has claimed as its own the practical instruction of awakening, which is at the heart of Buddhism.

Travelling along the bumpy, narrow road from the town of Patna to the village of Bodhgaya one is already discovering in the most palpable way the Buddha's central teaching. The human suffering and degradation in India's poorest state of Bihar leave one wide-eyed with horror and speechless with shame. It is no wonder the Buddha taught that detachment from the external material world is the path to inner peace. Detachment — or is it indifference? — probably is the only way to stop one's instinctive emotional entanglement with the scenes of human deprivation that unfold before one's eyes.

Bodhgaya is the most important of several pilgrimage sites for Buddhists. It was there, more than 2500 years ago, that the Hindu prince Siddartha ended his arduous spiritual quest and, under a local fig tree, experienced *bodhi* or perfect enlightenment. The fig tree became known as the Bodhi Tree, and the prince became the Buddha, soon-to-be founder of a new religion. Today the Bodhi Tree in Bodhgaya, which was sprouted from a Sri Lankan offshoot of the original, is a shrine. Two Buddhist nuns keep a chanting vigil there, while beggars pick up the fallen leaves of the sacred tree and present them to pilgrims in hope of rupees.

As the leaves of the Bodhi Tree grow, wither and die, they are an appropriate symbol of the Buddha's teaching that nothing in this world is permanent or of lasting value. Yet the transient nature and insubstantiality of things is a hard lesson to learn. Before long, Buddhists marked the spot for posterity, and surrounded the Bodhi Tree with a massive stone carved *stupa*, or memorial shrine containing relics, which, dating from the fifth century, is one of the oldest in India. Similarly, Bodhgaya today is something of a contradiction. Essentially a collection of recently built temples representing twenty-seven different national communities, ranging from Bhutanese to American Vietnamese, Bodhgaya is a shabby Buddhist theme park in the heartland of traditional Hinduism. The locals who peddle statues of the Buddha can make a convincing show of knowing Buddhist lore, but it is all for the sake of a sale. Their own lives are governed by the strict rules of indigenous tribalism, Hindu beliefs and a caste system so minutely ordered that it separates even the garden workers from the cooks. The anti-caste universalism of Buddhist teaching could not be further from their lives.

Nonetheless, in recent years, the locals have become used to living with a giant stone Buddha gazing down on them. Reaching some 20 metres in height, the Buddha was erected in 1990 by the resident Japanese temple authority, and blessed by the Dalai Lama. Like the temples in the town, the statue was intended to draw pilgrims and be a source of *dana* or donation. But coins tossed into the collection box give an empty ring, and it is not at all evident that the giant Buddha has benefited the locals. At any time of the day or evening, hundreds of emaciated men stand, sit or lie around their stalls, with no-one to buy their wares. It is the start of the long rainy season, and the pilgrims are down to a trickle.

This is all going to change if the Buddhist group promoting the Maitreya Project has its way. Named after the Future Buddha (one of the many manifestations of the Buddha), the project aims to build a Buddha that is more than seven times the size of the Buddha built by the Japanese temple. The brainchild of popular Tibetan guru Lama Zopa Rinpoche, the Buddha will reach a height of 152 metres — taller than the Sydney Harbour Bridge and three times the height of the Statue of Liberty. Scale drawings show it dominating the region of rice paddies, where locals still plant and reap by hand, and cows and water buffalo wander freely.

The project administrators have been working for several years to convince the sluggish Bihar government that the giant Buddha will significantly increase revenue from tourism. But the absence of a tourist infrastructure (there is no working airport, for example) makes the prospect of hordes of pilgrim tourists highly problematic if not unlikely. People still remember the utter chaos and rampant health problems that occurred in Bodhgaya when 250 000 people descended on the tiny hamlet in 1985 for a Kalacakra initiation celebration conducted by the Dalai Lama.

If the Maitreya Project goes ahead, it will have to be a self-contained compound, providing all of its own services, in much the same way as its present installations function now. A modest building, for example, houses the Maitreya School of Universal Education — an impressive service for around 400 children in what is obviously a caring, if experimental, environment, run when I visited in 2001 by Australian former businesswoman, Skye Holden. In fact, it is the grassroots focus of the Maitreya Project school and health clinic that has gained the confidence of some of the locals.

The free provision of these basic and much-needed services is supposed to demonstrate the compassionate loving kindness of Maitreya Buddha. Less convincing are the arguments put forward by the promoters of the proposed giant Buddha that the mere presence of the colossus on the landscape will communicate those values and help bring peace on earth. What is indisputable, however, is that, if successfully completed, the Maitreya Buddha will produce a lot more revenue for Lama Zopa Rinpoche, in the same way the pilgrimage destination of Dharamsala, in India, the home of the Dalai Lama, has done for the exiled leader of Tibet.

There is something deeply disturbing about the mad rush for the biggest Buddha. Hong Kong recently built what it claims is the world's biggest outdoor, bronze, seated Buddha on Lantau Island. Hyderabad in India has a 16-metre, 350-tonne white granite Buddha, which now stands proudly in the middle of a lake — but not before it fell and sank to the bottom during the delicate process of transporting it there. In 2001, South Korea announced that it would build the world's biggest Buddha, a proposal that has already caused violent skirmishes amid allegations of corruption. This is to say nothing of the world's biggest Buddhist stupa or temple, the Dhammakaya Citeya, built outside Bangkok in Thailand, which boasts a monthly Sunday attendance of 20 000 people in its enormous facilities. Its golden dome covered with 300 000 gilt Buddhas (with a further 700 000 inside) is visible from afar. But more people saw it on the evening news, when it was discovered that the selling of Buddhas to the public involved significant overselling and other kinds of financial corruption, for which the abbot was arrested. No-one expected that the Thai government would convict him, and they were right.

The Buddha taught that unnecessary suffering was caused by the attachment to things, including the 'self', which would soon pass away in the cycle of birth and death. As Prince Siddartha, he demonstrated this by walking away from the material wealth and stature of his inheritance and trading it for a simple life of contemplation and right action. What then would the Buddha say to some of his robed followers who seem intent on building a giant image of himself in a land that is regularly awash with monsoonal floods and floating corpses? It is doubtful that he would think they had grasped the teaching of impermanence when they explain that this giant image will be fashioned from a special bronze alloy made to last a thousand years. It is hard to imagine the man who rejected aristocratic luxury rejoicing in an image of himself which, by conservative estimates, will cost US$195 million to complete, and which will contain over one million works of art, most, if not all of them, images of himself.

While we can only speculate on what the founding sage of Buddhism, who lived to the ripe old age of 80, would have made of these excesses, the Dalai Lama, in a conversation with me during his Australian tour in July 2002, refused to speculate. A supporter of the project, he conceded that a case could be made for spending the money on more useful things, but then argued that Buddhism, like other religions, has always built shrines which function as focal points for the faithful, and that the Maitreya Project would be a great one. Given the democratic cast that Buddhism has taken in the West, it was worth asking several other of its spokespeople to comment on the Maitreya Project. Buddhist scholars Peter Harvey in England and Robert Thurman in America had no trouble coming to its support and responding to the obvious counterarguments with the same traditional answers the Dalai Lama gave. But the Maitreya Project has its detractors, and at Spirit Rock, Australian Sally Clough made it clear that it was a bone of contention amongst many Western Buddhists, who could not countenance the extravagant use of money and the ostentation of the planned Maitreya compound, particularly in a country so desperate for the most basic amenities. These concerns notwithstanding, Western money pours into the project.

That is because, unlikely as it seems, making a lot of money is an entirely Buddhist exercise. Especially if you are Michael Roach, the American of Irish descent who became a Tibetan *geshe* (master of Buddhism) and then made a hundred million dollars in the diamond trade — without, it seems, compromising his status or his principles. Never mind that his master sent him out to make a fistfull of dollars with strict instructions not to appear outwardly as a Buddhist monk, but to sport fine clothes and average-length hair, clearly in the days before shaved heads became the fashion! Ever since Roach published his own account of his rise and rise as a successful businessman in *The Diamond Cutter: The Buddha on Strategies for Managing Your Business and Your Life*, the barefoot founder of an ancient religion has been deployed as a get-rich guru for the ethically minded and spiritually sensitive. Somewhat ironically, the name 'Diamond Cutter' refers both to Roach's profession and to one of the most well known and also one of the shortest Mahayana Buddhist sutras, in which the Buddha teaches his disciple Subhuti the meaning of emptiness.

Emptiness is a central Buddhist philosophical concept, which is exceedingly subtle and an attempt to promote a non-dualistic outlook. Put in a very simple form, phenomena are regarded as having neither reality nor non-reality, but both simultaneously. What seems nonsensical is really a method of encouraging a mental non-attachment to things, including beliefs, even while cultivating a practical relationship to them. In the Diamond Cutter Sutra, the Buddha teaches Subhuti that the truth about the 'perfect worlds', which we work to make, is that they could never exist, which is why they can be called 'perfect worlds'. What the Buddha applied to the paradisical notion of a 'perfect world', Michael Roach applies to a perfect business: it too does not exist, although it can be said to potentially exist. In the wink of an eye, the doctrine of the emptiness of all things is transformed into a recipe for 'unlocking the hidden potential in things', particularly success in business.[7]

In the language of business, of course, potential really means profit, and Michael Roach makes perfectly clear that making money is consistent with running an ethical business as well as with leading a spiritual life. Not only is the person with abundant resources able to do much more good than one without, argues Roach, but also the key issues are how the money is made and 'how *to make it continue to come*' (his italics).[8] So long as one is running a business successfully, according to Buddhist principles, it becomes part of one's spiritual life. And this extends to enjoying the money, which is an essential sign that one is leading a healthy life, pursuing work balanced with pleasure.[9]

While this teaching may appear to clash with the perspective found in the ancient texts of Buddhism, and is certainly nowhere explicit in the Diamond Cutter Sutra, it certainly speaks to the many strung-out professionals and business people who have plied their trade in the hothouses of ambition without reference to any set of spiritual values, only to find themselves exhausted and in a state of personal confusion. Take that apex of achievement, New York, where, as the saying goes, 'If you can make it there, you can make it anywhere.' Along with the star performers, there are at least as many who get chewed up and spat out in the process, and Buddhism is helping some of them get their lives back together. In the Three Jewels, a Buddhist drop-in centre for addicts in Greenwich Village, a former solicitor, Elizabeth Prather, regularly meets with several other thirty-somethings to talk about their descent into substance abuse.

Elizabeth used to spend eighteen-hour days working on her cases, only to find sleep impossible without imbibing copious amounts of alcohol. Then she encountered Michael Roach (alias Geshe Lobsang) at a Buddhist retreat and found her cure in Buddhism. Now she is putting her impressive intellect toward directing one of the many projects which Roach funds, the Asian Classics Input Project, which is placing all the Tibetan Buddhist texts on CD-ROM. It's a long way from the high-flying life of the legal eagle, but for Elizabeth the full-time spiritual path came just in time.

Frank Schwartz had a similar dependence on alcohol, threatening his life and livelihood as a real-estate broker in Manhattan. He had other pressures to deal with as well, being a Black American with a Catholic mother and raised Jewish by his father. The answer to his identity crisis, the tensions of one of the most cut-throat jobs in New York City and his heavy drinking was Buddhist meditation, which he now prefers to martinis and teaches to others in the Three Jewels drop-in centre.

Western Buddhists on the whole prefer their well-cut clothes and good jobs to saffron robes and begging bowls. This has obvious benefits for the monks in Dharamsala and elsewhere who rely on their financial support. No-one understands the necessity of this relationship better than Robert Thurman, co-founder and President of Tibet House in New York City, one of a network of organisations under the patronage of the Dalai Lama dedicated to preserving the spiritual and artistic heritage of Tibetan culture. Thurman's relationship to Tibet's exiled leader goes back a long way, when he was the first Westerner to be ordained in the Tibetan Buddhist tradition by the Dalai Lama, in 1965. He also has the dubious distinction of having given up the monastic life for a beautiful woman, who then became his wife. Thurman did not give up his interest in Buddhism, however, and completed his studies at Harvard, and went on to become a scholar of repute at Columbia University. Now retired, Thurman is a full-time champion of the free Tibet cause, and raises money on behalf of the Dalai Lama. He admits that there is no better way of doing this than taking advantage of celebrity Buddhists, the most well known being Richard Gere, who attracts media interest and the financial donations of the public. The father of film star Uma Thurman, Robert Thurman has not been far from the limelight, but he insists that high-profile Buddhists are one thing, and 'real Buddhists', true to the exacting demands of the tradition, are few and far between in the West.

An exuberant person with a delightful sense of humour and a legendary capacity to say the unexpected, Thurman is perplexing for his purist stand on Buddhism, by which he champions celibacy and dismisses notions of a Westernised and demythologised Buddhism of the sort that Stephen Batchelor advances. Exchanging views on a panel with Zen priest John Daido Loori Roshi at a conference in New York on 30 June 2001, Thurman insisted that celibacy was an essential part, not an 'optional extra' of the true Buddhist life. In this, Thurman might have been insinuating that the Roshi's Zen Buddhism, which allows married priests and is known for its emphasis on simplicity, 'ordinary mind' and meditation, is inferior to the Tibetan monastic tradition, particularly the Galug lineage of the Dalai Lama, which entails rigorous scholastic debate and elaborate mythological belief systems.

As for Thurman's Buddhist practice, he falls clearly in the outer circle of the 'household' who, unlike the monk, is a long way from enlightenment and rebirth as a Buddha. In a conversation with me in Tibet House, Thurman argued that being Buddhist was not just about adopting a few religious practices or magical tricks or beliefs, as he alleges is the case with many Westerners who are enamoured with Tibetan Buddhism's exotic tradition. For Thurman, who has a profound academic knowledge of the tradition, being a true Buddhist consists of an entirely different outlook that incorporates radical compassion, reincarnation and mysticism as well as a different scientific and practical vision of life. All this, he claims, would greatly improve the world, which he believes is rapidly destroying itself with over-population, militarism and technological and economic progress. Thurman's is an apocalyptic vision of the West, but his affable personality and ready laughter gives one the impression that he only half means it. In fact when he makes the improbable recommendation that we should all take up the monastic life to curb the population explosion or, at the very least, to follow the example of ex-monks and ex-nuns who make gentle parents when they finally get around to leaving the *sangha* and having children, one gets the impression that Thurman is a fluid thinker. And while he is critical of Batchelor's denuded form of Buddhism, at an earlier conference in Berkeley, California, Thurman made it clear that Westerners do not have to be Buddhists to benefit from the general outlook that the tradition offers, a view which is certainly in line with what the Dalai Lama teaches his Western audiences. 'Buddhism,' said Thurman, 'is a therapy the Buddha elaborated for demented human beings,' who suffer primarily from selfishness.[10]

Perhaps because of that overwhelming tendency to individualism, Thurman's hope for the West to become thoroughly monastic is no closer to being fulfilled than the Christian hope that churches will be full to brimming every Sunday.

Nor does it seem very practical, as monastics are forbidden to touch money, indulge in entertainments and luxuries, and for the most part be gainfully employed. Although there are exceptions like Michael Roach, living in the mainstream defeats the purpose of monastic life, which entails devotion to study and service. Yet even this traditional ideal is gradually changing with the advent of an outlook that challenges the notion of the secluded life. 'Engaged Buddhism' was originated by the Vietnamese Zen Buddhist monk Thic Nhat Hanh, who roused his fellow monks and about 10 000 student volunteers to social action during the 1960s, through an organisation he founded called the School of Youth for Social Services, which set up schools and medical centres and organised agricultural co-operatives. Subsequently exiled from Vietnam, Thic Nhat Hanh travelled to the United States and persuaded Martin Luther King to oppose the Vietnam War. Continuing his political campaign, he later headed the Buddhist delegation to the Paris Peace Talks.

Although Thic Nhat Hanh has lived for many years in Plum Village, an idyllic religious community in the south of France, his original example was a defiant rejection of the passive culture that dominated Buddhist monks and made them easy targets for militant regimes. Today Engaged Buddhism is more popular amongst Western Buddhists, for whom it is a grab-bag term that covers a host of activities from genuine compassionate service, such as visiting prisoners and helping the homeless, to offering classes, publications, various therapies, and retreats for paying customers. Although Engaged Buddhism is shorthand for Buddhists who take their message and practice into the world in order to improve it, one could be excused for thinking that it is sometimes a pretext for raising money. But as Michael Roach says there is nothing spiritually unclean about making money, and in the West it is difficult to imagine religious life without it.

Despite the reformative aims of Buddhists like Jack Kornfield and his colleagues at Spirit Rock, who want to see Buddhism democratised, feminised and integrated into the mainstream of life and society, without which they do not see it as viable in the West, there are those who are committed to keeping the ancient tradition alive at all costs. For them, an adulteration of Buddhism would be no Buddhism at all. They have enthusiastically donned the saffron robes and picked up the begging bowls of the forest-dwelling tradition of Theravada Buddhism. At the Wat Buddha Dharma retreat on the outskirts of Sydney, Australia, one is likely to encounter one or two such dedicated monks or nuns, who spend most of their hours and days in solitary contemplation, each in their own *kuti*, or tiny hut, in the bush. For Sister Thanasanti, an American who trained in the forest-dwelling tradition of Ajahn Cha of Thailand and who lived for some years in its community in England, the journey to Eastern spirituality was forged, like so many others, during a trip to India, where she discovered that even in the grip of unfamiliar and dangerous circumstances a calm countenance and some concentrated meditation could save one's life — in her case, delivering her from a near-fatal encounter with a bear, whose scar still shows on her closely shorn skull.

Although Sister Thanasanti is characteristically modest about the miracle of surviving the bear, there is a fundamental truth which, in retrospect, it signifies for her: living the Buddha's teaching renders all external threats meaningless and void. Indeed, from the Buddhist perspective there really are no external threats, for there is no dualism of inner and outer existence. Given this classic Buddhist view, it is no wonder that Sister Thanasanti told me that the dream she hopes to fulfil one day is literally to go on the road with begging bowl in hand, and live as the Buddha did 2500 years ago.

While it is a logical extension of the Buddha's teaching, there is little doubt that the prospect of living such a dependent and precarious existence sits uncomfortably in the West where monks and nuns of Catholic orders are expected to be self-sufficient and most are fully integrated with society, providing much-needed services like education, social welfare and health care. Regardless of the value of the wisdom she might dispense along the way, an itinerant nun, dependent on the charity of strangers, is not a model of the religious life cherished in the West, and would be regarded not only as a folly but also as shirking her personal and social responsibilities. The reality is that she would be welcome mainly in the Buddhist communities that recognised the value of her teaching and the significance of her life of renunciation.

Renouncing material possessions, the hallmark of the unencumbered life that the Buddha lived remains, nonetheless, a powerful aspiration for some, perhaps because it is more of an ideal than a reality. Monastic life is no picnic; it's more like a pressure cooker, says Thubten Chodron, a former married teacher in California turned Tibetan Buddhist nun. A Buddhist for twenty-five years, Thubten is frank about the tough practice of living in close quarters with people she would never otherwise choose to spend time with. But it was a price worth paying, it seems, for the nun previously known as Cherry Green, who at age twenty-five attended a meditation course given by the Venerables Lama Yeshe and Zopa Rinpoche that would dramatically change her life. It was 1975 and for the young woman facing a future of teaching children in a suburban Los Angeles school, Tibetan Buddhism opened up a whole new world of possibilities. She went off to Nepal to study and by 1977 received ordination as a novice. Less than ten years later she took full ordination in Taiwan, which has revived the ancient practice of ordaining Buddhist nuns on par with monks. For the past twenty-five years Thubten Chodron has developed her teaching and leadership skills in Buddhist centres around the world, including India, France, Italy, Singapore and America.

Thubten believes that Buddhism, apart from providing a rich and exciting life, has helped her become a kinder person, and through systematic inquiry and practice she says she has come closer to the ideal espoused in the Bible of loving one's neighbour as oneself. For nine years, from her base in Seattle, Washington, Thubten travelled, wrote and taught a local group, which gathered once or twice a week for meditation and in exchange brought her food and donations. Although this may seem like the fulfilment of a traditional Buddhist life, she told me on my visit there in 2001 that she was looking forward to founding an American monastery where significant reforms would be evident, such as total gender equality, overturning centuries of Tibetan tradition in which nuns cooked and cleaned for monks, who spent their time studying. The planned monastery would be based on an ecumenical approach, which would involve monks from non-Tibetan Buddhist traditions. In February 2002 that vision began to be realised when she moved to St Louis, Missouri to start Sravasti Abbey at Liberation Park, described on its website as an innovative yet traditional Buddhist monastery, based on total gender equality and catering to the three major traditions of Theravada, Vajrayana (Tibetan) and Mahayana Buddhism. It is only a matter of time before this experimental pluralism effects changes in the traditions themselves.

Western Buddhists bound on reform frequently note that the tradition has always adapted to different cultures and times. It is a handy argument that has been used to jettison cultural accretions that are deemed unsuitable or no longer viable. The Dalai Lama himself has led the way, seeing fit to dispense with much of the ceremony accorded his position as the religious and political head of Tibet. Indeed, his insistence that the practical teachings of Buddhism can be disseminated to the West without imposing additional religious beliefs and customs is another demonstration of the separation of the core philosophical teachings from Buddhism's religious heritage. Yet for Thubten Chodron, as indeed for all Western reformers of Buddhism, the claim that the tradition has been subject to cultural overlays, which have included superstitious beliefs in magical deities (as in Tibetan Buddhism), is a claim that already announces its intention. The removal of some of those accretions makes way for their substitution by other more compatible and modern cultural forms. Democratic values, egalitarianism and a Western penchant for ecumenical cross-fertilisation are making their imprint on the Buddhism that is becoming the spiritual path that many new believers choose to follow in the West.

6. RENEWING JUDAISM
Jubus and Kabbalah

Twenty-five people, most of them women, gathered on a Sunday morning to participate in a retreat that began with each one sharing what spirituality meant to them. 'Intensely experiential,' said one; 'Connected to all of creation,' said another; 'Lifting the veil on my inner self,' said someone else. Qualities like stillness, clarity, peace and trust were mentioned by most of those present, as was the practice of meditation, but only one person equated spirituality with 'the love of God', and no-one mentioned the synagogue.

This omission did not go unnoticed by the leader of the Jewish Renewal retreat, and it demonstrated precisely why he was there. Robert Esformes knows all about the other kind of retreat—from Judaism—that has claimed many of the tradition's best and brightest over the last thirty years. In the 1970s, he was one of them, beating a hot trail to Zen Buddhism where his spiritual ardour and his intellectual curiosity found much food for his soul. Eventually, however, he found himself unsuited to the austere rigours of Zen, which, he said, strangled his emotional nature and his musical talents.

They were more suited to his becoming a cantor, singing the melodious prayers of the Jewish tradition. But it would not be the Jewish tradition of his parents' generation, whose hallmark was a suburban focus on lavish weddings and bar mitzvahs, capped off by the annual rush to the synagogue on the high holy days of Rosh Hashanah (Jewish New Year) and Yom Kippur (Day of Atonement). Having already experienced the altered consciousness of Zen meditation, Robert Esformes would search for the same sense of 'at-one-ment' in his practice of Judaism, and he found it in a contemporary expression of the faith.

Drawing heavily on the kabbalistic mystical tradition of Judaism, the spiritual practices of Eastern wisdom, especially Buddhism, and the large musical repertoire of Hassidic and Sephardic Judaism, Robert is now an exponent of Jewish Renewal or what has been called 'post-denominational Judaism'. It is a controversial movement that even some defenders of a more liberal expression of the faith, like Rabbi Dov Marmur, the international head of Progressive Judaism, do not accept, on the grounds that it is an 'excuse' to 'do your own thing', a kind of 'New Age Judaism'. But Marmur's view has the ring of an older generation, now in its seventies, for whom the survival of Judaism after the Holocaust was its single greatest achievement, not to be undermined by newfangled 'alien' importations, but supported through mainstream developments, such as feminisation of the clergy. Nonetheless, female rabbis did not prove to be enough for many of the spiritual seekers growing up in the cultural revolution of the 1960s and 1970s, who were uncomfortable with the rigidly defined denominational boundaries of Judaism, which kept Jews apart from each other and from other faiths.

The Jewish people make up only about 14 million worldwide, but their religion is divided into several major and some minor denominational expressions. Orthodox, Conservative and Liberal (including Reform and Reconstructionist) are the major ones, followed by Hassidic (often called ultra-Orthodox), of which there are several groups, the most well known being the Lubavitchers. There are also two major cultural expressions of the faith, each with its own liturgy, which have histories going back over a thousand years. Sephardic Judaism originated in the Spanish, North African and Middle Eastern communities, but also extended into India, while the Ashkenazic tradition emerged first in Germany and France, and spread to all of Europe and the New World. All these denominations and cultural identities coexist wherever Jews have settled, but that coexistence is sometimes uneasy. At its worst, Hassidic groups in New York and Montreal have been known to get into serious fights with each other and with other Jewish denominations, involving personal assault and the destruction of property. Orthodox and Reform Jews have such major differences in their approach to the binding nature of ritual and legal observances that for years their rabbis would not even appear on the same platform at a communal event. Sephardic Jews are appreciated for their music and other cultural forms, but they are often alienated from the largely Eurocentric Western communities, whose experience of the Holocaust most of the Sephardies do not share.

All these denominational differences and cultural identities of Judaism, which thrived in the post-war free societies of the West, would soon be in for a challenge they could never have anticipated. Unprecedented affluence, university education and the Vietnam War conspired to create a whole new generation of young people in America in the 1960s whose expectations were raised — but then let down with the prospect of dying for a cause they did not believe in. For others, it was not dying in a war that threatened their future, but the idea of suffering a spiritual death in the suburbs, resigning themselves to a hollow existence where they would go through the motions but not connect to the deeper meaning of living a Jewish life. They felt cheated and frustrated and were prepared to sweep aside the middle-class suburban lifestyle, which their parents had laboured to establish, for an alternate one they would fashion for themselves. The synagogue was part of the suburban idyll they rejected and, just like the parish church, it seemed far removed from the new religious ferment that was bubbling up on campuses across the English-speaking West.

That ferment came in the form of new religious movements, many of which were home-grown cults, while others were created by Indian or East Asian holy men who brought their ancient traditions' teachings of inner peace to a generation looking for an alternative to the peace marches that often turned into violent and destructive confrontations with the police. The sheer danger of political activism scared many young people away from the revolutionary cause, and prompted them to adopt an alternative ideology that promised to bring peace to the world — but from within: 'Change yourself and change the world.'[1] This is after all a traditional religious view, but there was little inspiration to be found in the suburban religious communities. College campuses comprised the most fertile mission-field for Asian holy men, and Jews, who were disproportionately university educated, would be among the most enthusiastic students of the Eastern traditions. Amongst the literati, Allen Ginsberg, the self-proclaimed 'Buddhist Jew', was certainly the most outrageous proponent of Buddhism, which at that time he largely conveyed through his poetry. It was when another pop culture phenomenon turned to the East, however, that the floodgates were really thrown open. The Beatles' adoption of Maharishi Mahesh Yogi as their spiritual mentor, and George Harrison's devotion to the Hare Krishna sect, gave popular expression to a development that was already taking shape in zendos, ashrams and university classrooms in the West.

The extraordinary involvement of Jews in Buddhism and Buddhist studies is frequently remarked upon, and has recently been the subject of a film by Bill Chayes, *Jews and Buddhism, Belief Amended, Faith Revealed*. Explanations range from the extensive presence of Jews in university life to their interest in a religious tradition that had no history of anti-Semitism. Both of these are undoubtedly important, but the affinity may have as much to do with the teachings of Buddhism itself. It was a hunch that was put to the test in an unusual event of interreligious dialogue that took place in Dharamsala in1990 between a delegation of Tibetan monks and nuns headed by the Dalai Lama and a collection of rabbis and Jewish scholars organised by an American eye surgeon, Mark Liebermann. The dialogue, which was recounted by Rodger Kamenetz in his book, *The Jew in the Lotus,* was prompted by the recognition that many Western Buddhist scholars and monks were in fact Jewish, known affectionately as 'Jubus' (Jewish Buddhists).

The list of prominent Jubus is very long, but it would start with Charles Strauss, who in 1893 became the first American to proclaim himself a Buddhist publicly, at the Parliament of the World's Religions in Chicago, and went on to become a leading scholar of Buddhism. Towering names in Buddhist scholarship like Alex Wayman, Matthew Kapstein and Robert Thurman of Columbia University come from Jewish backgrounds; so too do Charles Prebish and Steve Heine of Pennsylvania State University, as well as Anne Klein of Rice University. It is estimated that 30 per cent of the faculty in Buddhist studies in America come from Jewish backgrounds, and outside of the academy it is probably greater. Jack Kornfield, Joseph Goldstein, Jacqueline Schwartz and Sharon Salzberg, for example, set up the Insight Meditation Society in Barre, Massachusetts, which is considered one of the most successful Buddhist teaching institutions in America. Jack Kornfield also co-founded Spirit Rock Meditation Center in California with Sylvia Boorstein. The current abbess and abbot of the San Francisco Zen Center, Blanche Hartman and Norman Fisher, also hail from Jewish backgrounds. In the Tibetan tradition, Lama Surya Das (Jeffrey Miller), the first Jew to become a Tibetan lama, and Thubten Chodron (Cherry Green) are influential teachers and authors who travel the world giving lectures and leading retreats. Thubten is particularly interested in interreligious dialogue and was one of several Buddhists from a Jewish background who participated in the momentous event of Jewish–Buddhist dialogue at Dharamsala.

Although all the members of the Jewish delegation were there to learn more about Tibetan Buddhism and in exchange to share their own specific experience of Judaism with the Dalai Lama, it was Rabbi Zalman Schachter-Shalomi, the colourful and inspiring spiritual leader, who seemed to have connected most with the mystical dimension of Tibetan Buddhism. Already renowned for spearheading experimental Jewish communities in the 1960s and possessing an affectionate following that refers to him by the honorific term 'Reb', which traditionally the Hassidim reserve for their spiritual leader, Reb Zalman is the spiritual founder of Jewish Renewal. It is he who has dubbed it 'post-denominational Judaism'. Hailing from a Hassidic Jewish background in Poland, then acting as an outreach worker for the Lubavitcher Hassidim in Brooklyn, it is no wonder that the term comes easily to him. The Hassidic movement of the late eighteenth and nineteenth centuries was itself a revivalist phenomenon, which initially sought to rejuvenate Jewish practice for the masses by stressing the importance of joyful prayer and loving kindness over the meticulous observance of Jewish law. Hassidic Judaism achieved this by unlocking the door to profound mystical experience through the esoteric teachings of the Kabbalah (previously reserved exclusively for married men over the age of forty who were thoroughly versed in Torah study). It also had a genius for conveying its teachings through simple, often affecting and humorous stories, which were far more accessible to the Jewish populace than the learned forms of argument and analysis that characterised Torah study in the *yeshiva* (the Jewish seminary).

But all good things pass, and the openness, which characterised Hassidism's origins is largely lost to the modern era, and Hassidic groups (which formed around 'lineages' of famous rabbis) have become rigid, ultra-orthodox, and are largely rivals to each other — when they are not sworn enemies to the rest of Jewry whom they consider to be so far from the law as to be virtually apostates. Nothing could be further from the outlook of Reb Zalman, who has always cherished the freedom and personal focus that marked the teachings of the Bal Shem Tov (1700–60), the miracle-worker and storyteller who founded the mystical sect known as Hassidism. It would be a freedom that would cost Reb Zalman his affiliation with the Lubavitchers, who severed ties with him when his youthful experimentation involved the use of forbidden drugs and explorations into non-Jewish mysticism. So it was with some relish and a certain degree of familiarity that Reb Zalman anticipated his meeting with the Dalai Lama to talk about the Kabbalah and to learn from him about Tantra, the esoteric tradition of Tibetan Buddhism.

In one exchange with the Dalai Lama, Reb Zalman compared the Buddhist goal of becoming a *bodhisattva*, a living buddha, with the kabbalistic aim of nearness to God. While the Buddhists begin with a concept of the mind and its relationship to suffering, mystical Judaism begins with a cosmology which is directly linked to the unpronounceable Hebrew name of God, YHVH, each consonant being related to one of the four elements of fire, air, water and earth, and each of those being related to one of the four worlds of spirit, mind, heart and body, and in turn related to celestial realms, and so on. Specific meditations are used to direct prayers to each of the realms, and fervent prayer achieves its highest expression when it is done with *kavvanah*, a deep intention. As Reb Zalman related these ideas he mentioned angels, and it was then that the Dalai Lama's interest was obviously piqued. He questioned Reb Zalman on the elaborate angel-filled cosmology of mystical Judaism, which has parallels with the pantheon of Tibetan *devas*, or gods and goddesses. On the other hand, when it came to the Jewish belief in God the Creator, the seeming clash with Buddhism, which does not accept a creator, was not as had been expected. In mystical Judaism the highest realm of nearness to God, *atziluth,* is both full of God and is empty, because God is not a thing. God is referred to as *ain sof,* or no limit, but is also referred to as *ayin,* nothing. Here the Dalai Lama said there was 'a point of similarity' to the Buddhist concept of *shunyata*, emptiness, which is the fundamental basis of existence.[2]

It is always perilous to make simple comparisons between beliefs found in different traditions, because invariably they have evolved out of unique histories and systems of thought, even if they may have shared a common origin. (The six-pointed star, for example, which originated in Mesopotamia as a fertility symbol, is also found in Tibetan Tantric Buddhism as representative of the cervix, and in the late Middle Ages as the Jewish sign of King David's shield.) Yet there is within mystical Judaism much that has affinities with Buddhism, such as the complex kabbalistic male–female sexual symbolism that has parallels in Tantra, and more generally the Jewish belief in the transmigration of souls that has some similarity to the Buddhist belief in reincarnation. As Reb Zalman put it, the goal of the Jewish mystic is to achieve 'the annihilation of the personal, to be totally drawn in to the being of God,' which may be achieved over several lifetimes or reincarnations.[3]

It must be said that reincarnation, sexual symbolism, angels and the *ain sof* are not part of mainstream, common garden variety Judaism. After the Holocaust, which wiped out virtually all of the communities of Europe as well as the study houses that were steeped in Hassidic and kabbalistic lore, Jews became bent on survival in the present world. That meant a focus on issues like fighting for Israel's existence, securing the freedom of Soviet Jews and preserving Jewish communal life in the face of anti-Semitism and growing rates of intermarriage. It has been a hard road and one that has required vigilance and courage. But for Jews who have not been comfortable with a focus on community politics, and indeed have wished to escape from them, the non-political focus and the personal mysticism of Eastern traditions have been alluring. For them, the road back to Judaism, if they choose to take it, is paved with the teachings of the Kabbalah, as well as an acceptance of truths found in the mystical yearnings and insights of other traditions.

That was how it was for Robert Esformes and most of the people attending his Jewish Renewal retreat in Sydney. Their experiences of Buddhist, Sufi and Yogic practices marked them out as people who would agree with the late Buddhist teacher Chogyam Trungpa Rinpoche, who said that 'spiritual practices are not patented,' but available to all to reach spiritual states. Nonetheless, most of them were there specifically to reconnect to the Jewish tradition in a way that built upon their previous experiences, and Esformes was able to guide them with the ease of someone who had been through it all himself. Talking to the group about the meaning of spirituality, he dwelt on the notion of reaching above oneself to the Source, a term he preferred to God, because of its connotation of a wellspring of potential, containing 'what was, what is and what will be'. The idea of connecting to the Source suggested the Sanskrit word *yog*, to connect, the basis of yoga practice. Continuing on this theme, Esformes referred to the Jewish practice of keeping the *mitzvot*, the commandments, which, according to the Hassidic mystical tradition, connect one to the supernal world, because with each act one lifts the divine sparks which fell during creation back to the Creator whence they came. Robert Esformes presents the spiritual insights of Jewish religious life in a way that breaks the unsaid rule of keeping Judaism entirely apart from other traditions to preserve its purity and uniqueness. On the contrary, he seems to contribute to its truths by reference to other traditions, and by so doing reinforces its claim to universality.

One of the hallmarks of the Jewish synagogue service is that it does not vary: the same prayers are said every day, and the services for festivals and holy days do not waver from year to year. There is a tremendous sense of continuity in the knowledge that one is praying using the same Hebrew words as one's forefathers and foremothers. But it can also turn into a ritual by rote, in which one thoughtlessly repeats the words, with little sense of their meaning. For many people who walked away from the synagogue, never to return, it was this sameness that repelled them, and the knowledge that neither they nor anyone else would be able to contribute something new to the service. Jewish Renewal is different. When Cantor Esformes leads a service on Shabbat, he does not tie himself to a prayer book nor exactly follow a set service. He might include a Hassidic story, a teaching from the Kabbalah, or even a poem written by a non-Jew, like William Blake or Elizabeth Barrett Browning. The music is a mixture of Sephardic, Ashkenazic and contemporary melodies, and one might chant the psalms while sitting cross-legged on a cushion, Buddhist style. Hebrew is stressed as the sacred tongue, but is not employed exclusively. It is always used, however, in the most sacred prayer of Judaism, the Sh'ma, which is the succinct declaration of faith in the God 'Who is One'. In Jewish Renewal it has become a much-loved mantra for Jewish meditation. There is a sense that in adaptations like this, the Jewish tradition is rich, strong and welcoming of the many creative ways whereby one might experience and express its essential truths.

The Jewish people are known as the People of the Book. They also like to describe themselves as argumentative, a trait that is enshrined in the Talmud, where rabbis exchange views on what is the proper interpretation of a biblical word or phrase, and often agree to disagree. 'Two people, three opinions,' is both a joke and a truth, and its opposite, having nothing to say or no question to ask, is never seen as a worthwhile attribute. It is a view that is reinforced every year on the first night of the family celebration of Passover, when every child learns about the four sons: the wise son, the wicked son, the simple son and the 'son who wits not to ask' — in descending order; it is the one without a question who is the least of them and to whom the parents are instructed to give their concerted attention. The intellect plays a leading role in the formation of the Jewish religious consciousness, and it is in the Jewish seminary, the *yeshiva*, that a young man learns to memorise large portions of Jewish commentary and to argue legal or ethical points like the great rabbis of old. But this ideal holds less attraction to Jews who have experienced another kind of knowing, another state of consciousness, which lies in the path of silence. For some proponents of Jewish Renewal, it was the experience of long silent retreats, particularly the intense, ten hour a day silent meditation of the Vipassana school of Buddhist meditation, that opened up new depths of awareness. This was how it happened for Rabbi David Cooper, now one of the leading figures in Jewish Renewal, whose latest book, *God is a Verb: Kabbalah and the Practice of Mystical Judaism*, is something of a handbook of spiritual exercises, combining meditation and Kabbalah.

On his own account, David Cooper was an upwardly mobile businessman in 1960s San Francisco — an endangered species at a time when Eastern spirituality, the counterculture and every kind of drug were vying for the attention of young people, including those in grey suits. It seems he bit the apple of curiosity and embarked on years of spiritual searching in Buddhism, Hinduism and Sufism. He soon realised that long retreats of meditation and chanting led to experiences that were not contained by the usual modes of intellectual inquiry, but transcended the active mind. He sensed that within these experiences lay 'hidden teachings' that were within his reach. After a forty-day retreat at the age of forty-one (the age at which, according to tradition, married Jewish men are permitted to study the Kabbalah), he decided to immerse himself in Jewish mysticism.[4]

Were this the end of the story, David Cooper would have probably ended up a rabbi serving a community in the Lubavitch Hassidic branch of Judaism, which incorporates a fair amount of kabbalistic mysticism. He did study the complex theoretical metaphysics of Kabbalah, but found them at once fascinating and too abstract. Cooper's long experience of silent meditation pointed him in another direction, one that sought communion with God at an embodied experiential level. Putting to one side the strenuous intellectual activity that was prized in the *yeshiva*, Cooper realised that he was more interested in immersing himself in kabbalistic teachings through contemplative exercises from which mystical insight would arise and suffuse his every moment with the feeling of being surrounded by the Divine Presence. In effect, this is the aim of Jewish Renewal, as originated by Zalman Schachter-Shalomi and carried on by his students and others inspired by his example.

Elat Chayyim is a Jewish Renewal retreat centre in upstate New York, founded by the married couple Rabbi Jeff Roth and Rabbi Joanna Katz. It calls itself 'trans-denominational' rather than post-denominational, perhaps in recognition that the denominational differences in Judaism are here to stay, yet all are welcome to be 'renewed' by the courses and retreats offered by Elat Chayyim. As one of the seventy-five teachers who are listed as faculty, Rabbi David Cooper teaches other rabbis, educators and Jewish leaders how to use meditation as a means of deepening the experience of Jewish observances and personal prayer, as well as how to interweave contemplation into the existing liturgy. This is not as easy as it sounds. The introduction of silent contemplation into Jewish worship is radical. There is only one prayer in the Jewish liturgy that is silent, the Amidah, and it stands out for that reason. Yet silence is positively liberating as well as instructive. Rabbi Sheila Peltz Weinberg, who teaches meditation along with Cooper, described its hidden power, when she noted that 'within the silence the students witnessed the unfolding of Torah, and came up with stirring and magnificent teachings'.[5]

Introducing meditation to Jewish spiritual practice is just one of the ways that the Eastern training and experience of some of the teachers are felt in Jewish Renewal. Another way relates to the dynamic understanding of the individual's relationship to the universe. In Buddhist philosophy, there are no permanent things, just a constant interdependence of elements which are born, live, pass away and are reborn again. The individual is part of this interdependence and impermanence, since every act, every thought, has repercussions that affect the entire scheme of things. 'What goes around comes around,' is the most commonly quoted shorthand version of the Buddhist notion of reincarnation. What one thinks and does has cosmic effects, including determining one's rebirth. Not surprisingly, David Cooper writes in a similar vein about kabbalists, who teach that:

> ... everything we do stirs up a corresponding energy in other realms of reality. Actions, words or thoughts set up reverberations in the universe. The universe unfolds from moment to moment as a function of all the variables leading up to that moment. When we remain cognizant of this mystical system, we are careful about what we do, say or even think, for we know that everything is interdependent.[6]

This is a profoundly ecological spirituality, in which the human's impact on creation is a given, and every act must be mindful of the responsibility which goes with that knowledge. Like many contemporary Buddhists who like to mention scientific evidence for their beliefs, Cooper cites the discoveries of chaos theory, particularly the 'butterfly effect', whereby a seemingly innocuous movement of a butterfly's wing causes changes in the atmosphere resulting in a typhoon somewhere else. The mystic's tremendous attraction to chaos theory is perhaps an echo of the alchemist's much sought union of science and spirituality. Just as chaos theory has added a whole new dimension to our scientific understanding of reality as a constantly changing energy field, so does mysticism promise an astonishing new revelation about the nature of the world and our place in it.

> In Jewish mysticism, the instant we open our eyes to the true dimensions of creation and causality we find ourselves immersed in a sea of miracles ... At any instant, creation might unfold in a way that would be disastrous for us; therefore, each moment is bursting with the gift of life. Indeed, as a result of this awareness, the mystic loves life intensely and feels loved by it.[7]

The idea that life is a 'sea of miracles' in which we are born, and in which our actions can cause further miracles is not only a joyous outlook, but also a dynamic one. It is buttressed by the notion, first coined by Reb Zalman Schachter-Shalomi, that 'God is a verb'. In the same way that every part of the universe is in an active relationship with every other part, so too is God, who answers the call of the petitioner the moment it is spoken. God is a process, not a thing or a being. Rather than a God that simply exists somewhere, one can speak of God-ing, which entails an all-pervasive presence with which we have contact, an interdependent relationship between the individual and the divine.[8]

Just how that relationship is best served is the real focus of the religious life. Most traditions, and Judaism is no exception, dispense to each member something approximating a set of instructions on how to fulfil one's duties. From this perspective it is not God who is a verb, but the Jewish person. He is told to attend synagogue, keep the 613 *mitzvot* (the commandments that according to Jewish tradition are contained in the Torah) and keep the Jewish people going by making sure his spouse is Jewish and, it goes without saying, his children as well. The Jewish person is not only a very busy verb, but is also a transitive verb, one whose actions are directed to the remote object of God, performing according to his wishes, sending prayers in God's direction in the hope they will be heard. That, at any rate, is the conventional understanding, and it is not particularly conducive to an experience of intimacy between the believer and the Lord (*adonai* in Hebrew), a term, incidentally, that Jewish Renewal has largely dropped from its prayers because of its patriarchal connotation of 'overlord'.

The gulf between God and man in traditional Jewish practice could not be more at odds with the popular contemporary notion of divinity which sees God in the self. It is against this backdrop of spiritual alienation that one must see the significance of David Cooper's teaching. But one does not need to be a member of Jewish Renewal to sound the same note. The immensely popular author Lawrence Kushner, who has been a Reform rabbi for thirty years, has sought to bridge the gap between God and the individual by mining the mystical tradition of the Zohar and the Hassidic masters, and discovering there not just an intimacy but the very nexus of humanity and the divine. Paraphrasing one of the great sixteenth-century mystics, Kushner notes, 'God not only hears our prayers, God says them also.'[9]

The voice that speaks 'from the highest heavens and from the inner chambers of the self,' Kushner explains, is actually the One on account of whom we hear God say, 'I am . . .'[10] The separation between the individual and the divine actually closes altogether in the following interpretation of the Bal Shem Tov's teaching, in which Kushner relates a radically mystical, yet at the same time human-centred, understanding of the Messiah: 'The coming of the Messiah does not depend upon anything supernatural, but rather upon human growth and self-transformation . . . The world will only be transformed . . . when people realise that the Messiah is not someone wholly other than themselves.'[11]

In Jewish tradition the Messiah, which means 'the anointed one', the king who will usher in the Kingdom of God, still tarries, on account of the unreadiness of the Jewish people, who have yet to live up to the full measure of the law which was given to them at Sinai. Kushner takes a slightly different view of this chastening rabbinic interpretation, which enjoins the fulfilment of all the 613 *mitzvot*, or commandments, in the Torah. Kushner says it is not a matter of *doing* enough, it is a matter of *awakening* to ourselves. It is a matter of gaining God-consciousness.

> The more we become aware, the more we realise that we are in everything and everything is in us. The One we call the Holy One and the ones the Holy One calls us are the same beings, seen from different sides ... The question is not 'who makes who real?' People making God or God making people—for both make each other come to be. Both are One. *Yehido shel Olam.* The Only One of the Universe ... From the first person to the last person. From even you and me. Protoplasm and consciousness aware of their common source.[12]

It is fitting that the contemporary kabbalistic outlook stresses the importance of becoming aware of the depth and the breadth of God's presence, since it is imagined as a dynamic and changing presence. To be sure, the kabbalists developed a host of different theories about God's role in the process of creation, but as outlined by kabbalistic scholar Shimon Shokek in a series of lectures at the Smithsonian Institute in Washington,[13] creation is an ever-widening expression of God's desire to manifest. Shokek describes a gradual unfolding of the mind of God, in which God yearns to move from concealment to revelation, from the infinite state to the finite state, and from nothingness into being. As he puts it, 'It is God's *ambition* to be in partnership with His creation and creatures.'[14] Creation is, above all, an act of love, and kabbalists imagine that the fitting response to the Creator and to creation is also love. The eleventh-century Jewish classic, *The Duties of the Heart*, by Rabbi Bachya Ibn Paquda, put it this way: 'Love is the *telos*, the final aim of all noble qualities and the highest degree which men who worship God may achieve ... Beyond it there is no further stage and above it no further rank.'[15]

In kabbalistic thought the soul of man is female and is carved from the heavenly world, to which she longs to return. Bachya asks, 'What is Love of God? It is the soul's longing for the Creator, and turning to Him, so that she communes with His elevated Light ... she will turn to Him and commune with Him in her thought, and contemplate Him through her ideas, and cleave to Him and desire Him. This is the ultimate pure love.'[16]

It is in this dynamic circle of love from Creator to creation and from creation back to Creator that the new interpreters of the Kabbalah seek its lessons for the contemporary world. Today there are more than fifty Kabbalah Centers in North America and around the world founded by Rabbi Philip Berg and his sons Yehuda and Michael Berg. Although they have been the object of controversy and protest, especially by Lubavitcher Hassidim, who claim they distort Jewish teachings, and by others who have gone on record saying that they are essentially a big business masquerading as a religious organisation,[17] the Kabbalah Centers have nonetheless been highly influential in popularising some of the concepts of Judaism's hidden mystical tradition. The Beverley Hills location of the Kabbalah Learning Center has surely raised its stakes when stars like Madonna and Courtney Love are named among its students. Indeed, the endorsements emblazoned on Michael Berg's latest book, *The Way*, by Madonna and TV star Roseanne Barr are sure to boost sales.

But the wider appeal of this brand of Jewish mysticism is also owed to the fact that kabbalistic concepts frequently appear in occult publications on the tarot and witchcraft, and have a long history in non-Jewish esoteric circles, beginning in the fifteenth century under the influence of Giovanni Pico della Mirandola (1463–94) one of the leading minds of the early Renaissance. The scholar Robert Fludd (1574–1637), the mystic Jacob Boehme (1575–1624) and the author of *Kabbalah Denudata*, Knorr von Rosenroth (1636–89) are well-known occultists who adapted Jewish Kabbalah into a Christian version known as Christian Cabbala.

There is little doubt that the attraction to Kabbalah as a universal teaching lies in its focus on the act of creation, which predates the turmoil of religious history and the man-made institutions which have divided humanity against itself. Even the Bible is read by kabbalists in a way that lifts the veil on the human dramas it recounts, in order to reveal a hidden meaning which displays a transcendental unity and a healing quality that are not apparent to the ordinary reader. Rodger Kamenetz, who wrote *Gathering the Sparks* about his own quest for meaning in Kabbalah, finds in the mystical writings of early kabbalists a message far superior to that which the more analytical students of the Bible could offer:

> I know that the reading of Torah and Bible that we have inherited from the 19th Century 'higher criticism' is less interesting and perceptive and whole than the reading of Torah we get from a kabbalist like Gikatilla of the 13th Century ... I know that the scholarly intellectual way of reading Torah so common today only breaks the text down into bits, and that there's a deeper way of reading: a way that performs a *tikkun* [mending] on the text, and finds the light hidden in the text. I know this from Kabbalah.[18]

Returning to the primordial drama, before the existence of time and space, the kabbalistic imagination is fantastic as well as aesthetic. In his book *The Way: Using the Wisdom of Kabbalah for Spiritual Transformation and Fulfillment*, Michael Berg recounts the story of how the universe came into being as told in the *Zohar*, the Book of Splendour, which is the most important book of the kabbalistic tradition of Jewish mysticism. It is an elaborate story about what occurred before the first words of Genesis: 'In the beginning'. Then, God was manifest as an infinite positive energy, Light, *Or* in Hebrew, which we are told is a code word for divine love.[19] The Light wished to share its bounty and created a Vessel, which received the Light. The Vessel longed to become one with the Creator, but it could only receive the Light. Frustrated, it pushed back against the Creator, which abruptly drew back its Light, leaving the Vessel in total darkness. The withdrawal of the Light was indescribably painful, and the Vessel wanted it back. The Light then rushed back with full force in a single moment, and at that instant the Vessel shattered into an infinite number of fragments, which became the universe. Fanciful as this may seem, Berg reminds us of its parallels with the now widely accepted big-bang theory of creation.[20]

Whether or not the kabbalistic theory of the origins of the universe has scientific merit (a view that frequently appears in mystical circles, and one that Zalman Schachter-Shalomi also believes),[21] as a mystical teaching its purpose is spiritual and practical. Just which practical teachings will be drawn from its vast and highly complex theoretical speculations is wide open, however, and Michael Berg simplifies them to a couple of basic principles. First, that the duality of giving and receiving is the fundamental basis of being. Secondly, that as parts of creation, human beings carry the sparks of Light, which were cast asunder and whose only wish is to return and unify with the Creator. This is achieved through the acts of giving and sharing, the very things that the Vessel was not able to do. According to Berg, it is this teaching alone which must become the paradigm for how to live, and which is the true foundation of happiness. It is entirely counter to a prevalent ethic of society, which is to *get* things and *get* love. Berg argues that this self-serving desire, although part of human nature, is what cuts one off from the Creator and is the origin of all negativity. Instead, he makes the distinction between receiving for oneself and receiving in order to share. Although his critics would see this ethic as serving the financial interest of the Kabbalah Centers, there is an undeniable virtue in its emphasis on charity, a sacred value in Judaism: 'Kabbalah teaches us and empowers us to integrate the dual aspects of our being that are our legacy from the primordial Vessel by transforming desire to receive for ourselves alone into desire to receive for the purpose of sharing.'[22]

Michael Berg's popular guide to living a life according to Kabbalah even includes a twelve-step program, with echoes of the original by Alcoholics Anonymous, which undoubtedly is based on a premise that most people are addicted to living a life of self-serving desire. The features of trust, of asking for divine assistance and realising that we are always tested recall the challenges that face the addict. Berg's last three steps, however, have a relevance that goes far beyond the life of an addict. Step 10 teaches that death can be used as a motivation, such that envisaging our own deaths reminds us of how little time we have left; indeed, that every day is a 'near death experience'. Step 11 enjoins the individual to imagine the pain of others and to take physical action to help alleviate human suffering. Step 12 implores us to judge ourselves, but not others. Taken together, and in this pared down form, the affinity of these teachings to Buddhism is obvious. The focus on compassion, on not judging others and especially on the daily reminder of our own inevitable death is identical to the Buddhist outlook, and accounts for the fluidity that many new believers experience when their spiritual searches lead them to Buddhism and also to Kabbalah.

This is not to suggest that Michael Berg promotes a Buddhist form of Kabbalah. However, his example suggests the openness of the esoteric teachings of Jewish mysticism to creative interpretations that echo contemporary spiritual preoccupations. 'Mind Yoga' is the trademark of Australian Kabbalah teacher to the stars, Laibl Wolf, who travels the world, including a regular stop in Hollywood, teaching 'spiritual postures of the mind' as a means of gaining self-mastery and a sense of peace. His introductory talks are often elaborate explanations, with the help of projected graphics, which relate kabbalistic concepts (such as the ten *sephirot* or emanations of God) to psychological states or qualities. His long white beard, soft voice and gentle manner, topped off with his trademark black beret, give this educational psychologist a grandfatherly authority that has won him many loyal followers. Mind, body, spirit and the cosmos come together in Laibl Wolf's teachings, and although his book, *Practical Kabbalah: A Guide to Jewish Wisdom for Everyday Life*, boasts an endorsement by the Chief Rabbi of the United Kingdom, Jonathan Sacks, who calls it 'spirituality at its most life-enhancing', like Michael Berg's Kabbalah Centers, you don't have to be Jewish or even religious to benefit from its teachings.

Even Jungian depth psychology, which has often been characterised as having a Christian bias, has been woven into the analysis of the Jewish mystical texts by Shokek in his *Kabbalah and the Art of Being*. Berg, on the other hand, offers spiritual 'tools', ranging from breathing meditation that inspires one to live each moment with renewed commitment to meditation on sacred verses (akin to affirmations), in order to deal with negative emotions such as fear, anger or guilt.[23] David Cooper offers a series of visualisation meditations as a means of awakening to the Divine Presence. The language of personal transformation and unconditional love freely mingles with references to angels, who guide and support one at psychologically vulnerable periods in one's life.

It is this which is the most significant contribution that Kabbalah has made to the contemporary search for the authentic spiritual life — the insistence that there is no place and no part of the world in which God is not present. In the latest scientific discoveries or in last century's psychological insights, in the midst of the secular and in the very substance of nature, there is God. It is not that these newer innovations are inserted into the older mystical tradition, but that whatever humans create they do so against the backdrop of 'what was, what is and what ever will be,' the never absent Divine Presence. We need only open our eyes to it.

7. RE-SOULING PSYCHOLOGY
The Soul is Clinical

When Sigmund Freud wrote *The Future of an Illusion* he confidently asserted that the religious urge would disappear as the scientific world-view took hold. Little would he know how much his own work would contribute to that belief, and then just as swiftly how his heirs would contribute to its undoing. Today psychology and its practitioners are benefiting from the insights that have come to them via Eastern religions, indigenous spirituality and even the mystical traditions of Judaism and Christianity. Spiritual psychology is flourishing precisely because it assumes that the cause of personal anxiety and depression is as much spiritual as it is psychological, and in fact that they are one and the same. Nothing could have been further from the view that the originator of psychoanalysis promoted almost a century ago.

In the early twentieth century, Freud had great cause to predict that in the future religion would go the way of the dodo. Nature's mysteries were being explained by Darwin's descendants, and among their most important discoveries was that evolution went hand in hand with extinction. Species that once thrived on the earth had disappeared to make way for more viable ones. And so it would be with *homo religiosus*. As the new breed of self-styled scientists of the mind, psychoanalysts, revealed the mysteries of the psyche (the old Greek term for the soul), Freud's view, that religious beliefs were destined to be outgrown as the primitive remnants of man's evolution, gained ground. According to Freud, religious mythology had been an attempt by primitive man to gain control over the sensory world, but science was already demonstrating that its consolations deserved no trust. It was a view roundly supported by the burgeoning field of anthropology, which recorded the shamanistic rituals and superstitious beliefs of peoples in the remote parts of the colonial world untouched by modernity. Social scientists, on the other hand, documented the swift demise of religious practice amongst the urban-dwelling and newly affluent bourgeoisie. Freud saw this as the mark of natural progress: 'If one attempts to assign to religion its place in man's evolution, it seems not so much to be a lasting acquisition, as a parallel to the neurosis which the civilized individual must pass through on his way from childhood to maturity.'[1]

Indeed, attachment to religious belief was regarded as similar to obsessional neurosis. They functioned identically, according to Freud, neurosis (characterised by ritualistic behaviour, rules and a fear of breaking them) being akin to a private religious system, and religion being a universal obsessional neurosis.[2]

One cannot blame Freud, and he was surely not alone, for believing that religious beliefs imprisoned the individual in a false consciousness and a warped sense of reality. When Freud was twenty-five, an infamous anti-Semitic case had rocked Europe. Joseph Scharf, a Jew, had been brought to trial in the town of Tisza-Eszlar in Hungary on trumped up charges of murdering a Christian girl for imagined Jewish ritual purposes. This was a reappearance of the medieval Christian 'blood libel' legend, which regularly appeared at Easter in Europe as a pretext for mounting pogroms against Jewish communities and ghettos. The 'blood libel' held that every year at Passover, Jews killed Christian children and used their blood to make unleavened bread. The reappearance of this scurrilous accusation in modern society was a devastating blow to progress, and was accompanied by a rash of anti-Semitic activities, conferences and publications. That Freud showed interest in the psychiatric diagnosis of the chief witness in the trial is evidence he was not unmoved by the affair.[3]

A more primitive expression of religious belief would be hard to find, and it threatened to destroy the new-found freedom of Europe's Jews. It must be remembered that Freud was among the first generation of Austrian Jews who were given citizenship rights on par with their Christian neighbours. It was in Freud's lifetime that Jews were allowed for the first time to live wherever they wished, attend university and acquire public posts, although even these were limited by numeric restrictions. By dint of religion, Jews had been excluded from society, and by dint of a secular humanist ethos enshrined in legislation they were given freedom. Yet how easily was this freedom shattered by the religious delusions of the crowd and their support by the powerful. Near to the end of his life, Freud would experience it for himself, and would flee Nazi Germany on account of an uprising far greater in magnitude and more severe in its consequences for the Jews of Europe than anything that had preceded it. No wonder it seemed eminently more desirable to Freud to imagine a world where religion had been outgrown.

To be sure, there would be other reasons religion would come under fire at the beginning of the twentieth century. In a famous assessment of his former mentor and friend, Carl Jung interpreted Freud's attitude to religion as a vehement reaction to the repressive and moralising Victorian period. Jung suggested that the Victorians had frantically striven to keep alive the high religious principles of the Christian Middle Ages, although these were by then 'anaemic ideals framed in a bourgeois respectability', and already discredited by the French Enlightenment and Revolution. Jung argued that against the Victorian tendency to see everything in a rosy light and to perpetrate 'sentimental frauds, such as parents "who live only for their children"', Freud, like his 'much greater philosophical contemporary, Nietzsche', shattered the glass of respectability and subjected the religious culture of his time to thoroughgoing criticism. Both Freud and Nietzsche squarely blamed religion for many human ills.[4]

What was religious belief but the subjugation of the individual to a mythological invention, no more real than the 'Man in the Moon', who dictated one's values, outlook and behaviour? For Freud the derivation of religion lay in the child's helplessness and subsequent longing for a father, who was then projected into the heavens as God, and who permanently reigned through fear and submission.[5]

In Freud's reckoning the very existence of religion was proof of its infantilism, and only its demise held the promise of maturity. It seemed as if the forces of modernity needed to unseat the Father who Art in Heaven in order to realise the full potential of humanity on earth. But history is full of ironies. As the proverbial saying goes, when people don't believe in God, they don't believe in nothing; on the contrary, they believe in anything—which may account for the enormous interest in mediums, spiritualism and automatic writing precisely at a time when people in the West were falling away from traditional church attendance. In Europe, it would not be long before Freud and many others in the fledgling psychoanalytic movement found themselves not in a freedom-loving society permeated with rational inquiry and humanism but on the run from the most authoritarian regime in living memory, which used Aryan mythology to justify its aims for a *juden-frei* (Jew-free) Europe. God had been unseated by the Great Dictator, Adolf Hitler.

Where did that leave religion? There is little doubt that in America, where there was no such dark awakening to the dangers of a godless society, Freud's scepticism, contained in his short and eloquent essays on the psychological motivations for religious belief, met a ready audience. Freud's unseating of the 'Big Daddy' in the sky dovetailed with a widespread flexing of the muscles of individualism, to throw its weight around in the newly affluent free world. America's large and growing middle class was the perfect clientele for the flourishing trade of psychoanalysis, eagerly accepting the Freudian theory that old time religious conservatism, particularly around sex, was having pathological consequences. Soon a mass of psychoanalytic offshoots was reaching out to a receptive populace. But the religious culture was also keeping pace, often adopting some of the insights and practices of psychology. By the 1960s psychoanalysis was assuming all the attributes of a new religion itself, and the religious terrain had undergone a massive retrenchment. The merging of psychology and religion was inevitable.

Not that religion had been entirely ejected from the psychological paradigm of mental health. Freud's old rival would keep the burning embers of spiritual yearning alive in a way that would prove to be an attractive alternative to conventional religion. Carl Gustav Jung, who had broken with the Viennese founder of psychoanalysis and his circle, believed that Freud's criticism of religion went too far and had thrown out the proverbial baby with the bathwater. Jung, who developed his own rival brand of depth psychology, was a self-declared refugee from an oppressive Swiss Calvinism in which his father was a clergyman. Although Jung condemned in lurid language all expressions of 'repression-religion', for which his consistent term of opprobrium was that it was 'bourgeois', he did not accept that this was necessarily the fate of all religious experience. Unlike Freud, who was a thoroughgoing rationalist, Jung had a lively interest in the paranormal and made extensive studies of the hermetic, alchemical and Eastern traditions, even penning an introduction to *The Tibetan Book of the Dead*. Instead of the Freudian rejection of religion as a distorted emanation of unconscious desires that hindered the process of psychological wellbeing, Jung posited a theory that placed the eternal, immutable and universal 'world soul' at the very heart of the unconscious, without which development into a fully functioning 'whole' person would be impossible. It was a concept that had powerful religious and spiritual connotations.

Briefly put, Jung's notion of the unconscious was entirely different from the personal storehouse of childhood memories and experiences postulated by Freud. In Jungian analytic psychology, the unconscious attains mythic proportions because it contains the inheritance of the whole human species. Labelled the 'collective unconscious', it is pre-personal or transpersonal in that it has causal priority and does not arise out of personal experience, which Jung regarded as largely banal and uninteresting. The contents of the collective unconscious are recovered by deciphering an individual's dreams, which Jung believed were the vehicles that carried the symbols of universal significance and ubiquity that regularly appear in Eastern and occult traditions. Such symbols include the sun-wheel, the challis, the cross, the bent cross (or swastika), the mother-womb and so on, and are referred to as archetypes. Typically, the Jungian analyst guides the client on a journey into the mythic significance of his or her dreams, and in the process the client actively explores the mythic symbolism that is at the heart of all human culture and consciousness.

If it ended there, one might be forgiven for thinking that this was no more than an exercise in introductory symbolic anthropology. But Jung refused to reduce the mythic realm to a scientific category — it could not be confined to rational scientific ways of knowing by virtue of its ineffable and largely mysterious quality. Indeed, Jung's conception of the unconscious contained an assertion of transcendental reality, and his therapy kept alive the notion of the spiritual quest as a path toward wholeness. Also known as the process of 'individuation', the aim was a kind of self-knowing, which was like some ancient form of wisdom, rediscovered once the layers of bourgeois religion had been peeled away. On that account, Jungian therapy was not necessarily the choice of polite moralistic society, but had within it an edginess that often attracted those who had already been delving into the occult or avidly reading the religious texts of Eastern traditions. For Jungians, such clients, usually of middle age or older, were ripe for the analytical explorations that would lead to their psychological and spiritual enlightenment.

Although Freud and Jung were very different in their understanding of religion, both were agreed that its conventional expressions traded on fear and guilt, and that these were largely counterproductive for the individual's psychological wellbeing (although Freud conceded their positive social functions, in maintaining order, for example). In this observation alone, the worlds of religion and psychology meet, the former being the progenitor of the latter. Shaking off religion and its authoritarian hold on the psyche was one solution, and clearly the one that satisfied Freud. Another answer to the problem was to develop an alternative kind of religion, and that to some extent was what Jung offered when he brought the soul into the therapy room and invited his patients on a magical mystery tour of its far-reaching symbolism.[6] For many psychotherapists and their clientele that was a decisive moment in the history of the profession, which went on to develop a variety of new therapies aimed at healing the psychological and spiritual anxieties which threatened the wellbeing of the soul.

One of the leading figures in this burgeoning field is Robert Sardello, who admits that he had to unlearn much of the behavioural psychology he studied as a graduate student, since the concept of the soul, the original meaning of *psyche*, was not part of its lexicon. Sardello co-founded the School of Spiritual Psychology on the combined insights of Jung and Rudolf Steiner, the Austrian clairvoyant and contemporary of Freud and Jung who founded Anthroposophy, the esoteric Christian offshoot of Theosophy. If the scourge of the soul in old-time religion is the ever-present temptation to sin, in this new version of spirituality it is the temptation to be afraid. In one stroke, Sardello furnished the answer to Nietzsche, Freud and Jung, who blamed religion for instilling a crippling fear in its adherents. In a reversal of this formula, a new spirituality is envisaged that achieves the opposite: by banishing fear it emboldens the individual to face the slings and arrows of life. For, make no mistake, instilling fear is not the preserve of religion alone.

Like an itinerant preacher with a kindly demeanour, Sardello writes and teaches extensively on the practical ways to free the soul from fear, which he is convinced is a pervasive malaise of our society, perpetrated by the media, politicians, the business sector — in fact, by just about everything. The spiritual implications of this fear epidemic run to 'contracting the soul' and destroying humanity's ability to engage positively in the world. Like Jung's 'shadow', by which he meant 'the inferior part of the personality'[7], fear is the constant dark companion of the soul, and destroys our sense of who we are. In order to conquer fear, Sardello urges us to enter into it and turn it into a virtue, one that has the power to teach the true meaning of love. Love is the antidote to fear in Sardello's equation. Put simply, he has posited two forces, fear and love, between which the soul must learn to grow, like a plant that benefits from the sun's rays and the moon's light. This may seem a little too neat, like a textbook formula, but Sardello introduces an element of mystery which presupposes a spiritual dimension of humanity: 'Our true humanity also consists of being oriented toward and experiencing the reality of something larger than ourselves — the mystery of otherness, the reality of the sacred, a sense of the holy.'[8]

This version of psychotherapy approaches what might be called a sacred science, if indeed it is any science at all. Its message is essentially psycho-spiritual, in that the ideally functioning human being is the one whose soul participates in the all-encompassing fear of the world and transforms it into a capacity for love, a love that is expansive and that is ultimately an experience of the holy and the sacred. It is the soul in its most natural orientation, poised toward the mystery that is the origin of itself. This view, although influenced by Rudolf Steiner's work, has strong parallels with the fundamental drama of redemption that is imagined by Jewish mystics, in which the soul seeks unity with its Creator by involving the individual in a process of raising up 'holy sparks' from the darkest corners of existence through acts of loving kindness.[9] This is exactly what Sardello imagines to be the ideal therapeutic situation:

> If I were a therapist working with someone, what would the essence of truly helping that person be? To love his soul and look on it without judgment, so that he can experience love without reservation. I would need to enter the darkest regions, the ugliest places, the scariest dimensions of the person's soul, and do so without the slightest bit of judgment or hesitation. Such empathy constitutes an act of redemption.[10]

If this passage has remarkable similarities to the writings of the Hassidic masters of Judaism, then it is also true that Sardello's eclectic thinking echoes other spiritual traditions as well, most particularly Buddhism. This might come as a surprise to anyone who is aware that Buddhism does not have a concept of the soul. Yet the practice of Buddhist meditation, which focuses on cleansing the mind of impurities through contemplation, has an affinity with Sardello's notion of the soul which can be purified of 'negativity', a term that covers a multitude of evils. This is achieved through 'soul work', which consists of being aware of the anger and hatred, for example, that wells up from time to time, and choosing not to act on that feeling, but instead holding on to the images that arise in one's mind. A process occurs in which the heat of the anger and hatred burns itself out, and this is akin to a poison that one absorbs in order to inoculate oneself or to an alchemical process in which substances turn into their opposites. (Here one sees shades of Steiner's interest in alchemy.) Sardello compares this method of neutralising anger in oneself as a way of rising above it to the three poisons identified by the great sixth-century Buddhist teacher, Bodhidharma — greed, anger and delusion — without which one cannot become a Buddha:

> The three realms are greed, anger and delusion. To leave the three realms means to go from greed, anger and delusion back to morality, meditation and wisdom ... The sutras say, 'Buddhas have only become buddhas while living with the three poisons and nourishing themselves on the pure Dharma.' The three poisons are greed, anger and delusion.[11]

Spiritual psychology shares with Buddhism the belief that the mind is the source of one's suffering as well as the instrument of one's spiritual fate, and in particular that exercising the mind to systematically deal with negative thoughts is a process of purification. It is this cognitive exercise which is the royal road to spiritual enlightenment. The mind and the soul, at least at the conscious level, are indistinguishable in Sardello's spiritual psychology. Like Jung, he prefers not to define the soul, but to 'characterise' it, so it is of little consequence if he draws upon the sayings of a Buddhist teacher who speaks of the mind rather than the soul. Whatever they call it, both the Buddhist and the spiritual psychologist are engaged in the development of inner resources, that are intended to result in a life in which repellent thoughts are nullified and compassionate love is the overwhelming response to the world. Jesus' love ethic, the Hassidic ethic of loving kindness and the Buddha's compassion all seem to melt into one another, and are, in effect, the moral dimension of this form of psycho-spiritual practice, which counterbalances the tendency to be exclusively preoccupied with one's self.

That is the ideal, but as it turns out, compassionate love is not a sure thing even among the most disciplined Buddhists. And this realisation has compelled a movement in the opposite direction, from the meditation mat toward the psychotherapist's couch. Former Buddhist monk Jack Kornfield, one of the founders of Spirit Rock Meditation Center, concedes that spiritual leaders, whether Buddhist, Hindu or Christian, have been known to be cold and unfeeling, even severely neurotic, despite being adept at contemplative practices. Similarly, students seeking tranquillity through meditation often discover that their emotional problems, if left untreated, may result in further distress and unsatisfactory spiritual practice. Kornfield is one of the chief promoters of co-operation between psychotherapists and meditation teachers, because, as he points out, being spiritually aware in one area does not necessarily transfer to other areas of existence:

> Thus, we encounter graceful masters of tea ceremonies who remain confused and retarded in intimate relations, or yogis who can dissolve their bodies into light, but whose wisdom vanishes when they enter the marketplace ... Just as deep meditation requires a skilled teacher, at times our spiritual path also requires a skilled therapist. Only a deep attention to the whole of our life can bring us the capacity to love well and live freely.[12]

The truth is that spiritual practice of any description is not the answer to all one's psychological and emotional deficits. This observation would occasion no surprise were it not for the fact that meditation is often touted by gurus and yoga schools as a panacea for all psycho-spiritual ills and bodily ailments. This is one of the most important areas of discussion and research in the now regular conferences that take place among psychotherapists and spiritual teachers. For example, a well-known form of Buddhist meditation, which involves a gruesome exercise of mentally dissecting the human body, may achieve its aim to de-sensitise one to bodily lusts, but it also can mask and repress normal feelings and needs. Australian clinical psychologist Mark Blows has reservations about the use of spiritual philosophies that urge one to simply 'drop the ego,' a popular catch phrase amongst Indian gurus that can lead to zombie-like behaviour.

Blows nonetheless advocates the blending of insights from Buddhism and psychotherapy, a project he has pursued for more than a dozen years in the context of the annual international Conference of the Transnational Network for the Study of Physical, Psychological and Spiritual Wellbeing. He is a proponent of the considered, common-sense approach, sensitised to Western culture, which he discerns in some of the teachings of the Dalai Lama.[13] One such teaching which Blows believes is helpful is the practice of reciprocal inhibition, or matching a thought with its opposite, such as when you are down in the dumps thinking of your successes, or if you are always putting people down, thinking of the things you have done in which you have fallen short. It is this homespun wisdom, always delivered cheerfully yet with its undeniable practical challenge to the individual, that has endeared the Dalai Lama to the many audiences he addresses around the world.

This straightforward use of the conscious intellect is also appreciated by Robert Sardello. He knows too well the allure of mind-altering practices, and warns against the use of hypnotic techniques, such as shamanic drumming, which put one into a light trance state. He argues that this does not deepen one's consciousness but dissociates one from it. Freud had similar reservations when he acknowledged that 'the worldly wisdom of the East' and the practices of yoga could suppress the anguish of suffering and induce a 'happiness of quietness'. But he considered the 'killing of instinctual drives' too high a price to pay, since suppressed instinct would always leave its mark in the unconscious mind and produce neurotic symptoms as a result.[14]

Having said that, the old Viennese master has been hard to keep down even in this new psycho-spiritual universe. According to some of his current interpreters, Freud was more Buddhist than he realised. The leading advocate of psychotherapy from a Buddhist perspective, New Yorker Mark Epstein, has credited Freud with inventing a method of analysis that is virtually identical to the Buddhist practice of giving impartial attention to thoughts as they arise. Freud stumbled upon this method when he analysed his own dreams, realising for the first time that it was possible to 'suspend ... judgement and give ... impartial attention to everything there is to observe', thereby gaining a unique insight into psychic phenomena.[15] What Epstein calls 'bare attention' is a challenge that faces all therapists 'to put aside their desires for a patient's cure, their immediate conclusions about the patient's communications, and their "insights" into the causes of the patient's suffering so that they may continue to hear from the patient what they do not yet understand'.[16] As Freud described the technique, it is no different from the meditator who attends to his thoughts and remains in the present, neither clinging to nor condemning what arises in one's consciousness. Advising the therapist to remain impartial, Freud declared, 'He should simply listen, and not bother about whether he is keeping anything in mind.'[17] Not only is this openness to the flow of information similar to Buddhist meditation, but, as Mark Epstein points out, even Freud's approach to 'remembering' is rooted in the present, in so far as Freud described the therapist's method as 'studying whatever is present on the surface of the patient's mind'.[18]

The similarity between Freudian listening technique and Buddhist meditation undoubtedly accounts for the upsurge of interest in Buddhist psychotherapy, a field that has grown into a subdiscipline of the profession. The aim is always to allow a person's life story and relationships space for exploration, remembering, 'working through' and healing, in the hope that a person's past loses its damaging hold, and a happier, freer pursuit of life and spiritual practice is assured. Self-understanding is both the process and the aim.

But is this really the goal of spiritual life, or is the very notion that we can know ourselves its undoing? How can one experience the mystery that transcends one's self if it is pursued in an endless round of rational inquiry, centred on the self? Indeed, even Buddhism ultimately disavows the self, so Buddhist psychotherapy must always accept a high degree of paradox, which after all is central to Zen Buddhism.

Perhaps this is why Thomas Moore, the former Catholic monk turned psychotherapist and popular writer on spirituality, is fond of Zen Buddhist sayings. He is no stranger to paradox. Twelve years as a monk taught him the limitations of the cloistered religious life, while his profession of psychotherapist has shown him that the 'cult of self-understanding', which dominates the therapeutic culture, promises more than it can deliver. Moore admits that a typical course of therapy, irrespective of how long and involved is the chain of events and interpretations that comprise a client's self-understanding, often has no effect on his or her quality of life. More often than not the exercise is evidence of a desire to interpret, analyse and reinvent oneself, but it removes the subject from a more authentic way of being in the world, which for Moore is living 'from the soul'.[19]

Clearly Moore has not entirely given up his monastic sandals for his psychotherapist's shingle. Rather, he stands at the apex of a trend in contemporary spiritual life which could not have come too soon. The explosion of the psychotherapeutic industry into countless schools, theories and models has generated both confusion and its share of turmoil, the latter prompted by the digging up of 'false memories', as Richard Ofshe has documented in his ground-breaking study, *Making Monsters: False Memories, Psychotherapy, and Sexual Hysteria*. It comes as no surprise therefore that Moore, amongst others, distrusts the use of clinical psychological insights alone as a tool of cognitive awakening: 'One day, instead of going to a therapist, troubled or searching people will pay a call on their theologican to consider the mysteries that have befallen them.'[20]

Psychology's emphasis on analytical understanding of events obstructs another kind of knowledge of the self, which is not especially rational but is deeply felt, undeniably experienced and passionately defended. As he puts it, you can know your dog very well, yet not understand what is actually going on in its head. The same can be said for one's closest relationships! Thomas Moore is urging his students and readers in a direction that is dynamic — he is saying there is a deep knowing in the doing, in the loving and in the living. Self-understanding in a clinical sense is not a necessary condition for unconditional love — the chief expression of the soul — and it may even stand in the way of it.

Here spiritual psychology is entering the realm of the mystics for whom bodily experienced and intuitive connection with the divinity form a central way of knowing. It can also be argued that it is through this mystical connection that the soul is discerned and becomes felt, as if it is only apparent when fulfilling its function. A Buddhist analogy to this abiding presence yet fleeting perception of the soul would be the ever-present waves of the ocean that only become apparent when the wind is up. Indeed, the Buddhist and Taoist predilection for experiencing spiritual wonder in the midst of nature, like Basho's poem of the frog, is especially relevant to spiritual psychology. To contemplate the sounds and the silence of a frog in a pond is possible only when you have taken the time to do so.

Old pond,
Frog jumps
Plop.[21]

For Moore, the contemporary version of this kind of knowing and experiencing of the divine is not the preserve of the monk alone, but emerges from the cave, comes in from the desert and occurs outside the monastery. It is played out in the ordinary person's daily actions, such as simply eating a grape, raising children, earning a living and making love. Even the multitude of disappointments and suffering which is our lot as human beings, Moore redefines as our 'mortifications' (more authentic than those that monks inflict on themselves), which should not be avoided but accepted as the constant testing of our capacity to love and live humanely. It is here on earth, and not resurrected in some rarefied heaven or channelled from an intergalactic realm, that our soul's life finds its fullest expression.

By now it should be abundantly clear that what drives spiritual psychology is a view that the individual is motivated by an instinct every bit as powerful as the sexual urges imagined by Freud. It is the instinct lodged in the soul to love attentively and unselfishly. Freud presumed that man was a rational materialist who wrapped his baser drives in self-deluding mythologies, which science and psychoanalysis had exposed as frauds. (Far from demythologising the human species, however, Freud was not above spinning his own racy myths, such as found in his two works, *Moses and Monotheism* and *Totem and Taboo*, in which he explains the sexual origins of religion itself.) Spiritual psychology, on the other hand, starts from the presumption that man is first and foremost an emotional being, a lover, and this quality is both good and god-like, the essence of Moore's 'original self'. It is the state of Adam and Eve before they were stripped of their cheerful innocence. (No wonder Moore puts limited store in the accumulation of knowledge, for was it not the tree of knowledge that was the compensation for the primordial couple's loss of innocence, the severing of their blissful union with God?) In a way, the difference between the two views centres on the chicken and egg dilemma as applied to sex and love: Which came first? For Freud it was undoubtedly the libido, the sex drive, whereas for spiritual psychology it is love. For Freud the religious life was but a cover, a prophylactic to the sex drive. For spiritual psychology it is an invitation to fully actualise the soul's natural disposition to love.

It would seem that spiritual psychology fits a world that no longer believes it requires an antidote for its sexual urges and baser drives, and has consequently lost interest in old-time religion's chastening function. Turning the spiritual life into a love affair with one's soul also has a certain economy of style and mobility that is perfectly suited to a world where autonomy is valued above all. But where does this leave the other major function of the religious life — to lead a moral life, not only for one's self but also for the sake of others? Can love fulfil this task? Would mystics like Bede Griffiths who experience 'pure consciousness which gives lasting peace to the soul' necessarily undertake the burdensome task of fighting for social justice or creating and administering a system of moral law that protects all of society, the great as well as the weak?[22] To whom will fall these responsibilities? At the very least, should not these responsibilities be articulated and urged upon us by the new believers in spiritual psychology? Or should we assume that such concerns have no necessary spiritual motive?

There is no doubt that the demise of traditional religion and its attendant moral authority has freed up the individual from the dictates of the superego, that father figure in service to religion, which psychoanalysis imagined was the gatekeeper of our conscience. Much has been written, not least the insightful work by Christopher Lasch,[23] which foresaw that the demise of religion and the superego would unleash a thoroughgoing culture of narcissism, a me-centred universe, in which an immature self-indulgence was converted into a new kind of ethic of self-justification. For Lasch, as for many culture critics, this state of affairs had monstrous moral and social implications. For what could one expect from one's fellow man if he was free to do as he pleased without any concern for its impact on society as a whole? Freud, for all his criticism of religion, conceded that it kept society fairly ordered and largely moral.

Freud, as it turned out, was proven wrong. When it came to the crunch, churches were weak opponents, when they were not collaborators, of the Nazis. But so too were some of the leading figures in the new kind of spiritual psychology that was going on in Europe at the time. No less than Dietrich Bonhoeffer, the brilliant German theologian, poet and anti-Nazi activist, who was one of the bravest critics of Hitler, saw through the self-styled pioneers of the mind and spirit like Martin Heidegger and Carl Jung who were nonetheless willing to make their own peace with the Führer. In the last year of his life, writing from a concentration camp, Bonhoeffer addressed the ultimate questions of death and guilt:

But what if one day they no longer exist, as such, if they too can be answered 'without God'? Of course, we now have the secularised offshoots of Christian theology, namely existentialist philosophy and psychotherapists, who demonstrate to secure, contented, and happy mankind that it is really unhappy and desperate and simply unwilling to admit that it is in a predicament about which it knows nothing, and from which only they can rescue it. Wherever there is health, strength, security, simplicity, they send luscious fruit to gnaw at or to lay their pernicious egg in. They set themselves to drive people to inward despair, and then the game is in their hands. That's secularised methodism.[24]

Hitler ordered Bonhoeffer's execution in April 1945. With his privileged background and international reputation, Bonhoeffer easily could have escaped Germany in 1939. But this option was not open to his conscience, for he was critical of his own Lutheran Church precisely for not living up to true Christianity. Bonhoeffer did not confuse the Christian life with the churches, which he regarded as moral cowards, along with university academics and the psychologists who were busily leading their inner journeys while the world around them was in flames. But if the academics, the clerics and the psychotherapists alike were guilty, what was it that made them pursue their beliefs without a conscience? Did they come to idolise their beliefs as ends in themselves, without care for their consequences in the world?

In *The Secular Mind*, the Pulitzer Prize winning psychologist Robert Coles reflects on the interplay between the secular and the religious mind, a subject which as a student at Harvard he first explored with his teacher, the great German–American theologian Paul Tillich. Coles quotes at length an extended interview he conducted in the 1970s with Dorothy Day, the suffragette and journalist turned devout Catholic. In a poignant account of her new-found faith, she told him that when she went to church each day she would tell the priest how anxious she was lest her faith become habitual, and the socially conscious, thinking person she was become submerged in a tide of ritual and tradition. The priest was impatient with her concerns, and on the contrary advised her that praying should become second nature, because its practice had an eternally sacred value all its own. But for Dorothy Day, as for Dietrich Bonhoeffer, the desire for a fully conscious faith in which she talked earnestly to God (and perhaps like Abraham of old argued with God) marked out the difference between a real religious life and a sham one. Indeed, for her, the concerns of her time had to be addressed by the eternal truths of her faith, which in that sense was firmly tied to the secular (temporal) world. In the same way, doubt was not some aberration of a newly unbelieving world, but was the constant companion to faith, the secular whetstone on which true faith was sharpened and cut deeper.[25]

It may turn out that redefining religion and experiencing spirituality is the easy part. Keeping it an active source of moral courage is something else altogether. While a sense of the spiritual is no longer exclusively or easily found in the churches or other religious institutions, locating it in the mind or the soul is no guarantee that it will possess a moral conscience.

8. REMOVING MORALITY
Morality is Dead

It is hard to imagine that a series of books in which the author claims to be having a conversation with God becomes a runaway best seller, but Neale Donald Walsch's *Conversations With God* I, II and III, plus the follow-up *Communion With God*, have been just that. Translated into twenty-seven languages and boasting sales of 70 million, Walsch's books have captured the imagination of people from all religious backgrounds and from none. At the very least, this phenomenon needs explaining. One would expect that opening a book with the claim, 'God began talking with you. Through me,'[1] would be likely to evoke one of two responses: 'Not another one!' or 'Who's he kidding?' But as it turns out, what God had to say was exactly what a lot of people wanted to hear. Just about everything we thought was true about God was a lie. And contrary to popular belief, we do not have to measure up to God.

For one thing, the God that speaks to Neale Donald Walsch is not poised above the human race, requiring obedience and prayers of supplication in order for his lowly creation to be redeemed. Nor is this God to be found embedded in the intricate religious systems and sacred mythologies of the world, the object of endless hours of study and worship. In fact, this God does not have a hint of aloofness at all. On the contrary, Walsch's God is only revealed to a person inwardly, because God is already known to each and every soul, and needs only to be remembered and experienced. According to this revelation, everybody's soul is all-knowing (in exactly the same way that we used to think God was all-knowing) and its singular aim is to experience and to bring into being all that it knows. This is consonant with God's one and only purpose, which is that every person would remember what they already know, and thus experience 'fullest glory'.[2] The *Conversations With God* CD appropriately intones over and over again the singular instruction to 'Go with the soul, go with the soul, go with the soul...' which sounds exactly like the 1970s hippy refrain, 'Go with the flow, go with the flow, go with the flow ...'

With this simple formula, Walsch rejects the prevalent opinion that people today are ignorant of God because they no longer read the Bible, and are hopelessly alienated from the religious life because they no longer attend worship services. It also follows that the decline in conventional religious practice is not a cause for concern, but for celebration, since it was based on the wrong idea about God anyway. He is not the Almighty who lords it over us, nor is he the King of Heaven and Earth to whom humanity is subordinate. The truth is that human souls have not realised that they have known God all along, as the voice inside their heads. But the news is even better than that. There is nothing for them to learn. 'Go with the soul, go with the soul, go with the soul ...'

If there is nothing for the soul to learn, then what is it that the soul needs to remember? 'Who You Really Are,' is Walsch's enigmatic answer. How did we forget who we really are? It seems that when we emerged into the physical universe, we relinquished the knowledge of 'Who We Really Are', which is also the soul's knowledge of God, the soul's remembrance of being part of the 'Divine Whole'.[3] But if that still leaves wide open the question of how to go about being 'Who We Really Are', then Walsch has the answer to that too: given that we forgot

'Who We Really Are', we must *choose* to remember, and thus we are free to be 'Who We Want to Be'. In a blink of an eye, a glance backward becomes a leap into the future. There is a certain familiarity about Walsch's teaching, which subtly introduces a creation mythology that resembles the kabbalistic belief in the soul as a part of the divine Creator from which it was separated at creation and to which it strives to return. Walsch has not merely revisited the 'myth of the eternal return' to the Godhead, made famous by the romantically inclined comparative religionist Mircea Eliade. He has taken his readers straight into the human potential movement, where the essence of a person is not to be found in a static notion of moral purity, like the sinless existence of Adam and Eve before the Fall, nor in a dynamic struggle with good and evil as evidenced in most of the figures in the Bible, but is found in the possibility of becoming a 'higher and higher' functioning being. This ideal state, as it turns out, has little to do with morality.

Being and becoming a better person is a large part of what the religious life has been about. Whether it is a Christian who believes that Jesus Christ died for her sins and is the greatest exemplar of true faith in God, or a Jew who follows the teachings and the commandments of the Torah, or a Buddhist who adopts the eight-fold path to enlightenment, the purpose of the religious life is to produce people and communities who are holy and who sanctify life by their spiritually motivated actions. The purpose is manifest in the process. In all cases moral teachings are paramount, because they demonstrate the values that are cherished in each tradition. A distinguishing feature of the moral teachings of any tradition is a system of dos and don'ts, prescriptions and proscriptions, observances and taboos, which form a standard against which to measure human action. To impose it is also to warn that ignoring the moral law will result in evil consequences, punishment and a cursed life. That is why in the Bible the commandments are followed by a list of curses.

For the reader of the *Conversations With God* series, nothing could come as a greater relief than discovering that the preoccupation with morality results from a giant case of misunderstanding. To start with, there is no evil, only fear. And fear is simply a lack of love. The edifice of morality based on good and evil is a mistake, because they don't exist as we have imagined them. Even worse, moral obligations only engender a sense of guilt and fear, which if anything are the real evil in this new ethic. The old God is also swept away. The Father God who loves us but punishes us when we are bad was merely the product of a childlike impulse to project onto the celestial realm a parental figure who judges us harshly.[4] So teaches Walsch's God, who has clearly read Freud and agrees with him, but has decided it is now time to come out of hiding and show us what he is really like. As it turns out, God never was interested in right or wrong or should or shouldn't. He emphatically denies that he ever set down any teaching that would restrict or prohibit people from doing anything they desire.[5] That would be a restriction of the unconditional free will that he gave to our souls, and which, tragically, we have forgotten. Hence, there are no human choices that elicit punishments from God. The dire effects of human actions may be attributed to a certain natural law of consequences, which is particularly unmerciful to people who live unfulfilling lives. Living unhappily delivers its own punishment; it is the true meaning of hell.[6]

Of those who have had truly miserable lives, few would argue with the prosaic truth of that last statement, although they might quibble about whether being happy is the sole measure of life's worth. But what about the rest of it? Maybe it is not as radical as it sounds and merely reflects the prevalent attitudes of the middle class in a free and affluent West. For who today believes that doing whatever they desire is theoretically not open to them or might be swiftly punished by the God of justice? There is little evidence that people believe in a God who keeps them in check, like a lion tamer his unruly brood. That in any case is left to the law and courts, which deal with individuals who have been caught seriously misbehaving. For those who get away with it, maybe their consciences will trouble them. But even that is overrated, for what constitutes a conscience, if not the internalisation of moral standards?

This question is already out of date, since another kind of conscience is in the making and it promotes an idea, already made famous by Nietzsche, that good and evil, morality and immorality, are mere conventions that strangle the spirit, and are counterproductive to the superior functioning of the individual. This, of course, is the central tenet of Nietzsche's *ubermensch* (or superman) who alleged that the masses venerated conventional religion merely because it was old, not because it was true.[7] Against this characterisation of popular religion, and echoing Nietzsche, Walsch and others are creating an ethic that claims a truth precisely because it owes no allegiance to the remote past, but is founded in the immediate and future potential of one's self to realise the true power of one's own divinity. Like Nietzsche's Zarathustra, the new man and woman look to eagles, not angels, for sustenance:

> *On the tree, Future, we build our nest:*
> *And in our solitude eagles shall bring us nourishment in their beaks.*[8]

Nietzsche described his own writing as 'this labyrinth of audacious insights', which most of the people he knew, even forward-thinking feminists, could not bear to take seriously.[9] It cast him in a solitude that is the complete reverse of the fame that our current crop of iconoclastic thinkers experience today. The astonishing success of the *Conversation With God* series gives popular assent to the Roman general's instruction to his legions: 'The gods look with favour upon superior daring.'[10] The consequences of such an attitude are yet to be measured, but before we look further into its supporting ethic, let us cross the Atlantic to another radical theologian, Don Cupitt, who has taken the lid off old-time religion and believes he has released its spirit from the burdens of a moribund morality.

An Anglican cleric and Life Fellow of Emanuel College, Cambridge, Cupitt is an entirely different breed of religious thinker from the former radio talk-show host and best-selling author, Neale Donald Walsch. It is doubtful that any of Cupitt's numerous volumes, most of them slender and very readable, have ever raked in sales of the order of his American counterpart. Yet, in a spate of recent works, Cupitt has been every bit as dedicated to peeling away layer after layer of religious custom and convention in order to champion a type of spirituality that is entirely founded on the individual's capacity for happiness and living a good life. Like Walsch, Cupitt equates the spiritual purpose in life as self-affirmation, which he believes is best expressed through an uninhibited outpouring of 'being yourself', and compares it to the sun's unlimited light, shining due to its own energy. In a rereading of Matthew 5: 14, 'You are the light of the world,' Cupitt discovers a Christian endorsement and proof-text for his way to happiness: 'solar ethics'.

The impetus for this newly styled ethic of expressionism based on the sun's indifferent outpouring of energy is Cupitt's belief in a mortal trinity. God, tradition and morality are not only dead and buried, he alleges, but also largely forgotten. Cupitt is not mourning. Nor is he pessimistic about a world without these once central beliefs. As for a divinely ordained morality, its absence occasions no panic, since 'there is always already a moral order' which somehow arises, as if by a natural law, and takes care of itself. Indeed, Cupitt insists there is no 'One True Morality', just a lot of ethical systems, which he prefers to see as lifestyles not rule books, feel-good choices not divine obligations. The 'good life' takes on the meaning of the food and entertainment pages of the weekend press, not the Sermon on the Mount in the Bible. Yet Cupitt concedes that some of the various moralities on offer can be cruel and strange. How would he know? Perhaps his judgment is a holdover from the now moribund Christian moral system, which has left a faded imprint on his conscience. Whatever, in the world of solar ethics any such discriminatory judgments are destined to remain merely private opinions. For solar ethics denies the authority from which such judgments are passed on to others, as if they have some objective reality, to become imposed as a standard, a tradition or an ideal. Cupitt considers such an imposition to be plain moral tyranny, which only induces undesirable feelings of guilt and alienation. He declares such moral realism dead, and argues for a world where everything changes, fades away and has no lasting value beyond the moment. It is a kind of nihilism, which he accepts as inevitable: 'Nihilism has come and it is henceforth our permanent human condition. That is so: it truly is so.'[11]

This would be a dreary sentence for humanity was it not for a prosperous Western society that delivers a fairly comfortable existence to its inhabitants, for whom the allure of the 'new' remains far more enticing than the preservation of a past ideal, which is too much like last year's fashions. Nihilism has its consumer-friendly aspects, and allows the opportunity for an ever-changing stream of experiences, where brand loyalty is a distinct disadvantage. Nihilism may have emerged from the very prosperity it feeds. Of course, Cupitt does not use the language of retail shopping per se, but he does promote a spirituality that has dispensed with permanent and metaphysical values, such as a transcendent truth, a past ideal and an interior soul dimension, all of which, he argues, promote an 'ugly dualism', at war with the plain reality of physical life itself. In his philosophy, God is replaced, in fact, by 'Life Itself'. Just being, not salvation, is the sacred state, and moral superiority is banished in favour of joyful, liberating, loving action. Life is a party! Indeed, it was at a party that Cupitt witnessed a woman who was simply radiating, dazzling and shining— she was positively solar: 'Notice that when people are thus shining, absorbed in communicative expression, they are totally unaware of *morality*.'[12]

Notice, indeed! His description suggests he could not take his eyes off her! Expressionism is the bubbling high point of a life that has no other purpose than to pour out an individual's psycho-physical being in its own unique manner. Each person possesses a distinctive identity and its expression is the great and the small purpose of life. As Cupitt himself admits, he is only telling us what we already darkly suspect. The question is whether he is putting a brave face on defeat—the failure of the moral tradition to command the authority it once had. Or is he simply crowning the victor of biological necessity? Living according to an ethic of the 'contingency of life' has replaced the morally prescribed way of life. Meanwhile, the unpredictability of existence has itself acquired a certain degree of mystery, which elicits a wonder and a humility. At least, that is what Cupitt hopes, taking a cue from another romantic, D.H. Lawrence, whose radical secular mysticism required one to live as if continually launching oneself into the unknown: 'For real utter satisfaction, a human being must give himself up to complete quivering uncertainty, to sentient non-knowledge.'[13]

This is not a particularly easy way to live, but Zen Buddhists, for example, have honed it to a fine and difficult art. Without their disciplined meditation regime and communal structure, or indeed Lawrence's eccentric philosophical commitment to 'the mystery of life', the qualities of humility and wonder may give way to hopelessness and fear. Perhaps another source of strength closer to home is also up to the task of living with Cupitt's radical uncertainty—the good old Protestant ethic, which appears to have left its mark after all. 'Life is just what you make it!' proclaims Cupitt, sounding every bit as defiant as the Protestant reformers who launched themselves into the New World frontier on the optimistic promise of life, liberty and the pursuit of happiness. It is as simple as saying that the bounty of life is in your hands.

But the sunny side of the street also has its dark side. The country that gave us the American Dream fuelled by the Protestant work ethic is also deeply aware of the conflict with its other great Protestant inheritance, Puritan morality. It is this dual inheritance that chafes uncomfortably throughout much of the affluent West, and very probably provokes Don Cupitt's solar spirituality. It is also evident in that other great product of American life, the Hollywood movie, which occasionally offers brilliant commentary on our current preoccupations. As if it was an elegy to our subject, the film *American Beauty*, focuses on two men who 'choose life itself' over the dictates of morality. A young man wishes to escape from the funereal atmosphere of his home and the severe morality imposed by his ex-marine father, who beats him (when he discovers his son dealing drugs) and warns him, 'You've got to know there are rules, that in this world you can't just do what you want.' Unable to engage his surroundings personally, the young man watches the world through the lens of his camera and captures its beauty in moving images. He films a white plastic bag, whirling and swirling as it is lifted by a gust of wind, and declares it the most beautiful thing he has ever seen, 'a reminder of the force behind things'. He explains to his girlfriend, 'There is so much beauty in the world that sometimes I feel my heart would cave in.'

The girlfriend's father is the other main character in the film. He feels equally trapped in his predictable universe of suburban middle age. While his wife intones empowering mantras to help her sell real estate, he lashes out from his passionless marriage by making a play for a teenage beauty whom he imagines in a bathtub of red rose petals. Transformed by his desire, he nonetheless realises at the last minute that she is a virgin the age of his own young daughter, and refrains from making love to her, perhaps inhibited by the morality that Cupitt assures us 'takes care of itself'. Played by Kevin Spacey, the character's disembodied voice is heard to utter, as it surveys the scene at the end of the film, 'I can't feel anything but grateful for every moment of my stupid little life.' It is a statement of abject gratitude that is hard to fathom, because he has been blown away by the absurd and accidental contingency of life, gunned down by an assailant whom he could not have suspected. The murderer is the young man's father. The ex-marine was tortured by morality and guilt about his secret homosexuality and, deluded by false logic, he killed an innocent man. Morality, rationality and logic delivered death and destruction in this Oscar-winning film, while beauty, sensuality and risk embodied all that was good and worth striving for in life even if its fruits were transient, and ultimately beyond reach.

There is a remarkable irony, bordering on audacious humility, which asserts that truth is nothing more nor less than one's own puny life. Taking life on its own terms, without looking beyond it or deep inside it, in the way that the religious or philosophical imagination has always done, is a starkly limited proposition, and yet it possesses a potential to 'live for the moment' heretofore not realised. The trouble is that it's a potential that is by definition self-serving, and if it benefits others it does so only incidentally, not by decree or obligation. No-one advocates this view more consistently than Neale Donald Walsch, who provides a blow-by-blow denial of the moral imperatives normally associated with the God of the Bible and replaces them with a series of assertions about the limitless, unbounded capacity of the individual to be himself or herself. To be sure, Walsch would not see those old imperatives as moral at all. On the contrary, he sees them as a hypocritical construct imposed by a tradition which he believes has outgrown its usefulness and for which he has only the barest residual regard.

In *Communion With God*, Walsch asserts that the central biblical notion of human imperfection, traditionally understood as sin, is illusory, and is fatally connected to a series of other illusions, such as a requirement to do certain 'right things' (righteousness), and the existence of certainties such as judgment and conditionality. Walsch regards these as mental traps that cage one in destructive ways of thinking and delude one into a false reality of one's own making. For Walsch, life is a 'journey to mastery' that will 'lead you out of the nightmare of your own construction'.[14] In this he is reminiscent of Friedrich Nietzsche, who denounced morality and religion as a giant illusion which humanity imposed on chaotic reality with dire results, glorifying the weak in place of the strong, and in the process crippling the real potential of man's 'will to power'. Better to live in a jungle 'red in tooth and claw' to borrow Tennyson's phrase, with winners and losers, than on a farm where all the cattle are equally fed — as well as fated for the slaughterhouse. There is hardly a more dismal caricature of 'everyman' than can be found in Nietzsche's work. Of course, the ordinary person reading Nietzsche is scandalised by the cavalier disregard with which the building blocks of a moral and stable order are cast aside in favour of a vision that has a barely concealed contempt for the mediocre, the average and the weak — which would describe the vast majority of humanity. A hundred years after Nietzsche, Walsch declares that the time for this deluded obedience to an invented moral order is over, and human beings should just *be*, which he insists is possible only upon realising that you are God, indeed that you are nothing outside of God.

The assertion that one is God is not new to those who have some familiarity with Brahmanic Hinduism. The notion of the self within, who is Brahman and who can be fully realised, has been the most potent Eastern notion to infiltrate Western spirituality. Yet the path set up to realise this in traditional Hindu society is a singular, long and arduous one for the ascetic or the high born; it is not a highway down which the entire populace courses toward *samadhi*, the rarified state of consciousness resulting from meditation and yoga in which there is no awareness of the physical and material world and magical powers result. The *sadhu* or saint on his holy path leaves behind normal family relationships, while the guru or swami trades his family home for the pristine ashram. In most cases, an individual who assumes the mantle of God is contained in the highly ordered and circumscribed settings laid down by tradition, which itself signals the potentially explosive nature of living 'as God'. Just how such a radical claim to human divinity transfers to Western society is something we have witnessed to some extent in small utopian and sectarian expressions, many of them with tragic results, and some of them with positively catastrophic consequences, such as the mass murder–suicide perpetrated by two self-proclaimed messiahs, Jim Jones at Jonestown and David Koresh at his compound outside Waco, Texas.

Given its potentially chaotic consequences, what could be the impetus for this dangerous proposal for living life 'as God', according to one's own imperatives, in the midst of Western society? Is it merely to carve out more freedom and power in a society already drunk on images of it? Perhaps it is just a symptom of a culture saturated with cinematic escapism where illusions of awesome power are its stock in trade. If it is merely a reflection of popular culture then it has no significance other than to demonstrate how much of contemporary spiritual yearning is an epiphenomenon, a mere echo of a much more powerful secular culture, which is dictating not only the form but also the substance of its ideals. On the other hand, if the teachings of Walsch and Cupitt amount to a protest, then it may be against a felt sense of alienation from the 'absentee father' whose rules have to be obeyed but who is no longer encountered in the family home or in the parish church, let alone in the heart. Could it be a radical attempt to close that gap between man and God by simply assuming his mantle and claiming his authority as one's own? Rather than having to go anywhere in particular to experience God, it is simply enough to believe that God is beating in your own breast and resounding in your own thoughts.

Whatever accounts for the popularity of *being God*, which is what Neale Donald Walsch effectively is in his books, there is some precedent for that claim in the biblical tradition where humankind is made in God's image and the prophets trumpeted messages to Israel in his name. In Christian tradition, Jesus is said to be the Son of God, and speaks in his name to all who will listen. The path of the mystic or the monk who lives as if imitating Christ is also a part of the Western tradition. But these examples are carefully circumscribed by orthodox Christianity lest they become warrants for radical or heretical licence. According to the biblical tradition, humankind lost its godlike purity in the Garden of Eden, while Jesus' life was cut short just at the moment his true identity was revealed. Priestly powers were limited by ecclesiastical law while the monk's life is defined by monastic rule. Even the radical teaching of the Quakers, in whom the spirit of God is said to move and inspire speech and action, is tamed by its highly ordered method of communal consensus in which individuals claiming to be moved by the Holy Spirit are no more nor less authoritative than anyone else, in whom the Holy Spirit also resides. One can count on a natural dilution of individual power, regardless of its divine origin, in the community setting. Whether as a monk nor as a member of a congregation, living in a group where the communal interest is paramount is the usual safety valve for untrammelled claims to divine power.

But if Walsch and Cupitt, who both regard 'moral realism' as counterproductive if not dead in the water, are taken seriously, then how is community possible at all? For it is obvious that groups, communities and society in general cannot do without the so-called shared illusions of morality, translated into norms and laws. What is the possible basis of human co-operation if not the shared ideas and principles that embody those values we cherish most? Call them illusions, laws or revealed truths, in any case it is the belief in them and demonstration of them by a large body of people that provides the foundation for a fair and functioning society, in which citizens are not subject to the whims of autocrats and cultural continuity is possible. There are always competing pockets of culture and there are always dissenters—not to mention criminals who break the law—but none of these would be identifiable without a single overarching moral legal system, which makes the bare bones of society and culture possible in the first place. Otherwise, there is only anarchy (which nullifies the meaning of dissent), a situation, incidentally, which Nietzsche relished, so long as there was an aristocracy of supermen keeping the innately inferior peasants down. Is this what we are headed for?

The proposed alternative to the moral realism at the heart of society can only be a much shakier illusion. It is the belief that individuals who 'pour themselves out', doing whatever they can in order to be true to themselves, people who 'go with the soul', will make good citizens. It is reminiscent of communes in the 1970s which were founded on the belief that if everyone could 'do their own thing', then the sum total would be utopia. They were wrong. It did not take long for the open relationships and open bank accounts to devolve into authoritarian, exploitative and tragic pools of human suffering. If morality is a big lie, it's the lie we have to have to keep people from taking advantage of everyone else as they lever themselves into the stratosphere of their personal grandiose dreams.

The irony is that neither Cupitt nor Walsch believe in a non-moral universe. Both count unconditional love as a paramount value, for example, and regard it as a natural consequence of being or living according to 'who you really are'. One might say they are uni-moral, in that love really is the sum total of their moral conscience. All else melts in its path. It is a concentrated version of the Sermon on the Mount, Chapter 5, in which Jesus instructs his followers:

> But I say to you, do not resist an evildoer . . . Love your enemies and pray for those who persecute you so that you may be children of your Father in Heaven; for he makes his sun rise on the evil and the good, and he sends rain on the righteous and the unrighteous.

Echoing the opening formula of the Sermon on the Mount, but omitting the notion that there are 'the evil and the good', Walsch simply tells his readers to be an eternal bounty of love poured out: 'Now I come to tell you again that this is what is true: Love is unconditional. Life is unending. God is without need. And you are a miracle. The miracle of God, made human.'[15]

The real thrust of Walsch's message is that God and man are one, and they are love. Because this is simply what is, there is nothing to do, nothing to prove, no requirement to fulfil and no judgment to be made. That, so it seems, is the ideal state of affairs. Real life, on the other hand, is full of the opposite, so Walsch instructs his readers to believe the ideal but live in the world as if acting a part in a play that they know is merely illusion. It is as if we are angels who must tuck our wings under our street attire. We cynically pretend to play the part of poor dumb humans, all the while in the knowledge that we need nothing, fail at nothing and suffer nothing. Getting that truth is essential if we are not to be sucked in to the false reality that most other people are mired in. It is a Gnostic philosophy that reverses the biblical notion of the flawed human being who embarks on a path of righteousness and eventually enters the gates of heaven if judged worthy. On the contrary, in this version of the spiritual journey, it is as if we left the gates of heaven in the murky past to dwell in the houses of men, and now it is time to wake up to 'Who We Really Are' and start playing by our own rules.

Perhaps Gnosticism is too arcane a religious outlook to be mentioning in connection with a writer who has enjoyed such massive appeal. There may be another more popular philosophy that accounts for the particular outlook that sees the world as an illusion. The Israeli Zen Roshi and theatre director Gil Alon gave a clue when he was expounding Buddhist philosophy on a visit to Sydney in 2002, and cited Neale Donald Walsch's work approvingly. He found an affinity between the Buddhist notion that all phenomena are transient, reducible to energy and therefore not 'real' and Walsch's belief that there is only God, nothing else. Both the Roshi and Walsch accept that the world is filled with things and people, but their outward appearance is only an illusion. An enlightened consciousness according to them, therefore, is one that interacts with the world in the full knowledge that everything that we normally take as real is simply a construct of the mind.

This has profound moral implications, because the belief that something is good or bad is also a construction. For the Zen Roshi, the answer is to live in the moment, making choices that are authentically one's own. Don Cupitt would have a similar outlook, and concedes that much of his thinking about living with a radical existential consciousness is influenced by Buddhism. Science also comes to the aid of this perspective, with its findings that all matter ultimately is reducible to the tiniest particles of energy, and therefore cannot be assigned a value other than an abstract functional one. But what seems like the perfect ethic in a world that is infused with scientific knowledge is also forgetful of a salient fact. For all its sophisticated philosophical treatises on the nature of reality, Buddhism prescribed a set of 'thou shalt nots' because the founders of its monastic system realised that people are a bundle of self-seeking passions which cannot be given free rein. The moral order is plainly laid out in the eight-fold path and in the *Vinaya*, the monastic rule, which provides a blueprint for 'right action and right speech'. Whatever one thinks of the imposition of these rules, which in practice may be too extreme or too lax, their existence alone tells us something about the essential needs of any human community. Invented, biological or God-given, morality is the means by which people seek to regulate their vehement passions and channel them to more altruistic ideals.

While it is fruitful to compare the moral outlook of two of the most innovative religious thinkers today, the truth is that Cupitt and Walsch have radically different theologies. Cupitt would not be caught dead writing 'in the name of God'. The whole business of seeing God as a substance, as a person or as a lawgiver is anathema to Cupitt's bio-theology, in which God is barely discernible, like the skywriting that dissolves before one's eyes. After craning the neck to watch the last wisps of smoke fade away, there is nothing for it but to pull in one's head and get on with life. That is the present state of belief in God, which Cupitt rescues from total secular obscurity by sanctifying 'life itself' as the supreme expression of God's perfection — indeed, the only one left. And here Cupitt is more a scientific positivist than an idealist — life is finite, there simply is no proof that it will go on after death. Coming from a Cambridge theologian, a title Cupitt is less and less comfortable claiming, his is a refreshingly tender attitude that brims with compassion for the weary and browbeaten Christian, who is inadequate in the faith, faltering in belief and uninterested in church life. To this growing army of retreat from the Churches, Cupitt offers hope, not damnation. He sends a message that is gentle, comforting and almost whimsical — to delight in life and to feel the spirit all around us, as did the romantic poets like William Wordsworth.

> . . . *I have felt*
> *A presence that disturbs me with the joy*
> *Of elevated thoughts; a sense sublime*
> *Of something far more deeply interfused*
> . . . *and in the mind of man*
> *A motion and a spirit, that impels*
> *All thinking things, all objects of all thought,*
> *And rolls through all things.*[16]

And Elizabeth Barrett Browning:

> *Earth's crammed with heaven,*
> *And every common bush afire with God:*
> *But only he who sees, takes off his shoes* . . .[17]

To feel at one with both nature and the contingency of life means that death itself occasions no terror, only a benign picture of lying in the earth pushing up the daisies, fulfilling the biblical prediction, 'from dust to dust'.

No such humble resignation to the ebb and flow of life characterises the mood of Neale Donald Walsch's work. The reader of *Conversations*

With God I, II, III is on the receiving end of a new revelation, in which Walsch's God literally sweeps away the old beliefs and provides a new dispensation. Despite the antinomian message, in which the old world is turned upside down, there is a surprisingly authoritarian tone to his teaching. It is deeply ironic that a text which calls for its readers to free themselves from the shackles of their received beliefs about God should thrust upon them a new set of beliefs that insists it is the only way to be 'Who You Really Are'. Anyone deluded enough to believe in the old religion is swiftly reduced to the status of a poor fool, hopelessly tied, not to a sinking ship, but to one that has already sunk. Religion itself is full of holes, a vessel that simply cannot ferry humanity to the shores of salvation. To carry the maritime metaphor further, religion is nothing more than Captain Bligh's ill-fated *Bounty*, which according to Fletcher Christian's account was a ship run with such meanness and violence, instilling so much fear and resentment in the sailors that their only recourse was mutiny. Like the sailors, Christians are abandoning the Church, whose ancient symbol was the ship, and they are diving free-form into the sea of faith where it's every man for himself.

The Sea of Faith happens to be the name of the collection of groups in the United Kingdom, the United States, Australia and New Zealand which loosely follows Don Cupitt's version of a form of Christianity without a creed; that is, a creative quest for spirituality in everyday life. Cupitt and Walsch are among the many today who can be heard decrying religion as the dinosaur of the spiritual life. To be anti-religion has a certain elevating connotation; it automatically classes one among the new believers, the self-selected seekers who refuse to bow to the institutionalised cultural forms that masquerade as religious truth. While such critics caricature religion as little more than a bureaucratic enterprise, they presume a pure spirituality that descends like the Holy Spirit on butterflies and Buddhas alike. It requires no obedience, only an openness to receive it. There are no commandments imposed, only a willingness to experience its transforming buzz. Spirituality is like the orgasm of love; it is bestowed with grace and is only experienced if one is fully attuned to the divine. Religion, on the other hand, is the humdrum relationship that ensues when the bloom of love is past—it is full of expectations and mutual obligation. But can one really have one without the other? And is this dissection into parts truly representative of the whole?

What has this to do with morality? Perhaps it is just this: the moral imperative, by definition, does not serve one alone, it asks for a commitment to act on behalf of other people's needs. It is reminiscent of the quandary that faced the great German conductor of the Berlin Philharmonic Orchestra, Wilhelm Furtwangler, who served under the Nazi regime. The subject of the film *Taking Sides* by Istvan Szabo, Furtwangler explained his co-operation with the Nazis as a demonstration of his utter commitment to music, which he believed was so sublime that it transcended the world of politics and somehow miraculously offered a kind of redemption, perhaps only a glimpse, to a country overrun with evil. But the cold facts were different, as his American interrogator would remind him. The symphony concerts staged for the members of the SS served as distractions to the smell of burning flesh that could be detected four miles away, the empty seats in the orchestra once occupied by Jewish musicians, and the terror that reigned over a once civilised society. Did Furtwangler really believe that the celestial sounds of Beethoven's *Ninth* or Wagner's *Tristan and Isolde* could do anything more than provide a temporary escape for his troubled soul? Music, after all, can never do the work of helping another person in trouble, any more than the new believer's much sought after union with the divine can change the suffering of the world.

The fundamental ingredient of the moral imperative is the fact of life. When people and situations exist that require our constructive help or our straightforward relief, no amount of reflection on the metaphysical meaning of a situation will do. It is difficult to imagine any ethic of altruism or rescue directed at a world that is perceived as nothing more than a giant decoy.

> If you look at something—truly look at it—you will see right through it, and right through any illusion it holds for you, leaving nothing but ultimate reality in your sight ... There is nothing in your reality to hold onto.[18]

9. RECLAIMING MORAL SENSE
The Chimps Have It

The proverbial leap of faith by which sinners at a revivalist meeting are transformed into soldiers for Christ has its equivalent in New Age spirituality, but it is called the leap of consciousness. This is an equally mysterious process, yet lays claim to a concrete result every bit as miraculous as being saved. Ironically, it was a story drawn from the annals of primatology that became the basis of this New Age tale of transformation. *The Hundredth Monkey* was a book by anti-nuclear campaigner Ken Keyes, in which the story of how monkeys started to wash their potatoes on some Japanese islands was used as a model for collective 'ideological breakthrough'. Unfortunately, Keyes relied on a version of the story by New Age author Lyall Watson, who had added his own twist to the tale, claiming that when the practice of potato washing on Koshima Island had reached a 'critical mass', monkeys on other islands suddenly started to wash their potatoes, as if by monkey telepathy.

Since then the 'hundredth monkey' has become an article of faith in the New Age. It continues to make the rounds in change-management circles and is regularly cited by motivational speakers, proving once again that one should never let facts get in the way of a good story. The truth is somewhat different. Primatologists do not believe that the emergence of potato washing on the island of Koshima had any effect on events elsewhere, and there is no evidence to support the miraculous transference of the practice to other islands. In fact, the washing of food by primates has been observed in other parts of the world, such as among the lowland gorillas in central Africa, who wade into swampy pools of water to wash the soil from their favourite reeds before eating them. It is not an uncommon practice among animals.

Despite the allure of the hundredth monkey, which was meant to provide a graphic example of rapid evolutionary change, the truth about our propensity to coherent group behaviour and our links to the animal world may actually be more profound and, in one sense at least, revolutionary. The now well-documented evidence of primates expressing a significant degree of social organisation, compassion and even something approximating moral sentiment gives pause to the current trend of thought that regards similar tendencies by humans as either mere constructs and therefore not real, or the opposite: innate and therefore self-perpetuating. The reality, far more likely, is that human culture is possible because we are influenced, like the animal world, by a mixture of both our behaviour constructs and genetic determinants.

This would be a surprising statement to many people who are inclined to contrast the wholly instinctual life of animals with the cerebral inventions of human society. But in the same way that a century ago Freud turned this paradigm upside down and relentlessly uncovered the labyrinth of our libidinous urges and aggressive drives lurking under a veneer of civility, today a clutch of primatologists and zoologists is upsetting another paradigm by painstakingly documenting the deliberate social practices and the complex emotional responses of the animal world. Their work is opening up a sphere of understanding that has enormous significance not only for the way we value the animals with which we share our planet, but also for the way we assess the necessity or otherwise of our own moral culture.

Why go down this route of inquiry at all, when tomes of theology have explored the sinful inclinations and the moral imperatives of the human race, and have made their own recommendations as to the way forward? The answer is simple: many of the sins they identify as well as the remedies they prescribe are questionable by today's standards. St Augustine and St John Chrysostom, to take two of the early Church's most influential theologians, displayed such repugnance and condescension toward women in their own milieu, for example, that one could hardly look to them as exemplars of the kind of love and compassion that could extend to the whole of humanity, let alone to the non-human world. It is no surprise, therefore, to find the thirteenth-century theologian, Thomas Aquinas, citing Augustine approvingly on the subject of animals: 'When we hear it said, "Thou shalt not kill," we do not take it as referring to trees, for they have no sense, nor to irrational animals, because they have no fellowship with us. Hence it follows that the words, "Thou shalt not kill," refer to the killing of man.'[1]

Aquinas's reasoning, which uses an Aristotelian argument about the order of creation from lower to higher beings, concludes that, 'There is no sin in using a thing for the purpose for which it is ... it is not unlawful if man uses plants for the good of animals and animals for the good of man as the Philosopher [Aristotle] states.'[2] There is no human duty therefore to love animals, only to put them to use, according to their purpose. It was an attitude that was widespread both in the ancient world and in his time, though there were exceptions. The beliefs of most Buddhists and some Hindu sects, like the Yogi and the Jain traditions, encouraged vegetarianism, while Judaism has many ancient and medieval rabbinic sayings that not only counsel sensitivity and care for animals, but also occasionally depict beasts as loving God and being religiously observant.[3]

However much one wants to cast a benevolent light on these exceptional attitudes, the truth is that the Eastern tradition did not foster a culture of care toward animals,[4] and the Jewish tradition did not exclude killing them for food. The historical record shows that these examples of regard for animals made but a small dent in the common practices of treating them as little more than chattels, being indifferent to their suffering and generally affording them a low level of moral consideration.

It is with a superb sense of irony, therefore, that today we turn to specialists in the behavioural life of animals for inspiration and guidance in our quest for a greater understanding of our own moral nature. What has caused this turnabout? For one thing, the shrinking habitat of wild animals, leading to their endangerment and even extinction, has forced us to recognise that, contrary to Aquinas, we definitely have fellowship with them. And, no less compelling, specialists in animal behaviour are discovering strong evidence of a moral dimension to our partners in creation—which may amount to the primordial substratum of our own moral inclinations. It is a discovery that is not meant to remind us of our baser drives alone, but also to astonish us with the grandeur and the social complexity of the natural world, which is our inheritance. It is a lesson in humility if nothing else.

Everyone has their favourite story of animal compassion, like the account in Jeffery Masson's book *When Elephants Weep* of the elephant that repeatedly attempted to save a stranded baby hippo from drowning in a mud hole, and despite the angry protestations of the mother was successful. If you prefer monkeys, then it would be the story in Frans de Waal's *Good Natured* of Mozu, the macaque in the Japanese alps born without hands and feet, who dragged herself along in the deep snow at a much slower pace than her mates, yet was accommodated by the troop, and lived to become a mother of several offspring.

The most widely reported incident occurred in the Brookfield Zoo, Chicago, in 1996, when a female gorilla named Binti Jua rescued a three-year-old toddler who had fallen six metres into the gorilla enclosure. Within moments of the accident, Binti Jua walked over to the unconscious little boy, cradled him in her arms, took him to a place that she associated with humans, and laid him down in front of the zookeeper's door. While the tenderness shown to the child could be attributed to maternal instinct, the same could not be said about an incident ten years earlier at the Jersey Wildlife Preservation Trust in the Channel Islands, when a male gorilla, Jambo, reacted to a similar situation by standing guard over a child until zoo officials could come to its aid.[5] For every one of these examples there are scores more on record, demonstrating that the ability to empathise with another in distress and the desire to help are responses that are not restricted to humans, nor even to a creature's own species.

Perhaps the best known observer of the complex emotional and social interactions amongst primates is Frans de Waal, whose many books on the subject span a thirty-year professional involvement in the field of primatology. His patient documentation of chimpanzee relations has shown that the eruption of hostility between individual chimps — usually a minor affair like chasing or screaming, not physical violence — is either curtailed by others who maintain order or is followed by various acts of reconciliation. De Waal discovered, to his surprise, that it was not the hostilities he observed that were important but, on the contrary, the many ways in which the social group, and especially the leader of the troop, regularly minimised the full potential of aggression. Indeed, he would only come to realise how successful was the suppression of violence amongst primates when he suffered a major shock at the killing of one of his favourite male chimps by another. The communal harmony that was characteristic of the primate group had momentarily broken down.

This should not surprise us given the length of the learning period for a chimpanzee, which travels with its mother and siblings for the first eight years of its life and is only considered an adult at sixteen years.[6] During that time, the chimp is not only instructed by its mother in survival skills, but is also protected by her when play gets too rough or when more powerful individuals in the group are provoked and dangerous. Despite the importance of the mother and child union, keeping the peace in a community of primates involves much more than learning to avoid conflict. Acts of reconciliation between hostile parties, such as clasping hands with another and holding them high in the air, sharing food, grooming, rubbing genitals and kissing, were regularly observed by de Waal at the San Diego Zoo,

Arnhem Zoo and at Yerkes Primate Center in Atlanta, Georgia, as well as in the wild. Group harmony is therefore unimaginable unless chimps learn to conform their behaviour to expectations, and this is best achieved through imitation, something that is seen when immature chimpanzees copy their elders who use stones as tools to crush nuts, for example, or when youngsters follow an adult's display of beating the chest with a mock version of their own. That such juvenile mirroring, in the latter case, is tolerated and not punished by the adults indicates they understand its training function in their young.

Recognising typically human behaviours in the animal world goes back to antiquity, and there are plenty of examples in Greek thought, in biblical writings, such as Proverbs, and in Chinese and Indian sources. Indeed, it could be said that such close observation of our furry and feathered friends led to the universal tendency to produce animal fables as a means of imparting elemental wisdom. Vikram Seth's collection from several cultures, *Beastly Tales*, is a contemporary example. Of course, strict biologists view this line of thought as anthropomorphising animal behaviour. Their fundamental position, which sees all animal actions as driven by basic biological imperatives, rules out any explanation that attributes conscious virtuosity (or what de Waal, following Darwin, would call 'a healthy dose of fellow-feeling and kindness') to animals.[7]

Such fellow-feeling is the basis of empathy, which is able to both imagine the feelings of another and anticipate an ameliorating effect of an action toward that individual. Empathy requires some planning and forethought, but it is not always in service of altruistic ends. The same ability to imagine a feeling and anticipate a reaction is called upon in other situations, such as playing. Frans de Waal found himself the butt of a chimpanzee game which involved a mature female filling her mouth with water from a spigot, hiding behind the other chimps and then squirting the water on him when he walked by the enclosure. The obvious excitement and sense of fun that followed left no doubt as to the ape's playful intention and her expectation of de Waal's surprised reaction. When he scolded her, she sulked and stopped the game.[8] In another example of culturally evolved behaviour, Carel van Schaik has observed wild orang-utans on the island of Borneo 'snag-riding': climbing a dead tree, toppling it and 'surfing' it as it falls, then at the last minute grabbing a creeper and swinging to safety before the tree crashes to the ground.[9]

Playfulness is hard to account for in the strict terms of biological necessity for survival and goes some way to demonstrating the creativity that occurs amongst primates. Indeed, creativity is an essential element of culture, and it is the discovery of the rudiments of culture in the life of apes and other animals that makes the work of Frans de Waal and Carel van Schaik so significant. Van Schaik's observation of twenty-four different kinds of activities, including blowing good-night kisses-squeeks, according to traditions unique to specific orang-utan groups, shatters the illusion that man is the only animal to have ascended to the realm of making culture and passing it on.[10] And if culture is deeply rooted in the animal world, then its tendency toward patterns of authority, uniform or shared practices and even retributive behaviour is not an unnatural outcome. On the contrary, the human penchant for devising cultural forms and learning to pass them on may well be part of our natural inheritance, and not an elaborate system of self-delusion designed to keep our true selves buried in a web of self deceit, as is suggested by some New Age thinkers. It could be said that it is part of our nature to nurture and that cultural forms are indispensable if the human group is to survive.

The moral culture of a group is by no means based exclusively on displaying kindness to one's fellow creatures in a reckless outpouring of selfless love. Retributive emotions amongst animals were recognised as the foundation of moral culture by Edward Westermarck in the early years of the last century.[11] It should be noted that the biblical injunction to meet injury with punishment formalises this basic communal tendency. Far from being perceived as a divinely sanctioned formula of crude retribution, the ancient moral code, as biblical scholars often point out, was nuanced and elaborated, allowing its Jewish and Christian interpreters to exercise proportionate punishment, which is the real meaning of 'an eye for an eye, a tooth for a tooth'. This approach requires an intellectual assessment of the weight or seriousness of each crime and misdemeanour, and rejects a singular punitive reaction (such as execution) to every type of injury. One might expect this level of discernment to be exclusive to humans, but equally deliberate actions are witnessed amongst animals. De Waal cites the case of a macaque that was attacked by a dominant member of its troop, and then vented aggression on a younger relative of its attacker.[12] This indirect response suggests that the macaque made a strategic decision intended to deliver both an effective blow and a clear message, while avoiding getting involved in what could have been a fatal encounter with its more powerful attacker.

And yet, as noted earlier, monkeys and chimps are not doomed to endlessly repeat severe punitive measures to keep a semblance of order. In an experiment conducted by de Waal to test whether rhesus monkeys would learn the more easy-going and tolerant behaviours of stump-tailed macaques if the two groups were kept together for five months, the outcome was extremely positive and specific. The rhesus monkeys, though initially frightened of their new mates, nonetheless learned their reconciliation behaviours and eventually practised them at the rate of their mentors, but they did not pick up any of their other gestures.[13] Undoubtedly, one could explain the selective adoption of tolerant behaviours by pointing to the survival imperative of the slightly smaller rhesus monkeys. But how does that differ from the deliberate human practice of adopting conciliatory behaviour toward strangers, or people in general, because it is thought to be beneficial to the group? There is little difference if, in both situations, fostering social relationships is the means whereby survival together is achieved. From an evolutionary point of view, a related practice like helping others is very probably a strong survival trait, although an unexpected one. On the face of it, risking injury or death to come to the aid of others would seem to reduce the possibility of future offspring. Yet it cannot be as it seems, or altruism would be literally bred out of the human population, leaving only a collection of loners. Altruism, along with its accident-prone agents, would be extinct, as dead as the proverbial dodo bird.

It should be acknowledged that such a pragmatic interpretation of what is normally regarded as a religiously prescribed moral decision (to put aside self-interest and welcome strangers) as well as the not inconsiderable assumption that there is a link between primates and humans, is considered heretical in some circles. Regarding the latter assumption, it is safe to say that the world is divided roughly into two camps: those who accept an evolutionary and behavioural link of some kind among gorillas, chimpanzees and humans, which share between 97.7 and 98.4 per cent of their genetic make-up, and those who do not. Whatever side one takes, this chapter is not an attempt to reassert a direct evolutionary link with primates. It is more properly about recognising the existence of behaviours in the animal world which are analogous to the ordering of human society, according to what we might call rules of mutual obligation.

The suggestion that human beings might be duty-bound to be nice to strangers because it contributes to their group survival is cause for offence in some religious circles on the grounds that moral imperatives derive solely from a divinely revealed source, and their promotion or otherwise of human survival is therefore entirely beside the point and can never be the reason for their truth or force. This rejection of a utilitarian ethic is the stand normally associated with fundamentalists or biblical literalists, who hold that morality is commanded by God and responded to by human beings, irrespective of perceived consequences. The important elements are choice followed by faith and obedience, in precisely the same way that Abraham showed perfect faith and was duly prepared to sacrifice his own son, Isaac, in unquestioning obedience to God. True morality is performed with eyes turned heavenward and is blind to worldly concerns.

Anyone familiar with the earthy realism of the Bible knows that this unswerving and rigid attitude does not do justice to the nature of the sacred writings themselves nor to the ways they were interpreted in late antiquity and at various times since. (Even the case of Abraham was strenuously explained by subsequent generations, repulsed by the suggestion of human sacrifice, as an elaborate divine subterfuge that was never intended to put Isaac under his father's knife.) It is a simple fact that biblical imperatives were elaborated, qualified and interpreted in the light of historical realities, tastes and necessities as early as the setting down of legal texts.

One can see the developing process in the very first book of the Bible, where God's seven laws for mankind in the story of Noah in the book of Genesis become the ten commandments in the story of Moses in the book of Exodus. The book of Deuteronomy is a very considerable elaboration and update of the laws already given in Exodus, and it is in this latter book that the idea of centralised worship of the Lord in the Temple of Jerusalem takes precedence over and eventually eliminates local shrines.

In a supreme effort to make the Bible relevant to Jewish life in late antiquity, sages and rabbis produced biblical commentaries, which essentially comprised a body of legislation collected into the Mishnah at the end of the second century. But even this was partly dated the moment it was codified. To give but one example, all the legal discussions between the famous rabbis, Hillel and Shammai, regarding the appropriate forms of dough offering and sacrificial offering to be made to the Temple in Jerusalem were irrelevant since the Temple was destroyed by the Romans in AD 70, never to be rebuilt. Since Jews were cast out of their land by the Romans the Mishnah's discussion of the proper treatment of the land is also, practically speaking, irrelevant.

Revisionism is especially evident in the prophetic books of the Bible, where, for instance, Hosea denounced the animal sacrificial cult of the Temple, which had been prescribed in detail in the book of Leviticus. In the later biblical prophets, Hosea and Amos, one sees a clear preference for ethical practices over priestly propitiations, as laid out in the book of Leviticus.[14] Hosea cries out in the name of God, 'For I desire steadfast love and not sacrifice, the knowledge of God, rather than burnt offerings.'[15] The prophet Amos echoes these sentiments when he speaks for God who despises the ritual feasts, takes no delight in solemn assemblies, rejects the peace offerings and orders Temple singers and musicians away, and instead commands the Israelites: 'But let justice roll down like waters, and righteousness like an ever-flowing stream.'[16] When it came to strictly moral rather than ritual injunctions, these too were modified, such that polygamous marriage, which was commonplace in ancient Israel and attested to in the Bible, was later banned by the rabbis.

A further reinterpretation of the moral–legal teachings of the Bible is evident in the New Testament, both in Jesus' sayings and in Paul's epistles to the fledgling communities of followers. It could be argued that the early Church was busily revamping God's commands to Israel to suit its own expansionist aims and make the adoption of Greeks and Romans into the fold a great deal easier. Hence the large number of sacred taboos that were clearly spelled out in the Holy Book, such as the laws of table purity and the prohibition against the making of idols, which were simply jettisoned by the early Church. This, despite Jesus' warning that not a jot or tittle of the law would be removed. Instead, with an eye to the mission field, new taboos from the Hellenistic world were adopted. The pervasive Hellenistic belief that physical contact with women polluted male spiritual purity led to the early Church's practice and requirement of celibacy by priests. Such pragmatic concerns were serving more than survival itself — although given the Church's persecution by the Romans in its early period this was no small consideration. If the Church were to fulfil its claim to being the one true faith, then it would have to increase its followers amongst the Greek and Roman peoples, and that was best achieved by adopting some of the cultural attitudes of the majority. God's requirements of the faithful were therefore reinterpreted and applied in ways that served Church growth as well as stability.

Securing peace and comfort for most people in society, as envisaged in the Bible, is a primary moral duty. But as the Bible itself demonstrates, that particular obligation can and does periodically clash with the entrenched traditions of the Temple and the powers of the throne when both become excessively self-serving. The biblical prophets called this justice, and relentlessly insisted upon charity to the weakest members of society, such as widows, children and slaves, while they condemned ostentatious rulers lacking moral scruples. Many centuries later, from the late 1700s to the 1800s, the utilitarian brand of English philosophers, many of whom were either professed atheists or agnostics, called this the greatest good to the greatest number, and insisted upon fair laws that would not punish religious minorities or exploit children and the poor. It is patently clear that the arguments which the philosopher John Stuart Mill put forth in the English parliament on behalf of women, children and blacks in England's Caribbean colonies, and on behalf of Roman Catholic widows who were denied custody of their children, were motivated by a belief that their suffering was due to entrenched moral injustice, even if the Church, in these instances, had lost sight of it. Mill was also driven by an ideal vision of how society might operate fairly, and this involved a rejection of religious, sexual and racial intolerance of which there were many examples in nineteenth-century England. It is not difficult to interpret Mill's public efforts of moral revisionism, which blossomed into a tidal wave of social reform in Victorian England, as inspired by the biblical principles of justice and mercy. Although he would not describe himself as an obedient servant of God's law, Mill was well aware of the intrinsic value of these two central principles, originally etched as God's qualities in the Bible, and their material benefits to humanity. He would be their valiant champion in so far as they served the ideal to live peaceably with others while contributing to the prosperity of society as a whole. The best way of realising this moral culture was simply to make it practical, a view that is echoed by the contemporary moral philosopher James Q. Wilson, who observed that, 'moral behavior is more common when utility conspires with duty, and the strongest moral codes are invariably those that are supported by considerations of both advantage and obligation'.[17]

There is no straight line from monkeys to morality nor from primates to parliament (although de Waal devoted a book to *Chimpanzee Politics*), but there is an indisputable connection between the current interests of primatology and the social scientific insights that have enhanced our understanding of human society and its moral traditions. In both, the study of the social arrangements of group behaviour has identified their functional utility with their moral motivations. Indeed, sociology, which is the human science of group behaviour invented at the end of the nineteenth century to explain society to itself, has always been divided about one thing, and that is whether social structures generate religio-moral values, or the reverse, that they reflect pre-existing ones. It is impossible to answer this logical conundrum, but either way, a society's social structure and its moral values are seen to be inextricably bound one to the other, and are viable only in so far as they are mutually supportive. In philosophical terms, this is a simple teleology, a circular argument, but it is also the most enduring one around because it has become something of an ideal that societies aim to fulfil — but never achieve with complete success. It essentially affirms that morality is upheld when it is perceived to work broadly for the common good, and it breaks down (which is not to say that it is necessarily wrong) when it is palpably clear that it creates more conflict and individual suffering than stability. What happens then is anybody's guess, but trading off society's moral priorities, one against another, rests with those in power, whether in business, government, the Church or the people at large, and the relative strength of these sectors depends entirely on the type of political and economic arrangements of the society in question. In Western democratic societies, where all these sectors co-operate as well as vie with each other in an atmosphere of considerable freedom, moral prescriptions are challenged, revised or supplanted to reflect the ever-shifting power and position of the competing sectors.

Despite the great strides made in the academic sciences to map out and predict the complex relationships in nature and in human societies, it has always been an enormous challenge to incorporate this knowledge into a religious outlook. But that has never stopped Western man from trying to do so. To be sure, social scientists have come under fire every bit as much as evolutionary theorists for their attempts to explain moral culture. Critics label sociological explanations 'reductionist', in that they appear to reduce the religio-moral imperatives, properly the domain of divine revelation, to their practical consequences. The complaint is with the apparent suggestion that religion is ersatz, a mere epiphenomena, a second-order explanation for what is really going on, which is the rational ordering of a society according to relationships of mutual benefit. Defenders of religion as an unfathomable mystery reject the implication that if you scratch true religion, beneath it you find society.

The criticism is disingenuous, at least for the Western tradition. For all its pretensions to purism, it assumes that what is religious is necessarily irrational, impractical and not of this world. It is as if the story of Moses on Mount Sinai was about him climbing up the mountain in order to witness a burning bush and a pillar of smoke. Fortunately for the heirs of Moses, the meaning of Mount Sinai was not divine pyrotechnics nor Moses' personal account of his rapturous experience in the presence of the Lord (which did not even merit recording), but was the seminal act of receiving and propagating a moral and religious teaching of how human beings should relate to one another and to their God. The God of the Bible is principally a lawgiver and an ethicist, not a magician. The role of Jesus in the Sermon on the Mount in the Gospel of Matthew is consistent with the pattern already set down at Sinai and in the subsequent biblical books. For all their differences, the covenant of the Old Testament and that of the New directly addressed the domain of human relationships and each in their own way directed how individuals should conduct themselves according to high moral principles and under the eyes of God. Followers would be judged according to how well they lived up to those principles. This is also the message of the biblical prophets, who were unbridled in their attacks against the morally corrupt, finding fault with priests and kings as much as with the rabble and foreign powers. The heavenly kingdom was imagined as a place where these moral teachings would find perfect expression. Even the lion would lie down with the lamb, an image that undoubtedly was understood then, just as it is now, to be a metaphor of the strong and the weak, the rich and the poor, finding peace together at last.

Admitting that society is at the core of the Western religious tradition is not to say that it alone constitutes religion, but that it recognises that influencing for good the realm of worldly considerations is essential to its purpose. For example, to say it is harder for a rich man to get to heaven than for a camel to pass through the eye of a needle is to presume knowledge of a social structure where the wealthy are permissive and yield to the temptations of frivolity and self-indulgence and forget their duties and obligations to the poor and unfortunate.[18] In the Gospel of Luke the parable follows another one of a rich man who was clothed in the expensive colour purple, ate sumptuously day after day, yet ignored Lazarus the poor sick man at his gate, who desired only the crumbs that fell from his table. When the rich man died he went to hell, and he looked up from his anguish to see Lazarus in the bosom of Abraham, and he asked how this was possible, and the answer came swiftly, that his family would not be saved from a fate such as his even if Lazarus would rise from the dead and warn them because, 'If they do not hear Moses and the prophets, neither will they be convinced if someone should rise from the dead.'[19] The teaching clearly recognises that the rich man had forsaken the moral injunctions of his tradition even though he was in the greatest position to be of help to his fellow man, and miracles would not suffice for ignoring that personal responsibility. If leading a righteous life were not the core of the biblical tradition, and it was something else, like an aesthetic mystical experience or a divine visitation, then there would be no reason to make a bad example of the rich man, who if anything would be more available than Lazarus for these pursuits, as were the elite classes in ancient Greece and the educated alchemists and mystics of the Renaissance.

Just what comprises the true essence of the religious life is a perennial question, but the rise of science in the nineteenth and twentieth centuries was a catalyst to public debate on the matter, and it had ironic consequences. On the one hand, science generally dampened belief in the supernatural claims of religion, such that Darwin reported his gradual conviction that the miracles, the Gospel accounts and the claim to divine revelation of Christianity had no empirical truth.

I gradually came to disbelieve in Christianity as a divine revelation. This disbelief crept over me at a very slow rate, but at last was complete. The rate was so slow that I felt no distress, and have never since doubted even for a single second that my conclusion was correct.[20]

On the other hand, the view that the religious life was about moral conscience within human society was fanned into a flame by those who were content to let the supernatural embers grow cold. One of these was the eminent physiologist J.S. Haldane (1860–1936), who did not hold with those of his colleagues, like Thomas Huxley, who believed that science was incompatible with religion. Delivering the famous Gifford Lectures at the University of Glasgow in 1927–28, Haldane saw no necessary conflict between science and religion and noted that the rise of science had not diminished the popularity of religion. Incidentally, it is an observation that has not changed today if a 1997 random sampling of 1000 scientists, compared to a similar study in 1916, is anything to go by. It showed 40 per cent of scientists proclaimed a belief in a personal God and a further 15 per cent considered themselves agnostics.[21] As for Haldane, he explained his continued faith, and it went to the heart of the real relationship between religion and the 'secular' world: 'If my reasoning has been correct, there is no real connection between religion and the belief in supernatural events of any sort or kind.'[22]

Haldane seemed to intuitively understand that the miraculous accompanies the teachings of the great religions, but does not constitute them. As a Christian, Haldane said about himself:

> I can put my heart into this attempt [to formulate the proper relationship between science and religion] because no one can feel more strongly than I do that religion is the greatest thing in life, and that behind the recognised Churches there is an unrecognised Church to which all may belong, though supernatural events play no part in its creed.[23]

For many like Haldane who sensed that the 'unrecognised Church' exists without recourse to miracles but in the persuasion of its ethic, the discoveries of science, in medicine or in the cosmos, only broaden its realm of application. If the human world of good and evil is the proper domain of religion then it stands to reason that it is only on terra firma that its truths can be felt, expressed and measured.

It is no wonder then that this relatively friendly view toward science, together with an emphasis on religion as moral culture, would open the door to a theory that the survival of the fittest was identified with moral rectitude, such that the strong were naturally aligned with the right. The excesses to which Social Darwinism lent itself are well known, ranging from the Fascist ideologies of Mussolini and Hitler, who used it in their attempts to eliminate Jews and Gypsies from Europe, to the ideologies of the Marxists, who used it against property owners and anyone they deemed 'bourgeois'. In all cases, it was an unmitigated disaster.

In recent years, however, the theory has returned in modified form, although the memory of its abuse makes it an easy target for critics. Yet the evolutionary or biological explanation of morality is plausible, up to a point. As we have seen, Frans de Waal, over a thirty-year period, has documented the social patterns of behaviour in primates, observed their similarity to human ones and made cautious speculations about the presence of 'moral sentiments' in these and other animals. De Waal, however, stands at a significant distance from sociobiologist Edmond Wilson, who has argued that the selective adoption of so-called moral acts of altruism is based on the fact that it benefits the agent and his kin. It is a view that places far too much emphasis on the individual, according to philosopher Mary Midgley, who questions the assumption of selfishness in her discussion about the biological basis of altruism.[24] In her view, it is a utilitarian perspective gone wild, in that Wilson presumes individuals to be little more than calculators, plunging into the surf to save a drowning person because one day the rescuer, or his kin, may need to be saved.

According to Midgley, Wilson is guilty of an egotistical emphasis in his theory, which does not account for the numerous acts of altruism, big and small, that enjoy no reward, recognition, or payback, but are enacted out of an often visceral commitment to the value of caring for others. This is certainly how many rescuers of Jews during the Holocaust explain their actions — they could see no other possible way of behaving and to do otherwise was simply inhuman and unthinkable. (Given the Nazi reputation for threatening to punish anyone who helped the victims it remains an open question how many people were frightened away from acting on their natural impulse to help.) Many rescuers were uncomfortable at being specially recognised for their heroic acts by the Yad Vashem Museum in Jerusalem precisely because they did not feel they acted as heroes, but only as decent human beings who did what was right.

It calls to mind the last sane act of Friedrich Nietzsche, before he collapsed in a public square in Turin and was taken to a sanatorium. The man who spent his entire literary career denouncing pity as an example of the pathetic and weak Christian ethic, and who championed instead a new ethic of the strength and power of the *ubermensch* (superman), was himself overcome with pity when he saw an exhausted and starving workhorse collapse in the city square. He rushed over to it and threw his arms around the dying animal. All his philosophical ruminations about advancing a new moral ethic for humanity did not eliminate his visceral human trait to feel the suffering of another and offer comfort and tears of sympathy. It is this driving moral sentiment which is the very basis of our will to create moral cultures.

Fortunately, Mary Midgley is right about people not being calculators. If they were, they would soon discover most of their acts of altruism don't pay — at least not to the ones directly responsible nor even necessarily to their kith or kin. There is, however, a strong argument to be made for altruism's generalised value to the wider social group. When acts of charity and kindness are valorised or when they are barely noticed yet effectively pursued, altruism becomes a perpetually potential quality of society as a whole as well as an attitude of the heart. In this way, certain values are deepened or aroused, such that a moral sentiment to act kindly, for example, is given both public and private expression. Love, generosity and even weeping are sentiments which in and of themselves do not necessarily increase one's own prospects for survival, prosperity or happiness. From a rational point of view, most of the time these would pay few dividends. From an emotional point of view they would be expressed for their own sake, deepen bonds with fellow human beings and would regularly rehearse one's ability to respond in the same way to others in the future. To return to Nietzsche, who appears to be enjoying a new burst of popularity, he complained that he could find no-one with an identical grasp of the absolute truth as himself and he therefore resigned himself to being alone. But for the doting care of his sister in the last eleven years of his life when he was largely paralysed and demented, that would have been the case. History tells us that her motives may have been mixed with a personal desire to exploit his writings, yet the form in which she administered to his every need was nonetheless of intrinsic value as well as a familial duty. With Mary Midgley, one has to agree that the one impelling force, after all, is sociability, and it is a good thing too.[25] Even the primates have it down pat.

10. REDEEMING RELIGION FROM ITSELF
Cults Don't Think

The 1999 film *Fight Club* eerily ends with the collapse of several skyscrapers, which had been wired for meltdown by a cult that was bent on destroying the supreme icons of the affluent West. The story was not political, and could only be viewed as such from post September 11 eyes. Its subject was more familiar and reprised a theme that was memorably played out in the cinema classic of the 1950s, *Rebel Without a Cause*. In both films, the protagonist is attracted to a secret males-only club of daredevils who meet regularly to toughen themselves into fearless men. In *Rebel Without a Cause*, James Dean, like the rest of the boys, had to drive his car as fast as he could to the edge of a cliff and jump out in time; whereas in *Fight Club*, Edward Norton, who plays Jack, the mild-mannered executive of a company that makes unsafe cars, learns to fight, to inflict major bodily harm, and take it too. Senseless and destructive as these activities are, they are motivated by a gaping hole in the meaning of both protagonists' lives. We learn that both young men are haunted by their parents' loveless marriages, and in particular resent their morally unimpressive fathers.

And most obvious of all, they feel trapped in boring, pointless lives, in which people they once looked up to cause them to give up their idealism and forbid them to act on what they know is right. In the end, trashing property as well as themselves is a frenzied attempt to destroy illusions. But there is a final sting in the tail of both films. For all their attempts to prove otherwise, the two tough guys are little more than boys underneath it all, and they both crumple emotionally when faced with their own tragic fate.

Instead of exhibiting moral courage, they are swept into a tide of nihilism, into wanton destruction and the celebration of stupidity, epitomised by the cult characteristics of the fight club, which is sworn to secrecy and turns ordinary thinking people into sloganeering goons. These films are really about the perils of not acting on what you think and know to be right, and also about the desperation that ensues when you hand over your brain and moral instinct to someone else. In *Fight Club*, Jack's strange transformation, encouraged and facilitated by his alter ego (played by Brad Pitt), is caused by his inability to think or even stay awake, a result of chronic insomnia, which in turn is caused by his meaningless life. The spiral goes ever downward, until petty acts of vandalism against the establishment turn into an all-out attack on society itself. What is so astounding is how quickly a world one has taken for granted, including the very ideals that once beat in one's heart, can be reduced to rubble.

The attack on the World Trade Center and the Pentagon, and the subsequent attacks on other Western targets, including the devastating explosion in Bali in October 2002, all by Muslim extremists, throw a great deal of the world that we assumed was unassailable into a new light. They reveal literally in a flash how important and precious are the religious reforms and freedoms that Westerners have secured over hundreds of years. And yet like the vanished twin towers these freedoms suddenly seem, as in some apocalyptic nightmare, on the brink of oblivion. Now is not the time to panic, however, but to calmly reassess where we have come to and how we got here.

The non-violent co-existence that marks out the religious culture of the West is a supremely valued characteristic of Western social life, but its achievement has been far from smooth and its mandate is never finished. Yet it is unlikely that these precious freedoms in the future will be maintained without bloodshed, harking back to their origins when they were forged in revolution and civil unrest, which divided families and spilt blood. The Reformation, the English Puritan Revolution, the French Revolution, the civic revolts in much of Europe in 1848 and the American war against the British all had profound issues of religious freedom at their core. Most of us today would say that they were worth the struggle if they resulted in the constitutional freedoms, including religious freedom, that we enjoy by right. But there is one freedom equal to this that would benefit religion in an unanticipated way. It is the freedom of conscience which is protected by secular laws that would subject religious traditions and their institutional heads to the kind of scrutiny and accountability that would be required and expected in other spheres of society, and would be exercised with impunity.

The reason this critical scrutiny is so important is not, as some might think, to debilitate religion in general and erode its authority in the spirit of Denis Diderot, who proclaimed: 'Men will never be free till the last king is strangled with the entrails of the last priest.'[1]

The reverse is true for those who take religion seriously, because the very qualities of rational inquiry and transparency are part and parcel of the religious life itself; they are not the obsession of a carping chorus of hecklers in the gallery. The gallery is in the Church and its occupants are the faithful. The very revolutions that forced secular freedoms also directly influenced the substance of religion itself. The emancipation and education of women, for example, and their representation on church councils and synagogue boards eventually produced a burgeoning of new scholarship, inclusive theology and ordained women as spiritual leaders. Education after the civil rights movement in America had granted full citizens' rights to African–Americans changed church culture such that even the highly autonomous Mormon Church revised its theology, which had deemed Blacks to be a lower order of humans, not eligible for the highest rank of elder in the Church. In Australia, recognition of

Aboriginal rights and an interest in indigenous spiritual heritage has produced Rainbow Spirituality, a theological fusion of Christianity with Aboriginal beliefs, allowing not only a more comfortable assimilation of Western ideas, but also continuity with an ancient and treasured ancestral tradition. The most passionate articulators of modern faith have been keen to preserve and even expand the possibility of an existential encounter with God, the mystery at the heart of individual faith, while at the same time they have acted on and reinforced the eternally valid truths for a free and democratic society.

One of these truths, which was articulated by all the political proponents of the Enlightenment, is the importance of education and the cultivation of the mind. Disraeli proclaimed, 'A university should be a place of light, liberty and learning,' carrying the promise of a good and a fair society. He echoed the ideals of an educated public already advanced by Napoleon Bonaparte who declared, 'Public instruction should be the first object of government.' Across the Atlantic another great social architect, Thomas Jefferson, declared, 'Enlighten people generally, and tyranny and oppressions of both body and mind will vanish, like evil spirits at the dawn of day.' These statements by the political leaders of their day were premised on the confident belief that education would reflect the basic values of the newly forming democracies, which rewarded industry and self-responsibility, law-abiding probity and, in America, voluntary participation in communal organisations. Jefferson's belief that education could preserve society against evil was undoubtedly the reason that by the late nineteenth-century one social observer noted that in every village in America, 'the school houses were larger than the churches'. The same was undoubtedly true in Australia and Canada, where schools did not have to compete with centuries of cathedrals dotting the landscape.

The importance of the education movement cannot be gainsaid, for its fruits contributed in manifold ways to the progress of society, especially in the field of medicine and public health. But concerning religion, the free and rational inquiry of the university was sometimes regarded as an unwelcome challenge. This was dramatically played out in America around the controversial theory of evolution, the famous Scopes 'Monkey' trial in 1925 being an exemplary case. It crystallised the division between conservative and liberal Protestants, the latter having established themselves at Yale, Harvard and later Princeton universities.

Against these, the conservatives banded together in a movement to promote the fundamentals of Christianity, including the inerrancy of the Bible, the divinity of Jesus Christ, the Virgin Birth, a substitutionary theology of atonement, and the physical resurrection and bodily return of Christ. These five cardinal beliefs were popularised in twelve tracts entitled *The Fundamentals*, published between 1910 and 1914, which became the basis of what was known as the fundamentalist camp of Christianity. As against the modernists, who were reformulating doctrine in light of contemporary philosophical and scientific research, the fundamentalists wished to return to 'original' Christianity. Although the fundamentalist movement is often dismissed as conducive to closed-mindedness, it bore some surprising fruit, for the assiduous reading of the Bible was partly responsible for the social gospel movement, once dubbed 'the praying wing of Progressivism'.[2] The desire to live in a way that is faithful to the teachings of Jesus extended beyond an inward spirituality to a belief that society should be ordered according to socialist principles. While a number of failed co-operative and communitarian social experiments ensured, the social gospel agenda became more generalised and was summed up by Washington Gladden in 1905: 'If the kingdom of heaven ever comes to our city, it will come in and through the City Hall.'[3]

The social gospel movement, especially as articulated by Walter Rauschenbusch in *A Theology of Social Gospel*,[4] would be influential amongst intellectuals, but in the end its political ambitions, when not actually achieved, were overshadowed by the domestic prosperity that churches would enjoy by virtue of the evolving middle class of their followers. The rampant industrialisation of society, which the social gospel movement partly blamed for the misery of the poor, also brought unprecedented wealth in the late nineteenth and early twentieth centuries. Many factors, including immigration of specific language groups, like the German and the Dutch, and the increased financial prosperity of the population caused a rapid increase in denominational divisions and the diversification of church organisations to serve growing communities.

It is an open question whether this contributed to the strength of the dominant Western tradition, but the multiplication of church divisions came under fire, and not only from the poison pen of the founder of Theosophy, Madame Helena Blavatsky, who devoted a section of her massive volume *Isis Unveiled* to an unbridled attack on the thousands of churches and hundreds of divisions extant in late nineteenth-century Christianity. The great German–American theologian and social historian at Harvard, Richard Niebuhr, would also subject the phenomenon of denominational establishment to a sociological critique, claiming it tended toward a watered-down social conscience.[5]

This was also the concern of the twentieth century's most remarkable Christian, a man of immense personal courage and learning, Albert Schweitzer. In his view, prosperity could never do for Chrisitianity what thinking could. Schweitzer deeply valued the pursuit of knowledge not only to better serve the world, but also as an abiding partner of faith. Today this conjunction would seem oddly out of place with the way we have come to mark out faith and piety on the one hand and the pursuit of higher education on the other, as if they were separate domains. Nothing could have been further from Schweitzer's experience and message.

To be sure, Schweitzer was no ordinary Christian thinker. A scholar of the philosophy of Immanuel Kant, Schweitzer produced his own *Philosophy of Civilization*. In the field of theology, he wrote one of the most influential works of biblical criticism, *The Quest for the Historical Jesus*, as well as *The Mystery of the Kingdom of God* and other works including a major study of Paul's theology. He was a Lutheran minister who preached widely throughout his life, an accomplished organist and one of the great scholars and interpreters of Bach. All these faded into insignificance, however, beside his one true calling. He was a medical doctor and missionary who went to work in Lambaréné in the Republic of Gabon, Africa, where he was architect, builder, administrator and chief doctor for over thirty years. He received the Nobel Peace Prize for 1952. As his work as a medical missionary attests, Schweitzer would not use his brilliant intellectual gifts to simply grace the halls of a university or the Sunday pulpit. He was convinced that a commitment to knowledge and meditative thought was the duty of a Christian, and that it contributed mightily to a sincere living-out of his faith, which for him was meaningless without outward expression in an ethical life.

It is almost a cliché today to hear educational professionals emphasise the importance of knowledge in a world that is increasingly complex and requires our informed response. For the German-born Schweitzer it was no facile plea. In 1931, he wrote an epilogue to his autobiographical work, *Out of My Life and Thought*, which could not have been more prescient, given the malevolent whirlwind that started from his homeland and was to overtake the Christian communities of Europe, leaving six million of their Jewish fellow citizens dead. He could not have known what was to come, but his belief that the individual was the foundation of personal moral agency and responsibility would be too heavy a burden for many of his countrymen, who preferred to retreat into the silent collectivities of the Church. He wrote that Christianity had become excessively worldly, building up its organised bodies and deluding itself that it was growing stronger because of it. He claimed, on the contrary, that the Church was growing spiritually weaker. He accused it of hardly acting on its spiritual or ethical principles, and he cited the renewal of torture in many countries, to which Christianity offered no opposition, 'even in words, much less deeds'.

The theologian, philosopher, musician and medical missionary was not just complaining about the dead hand of bureaucracy which can place a blanket of inertia over organisations, including Churches. He was specifically faulting the Church's members with a failure to think, a failure to apply the gift of rational thought and observation to their own faith: 'Christianity cannot take the place of thinking, but it must be founded on it. In and by itself [Christianity] is not capable of overcoming thoughtlessness and scepticism ... I myself owe it to thought that I was able to retain my faith in religion.'[6]

Not a blind acceptance of an otherworldly promise of redemption for Schweitzer, but a combination of rational thought and religious faith was essential to the power of a true, living Christianity. His was not some vain quest to apply rational scientific inquiry to the eternal metaphysical questions. As a Christian he believed that the connection between himself and the Infinite was manifest in love, and that was all the metaphysics one needed to know about God. All the other big questions could remain unanswered, for they could never provide the reason or the will to live as a true Christian. Schweitzer was certainly taking his lead from Jesus himself, who discouraged speculative questions from his apostles and the crowds alike. Indeed, Schweitzer claimed, 'the deeper is piety, the humbler are its claims with regard to knowledge of the metaphysical'.[7] For Schweitzer, the aim of the religious life was, after all, a deep elemental piety, which expressed itself in a reverence for life and the power of love. It was directed to the human and animal world, and tested in the ethical life: 'The First Cause of Being, as he manifests himself in nature, is to us always impersonal. To the First Cause of Being that is revealed to us in the will to love, however, we relate as to an ethical personality.'[8]

'Reverence for life' would become the ethical expression of Schweitzer's philosophy, and it also encapsulated the Christian ethic by which he lived. It came to him in Africa, as he was on the third day of a wearying journey, on an island in the middle of a wide river. He noticed across to his left, on a sandbank, four hippopotamuses with their young plodding along in his direction. He must have felt a sudden sense of common purpose with these great hulking creatures lumbering to their destination.

Just then, in my great tiredness and discouragement, there flashed upon my mind, unforseen and unsought, the phrase, 'reverence for life' ... Now I had found my way to the idea in which the affirmation of the world and ethics are contained side by side! ... Only by means of reverence for life can we establish a spiritual and humane relationship with both people and all living creatures within our reach.[9]

We have already encountered similar sentiments in Don Cupitt's version of a 'religion of life', but it bears only a little resemblance to Schweitzer's thinking. His was an ethic to be found within Christianity, not invented from secular sources as an alternative to it. Nor did Schweitzer imagine his ethic in non-theistic terms, since it was the love of God which inspired it in the first place, and gave it a personal imperative. Schweitzer was keen, however, to emphasise Christianity's humanism which he found in the person of Jesus, the mediator of God's love. Far from being an enemy of Christian faith, humanism was already there in Jesus' Sermon on the Mount, in which Jesus issued a call to repentance followed by a detailed instruction of how individuals must act in righteous ways toward each other. There is no mysticism here. Indeed, mysticism was problematic for Schweitzer. Although evident in all religions, it was insufficient in itself as a basis of either religion or life, and held little attraction to Schweitzer, who was impatient with its lack of social conscience and its inability to give practical assistance. Yet mysticism did have significance for ethics, and in a sense was its ultimate reward, though not its purpose. In the act of serving what he regarded as the universal ethic of the reverence for life, Schweitzer conceded that 'a mystical union with the Universal Spirit' ultimately would result. It would put one in harmony with the 'Creative Will'.[10]

But all was not well in the Christianity of his day, and Schweitzer believed it would be a misfortune for the faith and for humankind generally if, as he warned, 'it refuses to let itself be interpreted in terms of ethical religious thinking ... I demand from Christianity that it reform itself in the spirit of sincerity and with thoughtfulness, so it may become conscious of its true nature'.[11]

Three generations have passed since Schweitzer wrote those words, but the task of bringing to bear a powerful ethic that will heal the world yet remain an individual expression of elemental piety remains as urgent today as it was in Schweitzer's time. If the world was verging on collapse then, it has suffered several catastrophes since, without, it seems, any hope of Schweitzer's ethical challenge to Christianity being fully met. To be fair, it was a command that could never be fulfilled, not least because his terminology was too sweeping. Christianity could hardly be addressed as if it were an entity with a central will and a singular mind, any more than Catholicism could be, even with the benefit of its centralised rule under a pope.

It is ironic therefore that the man who stepped up to assume the mantle of prophet for a new global ethic would be a Catholic, whose very inclination to question the direction of his Church would land him in purgatory. Hans Kung, the Swiss–German Catholic priest, scholar and theologian set himself the task of developing a universal ethic that might galvanise the religious communities of the world into a common purpose. His newly found role as the ecumenical architect of ethics would emerge after the Vatican's Sacred Congregation for the Doctrine of the Faith issued a censure in 1979, which banned him from teaching Catholic theology because of his strident criticisms of the papacy. Perhaps fired by the disappointment and frustration of seeing his Church turn its back on the liberal and democratic ethos of the Second Vatican Council (1962–65), for which he was a theological consultant and writer, Kung turned his efforts to articulating an agenda that would be bigger than the Church itself. He chose the one-hundredth anniversary of the Parliament of the World's Religions, held in Chicago in March 1993, to launch the outline of his New World Ethic for Global Responsibility. It was a momentous occasion, with six thousand delegates registered at the week-long conference, most of whom had come to hear his address. Afterward, he spoke to me about his project for a 'global ethic', which he was keen to point out was not a legal document, like the United Nations Declaration of Human Rights, for example, but a statement of values which could only persuade individuals to change their attitude, alter their inner convictions and eventually transform whole cultures. The urgency in his voice was palpable, as was the necessity to avert the coming conflagration, which in 1993 had also prompted Samuel

Huntington to write a paper called 'The Clash of Civilizations', published by the journal *Foreign Affairs* and destined to become one of the most talked about books of the decade.

Kung could not have set himself a more formidable task, which aimed at nothing less than creating the basis of world peace. This he believed could not occur without peace amongst religions, hence his immediate task of formulating an ethic that all religions could accept. Having canvassed alternate routes, he did not believe any of them would work. He was under no illusion, for example, that religious conflict would be solved by a post-modern ethic of tolerance whereby all religions are accepted as equal to one another. That would yield nothing but a willing indifference to the very things that divided religions, and do nothing to ease the conflicts it claimed to solve. Nor was he convinced that religions could be integrated in some overall unifying scheme, which assigned each of them a rank according to a hierarchy of truths (as found in the Baha'i Faith), which he recognised no religion would accept. It goes without saying that no one religion could be triumphantly held up as the one true religion, before which all others would have to bend or ideally be eliminated.

Kung finally proposed an ethical agenda which he argued could be applied to all existing religions, yet transcend their particularities. Inspired by the First Colloquium on Religion held by UNESCO in Paris in 1989, he broadly identified the dignity and autonomy of the human person as central to religion; self-criticism as necessary for interreligious dialogue; and a theology of peace, which would transcend religious divisions, as the hope of the future. These are sensible if not self-evident solutions, but in truth they seem all the less likely for having been uttered because they are so far away from the religious realities they seek to address. Kung's *Global Responsibility: In Search of a New World Ethic* strikes one as a document that was conceived by a number of committees as a series of solutions to a host of problems, none of which are practically based. Its highly rational tone and confident optimism seem to have germinated in university classrooms and cordial international meetings, both of which are worlds away from the coalface of religious conflict, like the Sudanese villages and the Pakistani and

Indonesian churches where Christians are massacred simply because of their faith. Despite Kung's profound awareness of the complexity of these issues, *Global Responsibility* reads like a list of thoughtful recommendations based on the belief that rational argument will solve some of the world's most irrational hatreds.

Yet for all its weaknesses, the fact that the strongest message remains an abiding and unapologetic advocacy of humanism, human rights and human values, which are given absolute sanction, is testimony to the modern, post-Enlightenment cast of the ecumenical agenda. It could not be otherwise, for the projects of interreligious dialogue and religious pluralism, not to mention the insistence on self-critical reassessment of religious teachings, are the products of the Enlightenment and remain its most precious contributions to religion in general. The West is the laboratory par excellence of religious traditions living side by side, not only sharing the same territory, but also the very same citizens' rights and opportunities, legal protections and economic possibilities, as well as, for the most part, the same education system. It is no surprise that the West should also lead the way in thinking through a possible theology of peace.

At the moment, however, such an ambitious ecumenical project seems as close to fulfilment as the proverbial coming of the Kingdom of Heaven. What is at the forefront of the religious scene today is an epidemic of hatred that has spread throughout the Muslim world and has gripped clerics, congregations, schools and mobs alike. It has been growing for decades and has identified its enemy as the triple-headed monster of the Jews, America and Britain. Its reading of choice is *The Protocols of the Elders of Zion*, the nineteenth-century Tsarist Russian forgery written to incite pogroms against the Jews. In the language of conspiracy and surreal imagery *The Protocols* purports to be a secret document of a Jewish cabal planning to take over the world. Hitler and his chief propagandist, Joseph Goebbels, used it to great effect, accompanied by repulsive cartoons, to stir up the German populace into a frenzy of hatred. They passed it on to Arab Nazi sympathisers, like the grand mufti of Jerusalem and the leader of the Palestinian Arab national movement, Haj Amin al-Husseini, whom Hitler invited to wartime Berlin. On 2 November 1943, a year after the Nazis began implementing the 'final solution' to exterminate Europe's Jews, Al-Husseini enthusiastically declared that, 'the Germans know how to get rid of the Jews' and insisted that their friendship with Hitler was 'a permanent and lasting friendship based on mutual interest'.

It is a sentiment that finds many contemporary echoes. Muslim nations continued to greet propaganda like *The Protocols of the Elders of Zion* with enthusiasm and are its most avid publishers, distributors and readers. Easily picked up in bookstores across the Muslim world, it is cited authoritatively in the Palestinian Hamas Covenant of 1988 (Article 32), is taught as history in Saudi Arabian schoolbooks and has recently been translated to the silver screen. 'Horseman Without a Horse,' a multi-million dollar thirty-part adaptation of *The Protocols of the Elders of Zion*, featuring a cast of 400 and presented as historical fact, was shown on Egyptian national television in 2002. This in a country with a government-censored media, which does not air material offensive to the authorities.

One could perhaps dismiss television as a ready conduit of sensationalism and fiction dressed up as fact, confident that in the hallowed halls of academe a serious regard for historical evidence would prevail. But when Dr Umayma Jalahma, Professor of Islamic Studies at Saudi Arabia's King Faysal University, lectured to the Arab League Think Tank on the 'US War on Iraq Timed to Coincide with Jewish Holiday Purim', grotesque fantasy gained academic credentials and a political audience. Dr Jalahma's address to the Zayed Centre for Coordination and Follow-Up, established by the Arab League in 1999, followed from her article published in the Saudi daily *Al Riyadh* on 12 March 2002, in which she claimed that on 'the Jewish holiday of Purim ... the Jewish people must obtain human blood so that their clerics can prepare the holiday pastries ... that affords the Jewish vampires great delight as they carefully monitor every detail of the blood-shedding with pleasure ...'[12] Jalahma's lurid imagination extends to gory details that would be thought unprintable, except that now she writes for the Saudi daily *Al Watan*, where her anti-Jewish invective goes unchecked and unchallenged.

While there are glimmers of hope among some Arab intellectuals, a few of whom publicly denounced the plan to hold a Holocaust Deniers Conference in Beirut in March 2001, saying they were outraged by the anti-Semitic undertaking, it is difficult to see how influential they will be in turning the tide of a vast sea of hate literature that pervades the Muslim world and finds its way into the publications of the Muslim diaspora in the West. As historian Robert Wistrich has pointed out in his monograph on Muslim anti-Semitism, it is no surprise that the September 11 terrorist attacks against the United States were greeted with rapture in many parts of the Muslim world (while the conviction in a British court of Holocaust denier, David Irving, on the other hand, enraged the Arab world).[13] Wistrich cites the mufti of Jerusalem who preached his regular Friday sermon at the Al Aqsa Mosque, calling for the destruction of Israel, Britain and the United States: 'Oh Allah, destroy America, for she is ruled by Zionist Jews ...Allah will paint the White House black.'[14]

It is hard to imagine anything that needs a major dose of self-criticism more than the pervasive religious hatred that sees the West as a joint 'Crusader–Zionist conspiracy' bent on the destruction of the Arab world. It is a disposition that no amount of assurances from America and Britain of Iraqi self-rule following the war against Saddam Hussein's regime is likely to change. The Christian–Jewish conspiracy is a powerful belief of a host of Muslim organisations, including the thousands of *madrassas* (fundamentalist schools) of Pakistan that churn out zealots ready to die in a *jihad* (holy war) against the West. It is the central message of Osama bin Laden, who organised the terrorist attack on the World Trade Center and admitted that it was a Jewish target, New York being the city with the highest Jewish population in the world. Such an attack on New York was a dream that Hitler himself cherished and often spoke about to his architect, Albert Speer.[15] When fewer than the expected number of Jews were killed on September 11, a further layer was added to the Jewish conspiracy, alleging that the Jews who worked at the World Trade Center got wind of the attack ahead of time and stayed away. Polls in the Middle East showed that this story, published in newspapers throughout the Arab world, was widely believed, as were others that blamed the Jews themselves for organising the attacks on America in a bid to stir up anti–Arab sentiment.

It is the nature of a conspiracy that it is never open to disproof by evidence of any kind. Conspiracies are always alleged to be secret, even when they are apparently 'out in the open', which explains why so many people are unaware of their dark designs. It is also why they are always at odds with the observable world, which can never be read as anything but a decoy wilfully deployed to keep people from knowing the diabolical truth. Above all, conspiracies are elastic and always stretch to cover new situations. That way no matter what develops the enemy is always the enemy. In the face of this solid wall of self-made delusion, it is hard to imagine rational analysis cutting through the propaganda that is propelling young Muslim men and women around the world to launch themselves at Western targets in a fiery inferno of *jihad*. It is hard to imagine how they will see through the dark lenses of anti–Western and anti–Jewish hatred (which to them are the same thing) to the religious, social and political problems that have dogged their own societies and now make young men and women seem worthy of little more than acting as vehicles for sticks of gelignite on their way to holy oblivion. It is a nihilism worthy of the *Fight Club* goons who parrot each other's slogans and believe destruction is their sacred duty and only path to glory.

But it is not a situation that is likely to change for some time. In Saudi Arabia, for example, the home of Osama bin Laden, there are limited prospects for the kind of enlightenment that would celebrate humanism and the critical analysis of religion. Long forgotten in the history of Islam are the Mu'tazila of the ninth century, a period often referred to as the golden age of Islam. The Mu'tazila mixed the teachings of Aristotle, Democritus, Empedocles and other Greek philosophers with their own speculations and came up with a humanistic Islam that gave primary place to reason, asserting that God's being, the universe, and human nature — that is, all truths — are knowable to human reason, while revelation is of secondary importance.[16] They lasted thirty years and produced many writings, but their memory is expunged by latter-day *imams* and *mullahs*. Today while the petro-dollars pour into the purses of the Saudi royal family, who control the country's natural wealth, the people are ruled by Wahabism, a strict puritanical strain of Islam. The result is an oppressed populace with few hopes for an enlightened future. Abdalrahman Munif, the exiled Saudi writer reflecting on his native country at the end of the twentieth century, told the London-based journalist Tariq Ali:

> Saudi Arabia is still without a constitution, the people are deprived of all elementary rights . . . Women, who own a large share of private wealth in the country, are treated like third-class citizens. A woman is not allowed to leave the country without a written permit from a male relative. Such a situation produces a desperate citizenry, without a sense of dignity or belonging. All our rulers do is to increase their own wealth while investing as little as possible in the intellectual development of our people. Why? Because they fear education. They fear change.[17]

No wonder young men in Saudi Arabia, and other similarly malfunctioning Muslim nations, want to join Osama bin Laden's Fight Club.

What Hans Kung's urgent plea for a global ethic does is remind us above all that the religious life, just like the non-religious life, is always in danger of descending into an anti-human system when it insulates itself from thinking and protest. These natural wellsprings of reform have brought an end to practices which no humane person could countenance today. Inquisitorial torture could not possibly be regarded by the thinking Christian as a tool for defending the faith. Slavery and bondage could not possibly co-exist with the dignity of human beings made in the image of God; likewise, the treatment of women as subhuman is anathema to educated Christianity. The list goes on, but Kung specifically calls upon Islam to pursue religious change, including developing a more humane doctrine of *jihad*, which remains the highest religious calling to young Muslims, and changing the medieval sacral law, *shariah*, which often contradicts the 1948

United Nations Declaration of Human Rights, in particular regarding equal rights for women and for non-Muslims. There would be little hope for women in societies ruled exclusively by *shariah* law without Western organisations such as Amnesty International, which defends cases like that brought against the Nigerian woman, Amina Lawal, condemned by *shariah* law to death by stoning on 3 June 2003, because she became pregnant after being raped by her father. Meanwhile Amnesty can only gather the horrifying statistics of thousands of deaths each year, the so-called 'honour killings' of women who are murdered by their male relatives when they are discovered or even suspected to be in a relationship not approved by the family, or in some other way deemed a source of shame.

What Hans Kung implies in his call on Muslim nations to bring the *shariah* law into conformity with the Declaration of Human Rights, but does not openly say, however, is that the culture of self-criticism has to be allowed free rein. Even in the West, Muslims are subject at times to stringent institutional control by their religious leaders. A Dutch Muslim woman, Ayaan Hirsi Ali, was forced to flee the Netherlands under a threat of death following the issuing of a *fatwa* for speaking out publicly against the oppression of women by Muslim men. It is, of course, significant that writers who have called for just this kind of change and have openly criticised the religious and political regimes in Muslim countries are, like Tariq Ali, M.J. Akbar and Salman Rushdie, conducting their campaigns well and truly outside Muslim strongholds. But not even this necessarily protects one from religious fanatics as Ayaan Hirsi Ali has just discovered, and Rushdie's own bitter experience of living in hiding for years indicates.[18]

Burning books and killing or imprisoning writers, artists and dissidents is not new. After World War II and the Holocaust, when the purges of intellectuals in Stalin's Soviet Union were just beginning and would cast the model for Castro's Cuba and Mao's China, the world was ready to embark on the greatest experiment of universal government since the failure of the League of Nations. The United Nations was conceived and then housed in a city that was a microcosm of what it hoped to achieve for the world. From as far back as the seventeenth century when Spanish colonials raped and pillaged the natives of the New World, the Protestant Dutch settlers who arrived on the island of Manhattan acquired the choice piece of land which they called New Amsterdam by paying the resident Indians for it. Soon they lost it to the British, who renamed it York, then New York City, and the island and surrounding land at the mouth of the Hudson and East Rivers would be the destination for a steady stream of religiously and linguistically diverse immigrants, including the Irish, the Italians, the Jews, the Chinese, the Blacks, the Hispanics and the Arabs. Indeed people from just about everywhere have made their mark on the city.

Notwithstanding the image put forward in Martin Scorsese's 2002 film, *Gangs of New York*, gang warfare would not be the hallmark of the most urbane city in the world. Just as the ethnic enclaves found that through legislative change, free commerce, and a reliable judicial system they could live side by side in peace (though no-one would claim in idyllic harmony), so the United Nations held out as its greatest hope the ending of war as a means of solving international conflicts and the elevating of human rights in all nations of the world.

A lot has changed since those heady days of idealism of the late 1940s, and today the UN's predominantly non-Western member states are just as likely to perpetrate and overlook human rights violations in peacetime as they are during war. There have been numerous revelations about waste and misuse of funds for personal enrichment by UN delegates, and of failures of administration of UN schemes, such as the oil for food program, which simply could not assure delivery of supplies to the people of Iraq under the regime of Saddam Hussein. This and similar opportunism and incompetence by UN apparatchiks brings to mind Albert Schweitzer's observation about Christianity. Its tendency to forget its original calling is every bit as relevant to this once venerable organisation, which has too often chosen to focus on its internal prosperity rather than the ethical imperative that gave it birth. Even the insistence by the UN during the Iraqi crisis that leaving Saddam Hussein in power would be more just than violently ousting him through armed confrontation rings hollow given the brutality and injustice of his dictatorship which left his people utterly disempowered and incapable of overthrowing him by other means.

Still, it is worthwhile recalling the courage of the UN's original vision, which was not without risk and foreboding. For the planes of war had only recently fallen silent and for those who knew the destruction they could wreak, the tall glass structure and lower one at right angles to it soon to be erected along the East River would loom as a provocative target. In the summer of 1949, the *New Yorker's* beloved essayist E.B. White cast his eye over the spot that would soon be graced by the architect's 'cigar boxes set on end', and with eerie premonition wrote these words:

> This race — this race between the destroying planes and the struggling Parliament of Man — it sticks in all our heads. The city at least perfectly illustrates both the universal dilemma and the general solution, this riddle in steel and stone is at once the perfect target and the perfect demonstration of non-violence, of racial brotherhood, this lofty target scraping the skies and meeting the destroying planes halfway, home of all people and all nations, capital of everything, housing the deliberations by which the planes are to be stayed and their errand forestalled.[19]

E.B. White was right about another thing: the ideal of nations and religions living in harmony is a provocation to some regimes and religions, particularly those that are unwilling to admit basic human rights and freedoms to their citizens or followers. Repressive leaders prefer their people to live in splendid isolation, where their thoughts and movements can be controlled and limited and their personal expectations never unduly raised by the example of others more fortunate or free. This is the characteristic of most cults, which find their only way of galvanising followers around extremist practices and bizarre beliefs is to rear them on a diet of thoroughgoing suspicion of others and an uncompromising hatred of those who criticise or question their practices.

Demonising outsiders is a typical tactic of cults, where there is no natural dignity or personal conscience allowed individuals. Cults permit only qualified representatives to speak about them. In effect there is no such thing as public disclosure, only propaganda, and those who challenge this rule are severely punished, expelled, sued, psychologically destroyed or killed. Cults brook no compromise and suffer no dissent even from those who have managed to leave them. Ex-members are loose cannons and have to be neutralised. The original teaching is preserved at all costs and any change is regarded as a corruption and an impurity. Whether they are political or religious, New Age or orthodox, minuscule or multinational, cults are the enemies of open societies. They make the true believer a term of opprobrium and a byword for the irrational.

Nothing could be further from the ethos of the new believers surveyed in this book and the environment in which they pursue their spiritual quest. The most significant ingredients in all the trends that are represented by the writers, researchers and thinkers whose ideas are discussed here is their open critique, their unfettered research and their daring exploration into new expressions of faith, all of which contribute to the richness of our religious culture. It is not only the challenge that they pose to the individual which is to be valued, but also the wake-up call they send to the religious establishment, which often can be impervious to the currents of change affecting its congregations and perplexed by demands it has not foreseen. But it is not as hopeless as it sounds. Sometimes the religious establishment cannot see the solutions that are being handed to it on a plate.

11. RETHINKING RIGID AND ROMANTIC RELIGION

Where We Are Now

The free-flowing exploration of spirituality and the charting of new frontiers might not be delivering all the answers, and indeed may be taking us into some dangerous waters, but they do provide something of a laboratory of thinking and practice that old-time religion is often much too cautious to engage in. Ex-priests, former psychologists, practising scientists, novelists and Hollywood script-writers who discuss the nature of the religious life have the freedom to innovate and even to express heretical thoughts that a parish minister usually does not. That is why the appeal of these new believers, through publications, retreats and the media, is often far wider than expected. Not that people are naturally drawn to heresy, but in many respects the preservation of old ways and rigid formulas is not serving a large and restless segment of the population, a great majority of whom are women.

Peter Cameron, the Presbyterian minister and distinguished holder of the Meldrum Lectureship at the University of Edinburgh, was one of those rare clerics who broke with conformity and was duly convicted of heresy by the Presbyterian Church of Australia in 1993. He wrote about his case in the book *Heretic*, but it's in his following book, *Fundamentalism and Freedom*, that he explores broader issues in the Church. He tells a story about sitting through a meeting at which two ministers from different parishes each gave an account of the reasons they were about to take their leave. One of them had done very well, significantly increasing both the numbers and the finances of the church he led, and was being rewarded with a post at one of the richest congregations in the country. The other had struggled valiantly but, it seems, hopelessly in a poor church that was beset by the endemic violence of the district, and with limited funds at his disposal and no visible prospect for improvement, the exhausted minister decided to go. Cameron reflected that it was the second example of ministry that was 'nearer to Christ', whereas the reality of Church life today is a preference for the prosperous, comfortable, even smug, community, which he compared to 'a watertight ark sailing undefiled upon the waters of the world'.[1]

Cameron, who practised law and worked in a parish ministry, is not a foolish idealist and he knows full well the necessity of financial viability, which can only come from the middle- and upper-class members of the community. He also is aware that religion will always reflect the values and lifestyle of the particular community it serves. But he was pointing to something behind the superficial success or failure of a church, which is the fact that appearances can be deceptive. While the social and spiritual deficits of the poor congregation are easy to see, those of the rich are merely submerged, masked by the comforts of affluence and perhaps even a veneer of piety. When this contradiction is starkly revealed — as when church members in good standing are found to be corrupt in their professional dealings and dishonest or immoral in their personal lives, bigoted and insular in their opinions and self-satisfied in their attitude — organised religion is thrown into disrepute. In recent years, there has been no lack of examples of public figures, from presidents to businessmen, whose personal and professional dealings have cast a shadow on the value of their professed Christian faith. President

Clinton's debacle with Monica Lewinsky followed by his evasive 'confession' on national television made a mockery of this Baptist churchgoer's religion. But carrying on a sexual affair with an employee is nothing compared to the spectacular damage done to innocent people by bad business dealings. Two very public examples of greed getting the better of faith have been provided by the CEOs of Enron and WorldCom, Kenneth Lay and Bernard Ebbers. With media reports foreshadowing an imminent indictment of Lay for his role in Enron, where the chief financial officer is facing 100 criminal charges for various counts of fraud,[2] and the revelation in an investigative report called by the new board of WorldCom that Bernard Ebbers was in meetings in which company officials discussed ways of artificially inflating revenue,[3] their claims in interviews that they were men of high Christian principles strike most observers as cynical or deeply misguided. In an interview before the sensational collapse of Enron in 2002, Kenneth Lay described his philosophy to Robert Darden, editor of *The Door* magazine: 'It is really always doing the right thing. Not bending the rules, not cutting corners, not doing things that are illegal or immoral ... I think a person of high Christian values, high morals and high standards, can be very successful in business.'[4]

For the people who read the vast numbers of executives who have so far taken the blame for Enron's demise, it is hard to see Lay as untarnished, given that he was the CEO of an organisation which is revealed to have engaged in phony transactions and sold off more than US$100 million in stock before the company's collapse, leaving thousands of employees without jobs or pensions. WorldCom also deceived investors, with the aid of 'accounting tricks', but Ebbers managed to convince the board to give him a personal loan of US$366 million to cover some previous bad investments (a mere pittance compared to the US$4 billion in accounting irregularities for which WorldCom was being investigated by a congressional panel). Nonetheless, Ebbers taught Sunday school, and according to the *Wall Street Journal* told church members: 'I just want you to know you aren't going to church with a crook ... I hope that my witness for Jesus Christ will not be jeopardised.'[5]

But of course it was, especially when the Church did not hold him and others of the same ilk accountable. Just as insurance companies which line their own pockets while letting policy owners and shareholders suffer the consequences of bad business practices and corrupt boards, so Churches, and indeed all religions, are judged by how well their true purposes are being served and exemplified by their most public representatives. It is an unavoidable equation. People reject religions when their members belie their true purpose. At the very least, they are moved to ask: what is religion for?

Occasionally the definition of a Church's true purpose becomes the focus of heated debate, and at least some of the parties to it believe those in power have obscured the essential teaching with their own set of self-serving values. Cameron was a critic of the Presbyterian Church's stand on women, whom at one time it ordained, but ceased to since its liberals left to form the Uniting Church. He was also a student of modern biblical scholarship, which tends to see the sacred text as reflecting its own time and therefore recommends the same temporal, that is contemporary, reading of the New Testament. It is an approach that easily incorporates women's aspirations for equality in the Church along with a number of other current values. Literal readings of scripture, on the contrary, are regarded as not in the spirit of its original intention, and evocative of the kind of fundamentalism and insularity that the New Testament ascribed to the Pharisees of Jesus' own day. For the record, the famous Pharisee, Rabbi Hillel the Elder, dating from the end of the first century BC, was always held up in Jewish tradition as the teacher who represented the ethical spirit of the Torah rather than the letter of the law. It was Hillel who, when asked by a precocious man to summarise the Torah while standing on one foot, answered: 'What is hateful to you do not do to your neighbour, this is the entire Torah. The rest is commentary. Go and study it.'[6]

In a similar spirit of 'essential' Christianity, Cameron, who was a visiting minister from the Presbyterian Church of Scotland and Dean of St Andrew's College at the University of Sydney, came under attack for his candid observations of the Church's elite men's college, where students behaved as if they had not yet emerged from the dark ages.

Unbridled physical abuse of freshmen students by their 'betters' as a rite of initiation, of the kind that reportedly still occurs in the armed forces, struck Cameron as a very serious and inexcusable part of student life that was born of a 'boy's own' culture gone mad. Hardly a reflection of the Church — or maybe it was. He saw the two issues of subjugation of women and brutal male culture as related distortions of Christ's message.

Given the clarity with which he saw and spoke about these and other important theological issues facing the Church today, the conviction of Cameron as a heretic was more a badge of honour than of shame. Not surprisingly it even prompted him to speculate on whether the disappearance of the Church, presumably in a general sense of that term, is necessarily a bad thing. That is a matter for posterity, but one thing is certain, the curry that is given the Church by new spiritualities, competing traditions and serious critics can only be a good thing.

Take, for example, the significant attraction to pagan spiritualities of women. There is little doubt that the Church views this as an unfortunate and wayward decline into pre-Christian tradition by feminists and lesbians. If the Church is right then it has been handed a clear message of what is wrong within its walls. By its theology and practice the Church has alienated a large proportion of religiously inclined women, and virtually driven them out of shared community with men and into one of their own making. It is probably true that the 'women only' brand of religion had to happen, if only to retrieve what is singularly feminine in the history of spiritual and pastoral traditions, and to reshape it into contemporary forms. But these are now having a wider influence on Christianity itself. Ordained women and younger men in the Church are not only reading widely but also engaging in innovative training, including eco-spiritual retreats, which inevitably incorporate strong feminist and pagan themes.

The same phenomenon is occurring amongst ordained Jewish women, for whom the Jewish lunar calendar offers a powerful feminine motif and the seasonal festivals encourage a heightened environmental awareness. In both traditions, it has become increasingly acceptable to speak about panentheistic theology, a nuanced variation of pantheism, where God is discerned dwelling in all of creation. While panentheists do not pray to tree gods and rock gods, as pantheists do, they pray to the God that dwells in each and every rock and tree. Even the Salvation Army's *War Cry* magazine, known for its urban focus and uncompromising Christ-centred faith, featured a front-cover story which extolled the spiritual benefits of getting back to nature and God.[7] Scaling the heights in Victoria's Grampians National Park, Alistair Paton discovered that the wilderness experience not only brings one face to face with God's creation, but has the power to put one in a state of being that is the Kingdom of Heaven as Jesus understood it. The Salvation Army's renowned welfare doctrine found support in the trying conditions of the Australian bush, where the windy gusts of the roaring forties lashed the tiny tents and reduced to insignificance the social hierarchies and class barriers of the inhabitants. Whatever one's particular frame of reference, the radical transcendent Father God of Genesis is mitigated by this panentheistic interpretation of God whose loving relationship with his creation is celebrated in the Psalms. It is an experience of God that is also more easily entered into by women, who are themselves deeply involved in the process of creation.

The challenges posed by women to the Church elicit a great many positive and creative theological responses, including new liturgies, which draw on the rich scholarship in religious history and also natural science. By comparison a tragedy perpetrated within the Church largely by men has shaken the very foundations of its moral right to speak for God, for that is what religious institutions claim to do. Sexual abuse and the significant failure to respond to it properly is a catastrophe for the Church. It is not just a scandal, a flash in the pan diversion from the Church's real work. Nor is it an epidemic, a rash aberration of its normally pristine state. The sexual abuse of minors is a long-standing, endemic condition that is all the worse for the Church's record of denying its scale and perpetuating the elements that give rise to it.[8] While it has been tried on, there is no solace found in glib comparisons to other sectors of society where the problem is also apparent, such as schools and child welfare organisations. The Church's unique role as the paragon of sacred truths and the guardian of morality as well as the last refuge of those most in need of comfort and solace is simply undone in the minds of the public by the now regular revelations of child abuse. If the Church's faithful stalwarts and hierarchy discern an ugly cast to the media attention, so be it. The public shaming is fully deserved and it is necessary.

The trouble is that the discernment of moral turpitude in religion does not occur enough and rarely strays from the predictable. In a free and open democratic society, targeting priests is relatively easy, even if they have a strong and powerful hierarchy behind them. Priests are a type of professional class who hold a privileged, if somewhat peculiar, position in today's sexually liberated society. And because of their vow of celibacy, Roman Catholic priests in particular are a perfect target for accusations of hypocrisy and moral failure when they are caught out. But they are by no means the only ones who are culpable. Orthodoxies in all religions have a crusty veneer of piety that provides a cover to a great many ills and cows even the fiercest critics. There is a deep resistance to launching inquiries into mainstream religions, just as there is into the judiciary and other pillars of our society, for the fear that in condemning the practitioners we are killing our most cherished ideals and sustaining beliefs. The truth is the opposite. By not calling religion to account for the evils it permits and the moral cowardice it demonstrates, we are allowing it to be killed off quietly from the inside and thus turning our ideals into mirages.

The compulsion to save face is one of the greatest enemies of religion, but one that is endemic particularly to sectarian and closed communities. Typically, apocalyptic or messianic movements that make less than accurate predictions are strenuously involved in image management. So too are enterprising cults, which regard all criticism and negative media coverage as a threat to their multi-million dollar businesses. Even without such sensationalist claims or dubious business interests, traditional religions can find themselves in regular face-saving exercises over relatively mundane issues. For example, despite the significant social and psychological problems that occur amongst ultra-orthodox Jewish communities, where families are unusually large (more than five children is the norm), religious demands are high and the contact with non-orthodox society is virtually nil, there is very little will to expose those problems and tackle them. Stereotypes of the Jewish community as highly educated, family-oriented, relatively sober and socially supportive have led to the assumption that the incidence of domestic violence, for example, is very low. But a growing bibliography of social studies on the Jewish population indicates that domestic violence is a problem, especially in ultra-orthodox groupings. Not that violence is greater in more religious communities — the incidence appears to be similar in all forms of Judaism — but seeking and providing help is significantly less frequent in ultra-orthodox communities because male authority over women is set out in scripture, and women's lives are entirely circumscribed by wifely and maternal duties as dictated by the Torah and interpreted by their husbands and rabbis.

The Jewish ideal of *shalom bayis*, the peaceful home, is legendary and romanticised, but it is not a true picture of reality. Women in ultra-orthodox communities are expected to uphold this ideal all the same, and rarely leave husbands who are violent. They stand to lose a great deal if they do, including their children and communal support. Suffice it to say, cultural barriers make it difficult for police and other secular institutions to address the problem. As for the larger Jewish community, it is loath to single out its ultra-orthodox brethren for their apparent failures in this area, perhaps out of denial, but more likely because deferring to those more religious is a deeply rooted principle that is designed to favour and preserve religious observance above non-observance. Who would think to point an accusing finger at a community that fosters large families of observant Jews when Judaism was nearly destroyed by the Holocaust and is considered to be in perpetual danger through anti-Semitism, assimilation and intermarriage? Just as serious breaches of the moral code in Catholic institutions have frequently prompted an initial strategy of discretion (or cover-up) lest the reputation of the Church be called into question, so ultra-orthodox Jewish communities are sensitive about revealing their internal weaknesses to a wider society they believe is unsympathetic to them.

They are left to their own devices, and the plight of abused women goes largely ignored and unremedied.

Criticisms like these are usually met with defensive statements by women who argue that their lives are wonderfully blessed, secure, fulfilling and utterly at odds with the pathetic situation described above. They may be correct — about their own lives. And it is certainly true that the ultra-orthodox Lubavitcher Hassidim, who patrolled college campuses and infamous districts like San Francisco's Haight-Ashbury looking for 'fallen Jews', provided a haven for a great many casualties of the drugs, sex and rock and roll generation of the 1960s, 70s and 80s, who would otherwise be lost to Judaism if not to the world. But a community and a society cannot be judged by the rescued and the comfortable alone, even if they are the majority, for they are also part of the problem. The narrow field of vision that prevents the ultra-orthodox faithful from seeing the moral and other failures within their own religious culture also prevents them from providing the kind of help required for people who are crushed by them. In such cases, it is always easier to blame the individuals, for they are expendable when compared to the larger edifice of tradition, which is not. It goes without saying that according to the ultra-orthodox, there are no traditional practices that can be regarded as wrong and in urgent need of change, for they were all ordained by God. This is how fundamentalism turns words on a page into brutal and inhumane acts, so that, for example, ultra-orthodox men at the Wailing Wall in Jerusalem throw wooden chairs at women in order to silence their prayers in a domain in which they believe women's voices must not be heard. To anyone watching this spectacle of physical abuse, such behaviour strikes at the heart of moral decency. And it makes the innovative feminist liturgies and prayer groups, which draw inspiration from the dancing and singing Deborah of the scriptures, a comfort and a necessity.

The rejection of feminism by the ultra-orthodox fortunately is offset by the majority of Progressive Jews who champion equality for women. But in other parts of the world traditions die hard. Nowhere are women more endangered by fundamentalist attitudes than in the

Muslim world. Their fiercest expression is the murder of women by their male family members, a practice that is meant to preserve the purity of the faith and preserve 'honour' among men. By conservative estimates honour killings claim 5000 women a year, according to reports submitted to the United Nations Commission on Human Rights.[9] Women who are suspected of breaking the elaborate code whereby they are kept under surveillance by male relatives and prevented from going out of doors improperly covered, without permission, alone or in the company of males who are not relatives, let alone not Muslim, are vulnerable to severe punishment. Although the Koran does not explicitly sanction honour killings, the Koranic text which is cited to support the practice, even in Jordan, a secular state, where honour killings go virtually unpunished, is Surah IV: 34:

> Men are in charge of women, because Allah hath made the one of them to excel the other, and because they spend of their property [for the support of women]. Good women are obedient, guarding in secret that which Allah hath guarded. As for those from whom ye fear rebellion, admonish them and banish them to beds apart, and scourge them. Then if they obey you, seek not a way against them. Lo! Allah is ever High, Exalted, Great.

Even though Surah IV: 36 counsels kindness to family, neighbours and strangers, it is the prerogative of the male to interpret the Koran as the custom dictates, and in societies where the Koran rules domestic life and women are considered the property of male family members and given little independence from men, it is easy to see how Surah IV: 34 becomes a device for suppressing the women who wish to live outside its dictates. As Surah IV: 36 warns, 'Lo! Allah loveth not such as are proud and boastful.'[10]

Norma Khouri's book *Forbidden Love* recounts the story of her closest friend, Dalia, killed by her father, who stabbed her twelve times in the chest, because she was seen in the company of a Catholic man. Khouri has dedicated her life to overturning this barbaric practice, which claims hundreds of women each year in her native Jordan. Khouri is in exile in Australia, because such a campaign would be impossible to carry out in a country that regularly interprets the last words in Surah IV: 34 as a licence to kill disobedient women. The interpretation fosters subterfuge and secrecy among women, who are forced to resort to every kind of bribe and deception to enjoy the simplest freedoms, like leaving the house or walking down the street unaccompanied by a male relative. Choosing friends, just like selecting a marriage partner, can only be done with the express approval of one's father, who is obliged to severely limit the possibilities. He, too, is imprisoned by the narrow customs of his tradition. The infantilisation of women, including mothers, who constantly defer to their husbands and sons in obedience if not fear, is the other side to this patriarchal society, and the reason it continues largely unchallenged. Mothers silently bear the brunt of losing their daughters to honour killings, and it is undoubtedly one of the reasons many of them hope they will not give birth to daughters.

Norma Khouri and others like her who want to break the shackles of women in Muslim societies are lifting the lid on an explosive and shameful issue, but it is precisely because of this that she is unlikely to garner the kind of support she deserves from Muslim women in the West. The obvious embarrassment of an inhumane practice prompts denials and protestations, and in a bid to protect the reputation of the faith it is argued that the problem is cultural, not religious, or that it is vastly overstated. (Given the euphemistic phrases used to conceal the real cause of deaths of many Muslim women, followed by the burial of victims in unmarked graves, it is more likely that the incidence is significantly understated.) The assumption is always that the Koran is unimpeachable. Even Norma Khouri, careful not to appear as a Muslim-bashing Catholic, couches her criticisms in careful language that sheets home the blame to ancient Arab customs, first forged in the sixth or seventh centuries BC. Although Khouri openly blames the *imams* who give religious sanction to the practice of honour killing, by pointing to its pre-Islamic origin she offers a way of explaining its appearance in the Koran (as scourging), and its customary interpretation in all parts of the Muslim world, including the non-Arab peoples of Africa and, especially, Pakistan, where the incidence of honour killing is highest. Yet there is no open suggestion for the removal or revision of this and other offensive passages, for this would presuppose a development in Muslim culture akin to the rise of historical critical scholarship in the West, which has not occurred to any significant degree.

It may be unthinkable to some, but the removal of problematic scriptures or words is not new in the biblical tradition, and during Victorian times it was done in order to clean up the Bible's lewd and suggestive imagery, which was thought to corrupt the congregation. The appearance of different names for God in the Bible raised other problems. Interpreting these as God's different qualities was the device used by theologians who had to make sense of peculiar phrases and prepositions in the Bible which on the face of it indicated that God is plural. In a bold move more recently, two Irish bishops made a controversial proposal to drop seven New Testament texts from the lectionary because they may lead to domestic violence. Bishop Larry Ryan of Kildare and Leighlin and Bishop Willie Walsh of Killaloe jointly issued a statement in November 2000 that some texts in the letters of St Paul and St Peter were open to being used, especially out of context, as a means to exercise undue power and authority over women. The use of inclusive language, which would always refer to women alongside every mention of man or mankind, has also been regularly advocated by American Catholics, and seven cardinals made a special delegation to Rome to urge it to approve such a revised lectionary of the Mass. With this as with many aspects of American Catholicism, the Vatican lags behind the will of the people, and no change has been approved yet.

These efforts, even in the putatively conservative Roman Catholic Church, signal an openness to secular currents that is surely one of the great strengths of Western religion. Yet the truth is that there is also very slow progress in some areas. The Church establishment's usual cautious counterarguments emphasise preservation of the status quo, but with a helpful suggestion to contextualise the offending passages in scripture. That, however, is a concession to the converted. With the supreme obligation being to preserve tradition as far as possible, it is difficult to hold out much hope for change and improvement when the wheels of reform turn so slowly. People who are hurt by the attitudes that certain scriptural passages perpetuate simply find their respect for religion waning, if not disappearing altogether.

That, however, is not the usual outcome. Most people with spiritual yearnings find other paths to consolation and inspiration. They become new believers in gods they can fall in love with, and enthusiastic participants in forms of spiritual practice that are new, exotic and sometimes still in the making. The result is often enjoyable and even hopeful, but not without its flaws. Falling in love, after all, is an idealised condition in the West, redolent with happiness and delight, joy and satisfaction. Is this the feeling that is meant to be at the heart of the religious life? Increasingly it is held up as the criterion of the new spirituality, with an accompanying emphasis on aesthetics. Thomas Moore, the ex-priest and psychotherapist who has popularised the soul as the locus of an anti-institutional kind of religious life, devoted a chapter in his book *The Soul's Religion* to women in India who paint their mud homes with designs that are intended to protect them against evil. With a pigment made from ground rice and cow dung, the women decorate the inner and outer walls of their huts with lotus flowers, peacocks and elephants, the goddess Lakshmi and other images drawn from Indian mythology. Thomas Moore came to know about them from a book of photographs by Stephen Huyler, *Painted Prayers*. They clearly touched Moore with their rugged simplicity and prompted him to reflect on the lessons they can teach the West.

While the indomitable aesthetic spirit is a wonder to see, especially in the most improbable circumstances, Moore draws too long a bow to make a point about the role of art in preserving the sanctity of home, hearth and family in India, which he favourably compares to the shallowness of the West. For Moore such shallowness is indicated by the West's denial of the world of evil spirits and its reliance instead on psychotherapy and other means of explaining and containing evil.

The painted houses of India, on the other hand, signal to Moore the women's sophisticated appreciation of the manifold functions of art in dispelling evil spirits and imbuing the home with a joyous and concrete expression of religion. He closes the chapter with the following statement: 'In these ordinary people, artists of rice, we behold the essence of religion and the secret of living without fear.'[11]

Are these painted houses a sign of living without fear? Who would dispute the lightness of heart upon seeing a gay design on the wall of a meagre dark mud hut, the usual dwelling of India's largely impoverished tribal people? It is more likely that the artwork is not a sign of living without fear, but an antidote to a life that is pervaded by fear, where rigid tribal laws dictate the regular starving of girl babies in favour of boys and where the incidence of rape of girls and women is epidemic (and for which the victims are usually killed). The living conditions in the mud-hut villages of India are miserable and hopeless for the more than 450 castes of untouchables who live there. Without even the barest sanitation and virtually no education, an extremely high mortality rate from diseases long gone from the West, such as cholera, continues to claim the population.

The belief in evil spirits by the tribal women of India may impress Moore, a self-confessed romanticist[12] and other Westerners searching for what they like to refer to as authentic religion, but such a belief is part of a world-view that has not come to grips (and is not likely to) with the real causes of their suffering nor with the means to remedy it. Moore's romanticised view of life in mud huts painted with cow dung (incidentally one of the substances along with urine, milk and ghee from the 'holy cow' that Hindus regard as purifying), which he contrasts to the naïve and technological West, may strike one as downright silly, but it is more than that. It is the kind of representation of religious life that capitalises on the insecurity of the West and its penchant for self-criticism, while it consciously ignores the ugly realities of living and dying according to misogynist and brutal tribal religious law, which according to UNICEF results in the killing of more than 5000 brides annually because their dowries are insufficient.[13] To suggest that simple faith is automatically deeper, richer and truer, not to mention ultimately more beneficial than that experienced in Western culture, would be harmless if it did not ignore the inhumane conditions in which people are forced to live by dint of their beliefs. Wall paintings that are meant to deliver one from evil are no more profound for being aesthetically pleasing to Western eyes.

It is precisely this kind of romanticising that dogs the quest for new spiritualities. Fortunately, there are thinkers who have guarded against it even as they push the frontiers of belief forward. For forty years, Charles Birch, the Australian biologist and theologian and recipient of the Templeton Prize for Progress in Religion, has promoted an alternative to both the materialistic world-view and the traditional concept of God. Taking inspiration from his one-time teacher, the great German–American theologian Paul Tillich, Birch refuses to let science expel religion from its home, which is everywhere: in the depths of the human spirit and in the expanding universe, in the microbe and in the ideas that form in our brain and that we enact in society. Birch does not advocate a return to pantheism, that is, identifying creation with God, nor does he suggest that God is the engineer of the universe. What he prefers is the notion of God as a 'persuasive force' that can be discerned in the responsiveness of nature and the process of evolutionary development and change, an understanding that was nurtured by his mentors, the Chicago University philosopher of religion, Charles Hartshorne, and the Harvard philosopher, Alfred North Whitehead. Birch's view that human beings are also evolving (which is both a very slow biological process as well as a relatively rapid cultural process) necessarily presupposes that there is always a certain imperfection, if not ambiguity, in their thoughts and decisions. Because of the fundamentally dynamic aspect of all life and Birch's scientifically open mind, he is cautious about making statements that anticipate a perfect state to be achieved, as was posited by Jesuit priest and scientist Pierre Teilhard de Chardin (1881–1955), in his Omega principle. For Birch there is always another step to go, anything less implies a point where ultimately one is left with a dead universe.

Birch's theological outlook is demonstrated by a considerate approach to the natural world, one that acknowledges it as being part of the unfolding presence of God. But he is wary of romantic ideas that misrepresent both nature and culture. There is little point in fostering benign affection for the universe if it perpetuates beliefs that are simply untrue. Birch[14] dispels the notion, for example, that there is some inherent 'balance in nature', a phrase that has become a mantra in eco-spirituality circles and is popularised in New Age magazines. As he notes, the ice ages followed by warm phases of the earth resulted in countless unadapted species becoming extinct. The vast majority of species that ever existed became extinct and that is the fate of all species, says Birch. Even the primordial period when the first living cells flourished was probably not some warm organic soup, a Garden of Eden paradise. Rather, on the latest reckoning by cosmologists like Paul Davies, life on earth probably got off to a false start when a barrage of asteroids and giant comets hit our planet with such impact and ferocity that its rocky crust melted to a depth of a kilometre and the oceans boiled dry. Life was annihilated and had to start again. There is nothing balanced about earth's beginnings nor its ensuing macrocosmic and microcosmic existence, where plagues and droughts, tidal waves and sand storms, epidemics and genetic disorders are regular occurrences across the globe.

It is relatively easy for Birch the scientist to expose the holes in pop science and New Age eco-spiritual arguments, but it is a much more sensitive task to tackle areas of belief that have metamorphosed into conventional wisdom. Birch, the scientist and theologian who has developed an ecological faith, is nonetheless critical of the popular assumption that indigenous peoples are superior conservationists. Evidence proves that the legacy is mixed. The writings of Jared Diamond on Papua New Guinean tribes reveal that in his thirty years of visiting the native peoples on three islands he did not encounter any examples of friendly or nurturing attitudes toward wildlife, with the result that many species have been depleted.[15] In Australia and in North America the disappearance of whole species of large mammals occurred at the hands of the then relatively newly arrived indigenous peoples, who hunted these easy targets to extinction. Australian Aborigines' use of fire as a method of hunting dramatically transformed the landscape as well as aiding the extinction of species. In national parks where the rights of indigenous people to hunt are recognised, their use of firearms in addition to spears and other traditional weapons has severely depleted native fauna.

These are just a few examples in the area of spirituality and the environment where more critical thinking is necessary even though it might be sharply injurious to long-held beliefs and trendy new attitudes. Indeed, that is the point of openly assessing religious beliefs and their impact on society, nature and the individual. It is to ensure that the ever-present temptation to ignore the faulty logic and the negative consequences of our beloved traditions and our new spiritualities will always meet with a free and vigorous response. Far from destroying the riches of the religious life, such thoughtful engagement with it is the highest mark of respect and an essential part of its always emerging nature.

In the 1980s and 1990s it seemed that the future belonged to interreligious dialogue and co-operation. Pope John Paul II held a ground-breaking interfaith meeting at Assisi in 1986 prompting many local and international organisations to be founded with great hopes of engagement across religious traditions. In the same spirit, the one-hundredth anniversary of the Parliament of the World's Religions was celebrated in 1993, bringing over 6000 delegates from every religion, big and small, to Chicago. Colourful processions and inspirational addresses, including Hans Kung's, marked each day, and even the Dalai Lama's faltering and accented English did not stop a huge crowd amassing to hear his talk, delivered with the aid of interpreters. It was a time of great optimism, in which religious teachings alone were thought to provide the antidote and the solutions to interreligious hatred, racism and political conflict.

With some notable exceptions and achievements, it has proved to be a much more difficult task than anyone anticipated. On the positive side, there has been a significant rapprochement between Catholic and Jewish leaders, in which the Church has acknowledged that its theologically embedded antipathy toward Judaism fostered a long and painful history of persecution. Through official statements and a great many face to face encounters, Australian Cardinal Edward Cassidy, for example, has been a great force for reconciliation with the Jewish faith and has inspired many in the Church to carry on his work.

But it is also true that religious communities are not monolithic. They are themselves hotbeds of the very kind of theological and political strife that they seek to eliminate between the traditions and in the secular sphere. Deep doctrinal and ideological divisions exist within the Christian Church, the Buddhist *sangha*, Dar el Islam and the Jewish people, to name but four main traditions. What can one hope to achieve when these houses divided against themselves engage in interfaith relations? One often wishes they would do more to repair their internal divisions. Still, there is good reason to pursue interfaith relations even if their outcomes are often equivocal.

Part of the difficulty is that religious communities tend to approach interfaith events as an opportunity to present an attractive face to others in the hope of engendering positive regard, which is, after all, the whole point of the exercise. In a cynical example of this, several infamous international new religious movements used the device of interfaith organisations to sanitise their images and develop a network amongst the major faiths. Usually, however, community initiatives focus on the simpler aspects of ritual practice, food and central beliefs, careful to avoid the contentious theological and political issues within any single tradition, lest the religious community in question appears less than united. In short, the result can be so superficial as to misrepresent the religions involved and create the illusion of peace and understanding, when below the surface hostilities boil and prejudices reign unchecked.

In a meeting that launched a new interfaith organisation in Sydney, a Quaker participant objected to the rule that excluded all political issues from discussion. She asked how one could speak about religion and not also be speaking about its political implications and involvements. Indeed, the political dimension of the religious life cannot be removed because it is part and parcel of its mandate, for good and for ill. After September 11 it is impossible not to seriously consider the political implications of religious beliefs. The women and girls who are cruelly abused by men and are forced into silence by tribal laws, the Church culture that protects its own clerics when they are known perpetrators of crimes, the extremist religious communities that believe critics should be 'rubbed out' and different religious communities subjugated, if not eliminated, are all acting politically. Equally, the religious community that refuses to either oppress women or protect criminals, that refuses to preach and fund terrorism and fosters friendship and dialogue with other religious communities, that examines honestly the social consequences of its beliefs and opens its doors to a changing society is also acting politically. Yet, precisely because of its wider ramifications on society at large, the inescapable political dimension of the religious life should always be the subject of scrutiny and open debate and thereby always recognised for what it is, the human voice of religion, responding to the demands which the secular world thrusts onto the human community, caught as it is in the torrents of history. To retreat from the temporal world and deny religion's political interests, for good and for ill, is simply dishonest and gives rise to the fiction, frequently encountered in matters of love, that its essence and reason for being is found in the experience of rapturous union with the beloved. In reality, the religious life is more like a marriage, where equality and accountability, humaneness and respect, sacrifice and courage are the very things that keep the love alive and are the measure of its worth.

ENDNOTES

Chapter 1 — Re-inventing the Self

1   *The Aberdeen Saturday Pioneer*, January 25, 1890

2   ibid.

3   ibid.

4   ibid.

5   ibid.

6   Joseph Campbell with Bill Moyers, *The Power of Myth*, Doubleday, New York, 1988.

7   Thomas Carlyle, *On Heroes, Hero-Worship and the Heroic in History*, Collins Clear-Type Press, London & Glasgow, 1840, p. 9.

8   ibid., p. 17.

9   ibid., p. 20.

10   ibid., pp. 20–1.

11   ibid., p. 21.

12   Jean Houston, *A Mythic Life: Learning to Live our Greater Story*, HarperSanFrancisco, New York, 1996, pp. 125–26.

13   ibid., p. 125.

14   ibid., p. 124.

15   ibid., pp. 126–27.

16   ibid., p. 127.

17   Jean Houston, *A Passion for the Possible: A Guide to Realising Your True Potential*, HarperSanFrancisco, New York, 1997.

18   ibid., p. 36.

19   Jean Houston, *Jump Time: Shaping Your Future in a World of Radical Change*, Viking, Ringwood, Vic, 2001, p. 128.

20   ibid., p. 38.

21   ibid.

Chapter 2 — Rewriting the Bible

1   Joseph Klausner, *Jesus of Nazareth*, Macmillan, New York, 1925.

2   Albert S. Lindemann, *The Jew Accused: Three Anti-Semitic Affairs — Dreyfus, Beilis, Frank, 1894–1915*, Cambridge University Press, Cambridge, 1991.

3   Robert P. Ericksen, *Theologians under Hitler*, Yale University Press, New Haven, CT, 1985.

4   Ernest Renan, *The Life of Jesus*, Prometheus Books, Buffalo, NY, 1991 (1863), p. 227.

5   John Dominic Crossan, *The Historical Jesus: The Life of a Mediterranean Jewish Peasant*, Collins Dove, North Blackburn, Vic, 1991, p. 422.

6   Albert Schweitzer, *Out of My Life and Thought*, Henry Hold & Co, New York, 1990, quoted in Meyer & Bergel, *Reverence for Life*, Syracuse University Press, Syracuse, NY, 2002, pp. 108–23.

7   Robert Funk, 2000, 'The Incredible Christ', talk given at Uniting Theological College, Sydney, 7 May.

8   Luke 11: 9–10; Matthew 7: 7–8; Thessalonians 2: 1–4; also the Gospel of Thomas.

9   John Shelby Spong, *A New Christianity for a New World: Why Traditional Faith is Dying and How a New Faith is being Born*, HarperSanFrancisco, New York, 2002.

10 ibid., pp. 2–3.

11 ibid., p. 8.

12 ibid., p. 145.

13 ibid., p. 137.

14 ibid., p. 138.

15 ibid.

16 ibid., p. 169.

Chapter 3 — Returning to the Mother

1   The Wisdom of Solomon 8: 3.

2   Jesus Ben Sira 4: 11–13.

3   Proverbs 8: 1–2, 30.

4   Proverbs 9: 4–7.

5   See Lucy Goodison & Christine Morris, *Ancient Goddesses: The Myths and the Evidence*, University of Wisconsin Press, Madison WI, 1999.

6   Elizabeth Cady Stanton (ed.), *The Woman's Bible*, Bell & Bain Ltd, Glasgow, 1985 (1895), Part 1, p. 10.

7   ibid., p. 53.

8   Genesis 1: 26–7.

9   Stanton, Part 1, p. 14.

10   ibid., p. 15.

11   ibid., p. 27.

12   ibid., pp. 139–42.

13   ibid., p. 143.

14   Alfred J. Gabay, *Messages from Beyond*, Melbourne University Press, Melbourne, 2001.

15   Stanton, Part II, p. 16.

16   Stanton, Part I, p. 11.

17   Margaret Hebblethwaite, *Motherhood and God*, Geoffrey Chapman, London, 1984.

18   Isaiah 49: 15.

19   Psalms 131: 2.

20   1 Peter 1: 23–2: 3.

21   St Augustine, *Confessions IV 1*, trans. R.S. Pine-Coffin, Penguin Books, Harmondsworth, 1961, p. 71.

22   Julian of Norwich, *Showings*, trans. College & Walsh;
      see Julian of Norwich website @ Julia Bolton Holloway, 1977
      www.meltingpot.fortunecity.com/ukraine/324/julian.html

23   Fay Weldon, *Godless in Eden*, Flamingo, London, 1999 (1976).

24   Fiona Horne, *7 Days to a Magickal New You*, HarperCollins, New York, 2001;
      Magickal Sex: A Witch's Guide to Beds, Knobs and Broomsticks, HarperCollins, New York, 2001.

25   Hosea 13: 8.

26   Phyllis Curott, *Book of Shadows*, Broadway Books, New York, 1998, p. 147; Fiona Horne interview, 1 September 2002, *The Spirit of Things*, ABC Radio.

27   Curott, p. 64.

28   ibid., p. 65.

29   ibid., p. 66.

30   ibid., p. 149.

31   Karen Jo Torjesen, *When Women were Priests*, HarperSanFrancisco, New York, 1993.

32   Curott, p. 152.

33   Joseph Campbell, Foreword to Marija Gimbutas, *The Language of the Goddess*, Harper & Row, San Francisco, 1989, pp. xii–xiv.

34   Richard Godbeer, *Sexual Revolution in Early America*, Johns Hopkins University Press, Baltimore, MD, 2002.

35   Kathleen Blee, *Inside Organized Racism*, University of California Press, Berkeley, CA, 2002.

36   thea Gaia, 'Goddess/Witch/Womon' in Doug Ezzy (ed.), *The Witch's Craft*, Allen & Unwin, Sydney, 2003, pp. 89–105.

Chapter 4 — Restoring the Earth

1   Fay Weldon, *Godless in Eden*, Flamingo, London, 1999 (1976), p. 139.

2   Leviticus 18: 22.

3   Timothy 2: 12.

4   Genesis 1: 26–8.

5   Deuteronomy 14: 3–21.

6   Leviticus 25: 1–5, 20–4.

7   Homer, quoted in David Suzuki & Amanda McConnell, *The Sacred Balance: Rediscovering our Place in Nature*, Allen & Unwin, Sydney, 1997, p. 84.

8   Brendan Mackey, 'The Earth Charter and the Catholic Church' in *Compass: A Review of Topical Theology*, vol. 37, Autumn 2003, p. 19.

9   Rupert Sheldrake, 'Really Popular Science', *New York Times*, 4 January 2003.

10   David Suzuki & Amanda McConnell, *The Sacred Balance: Rediscovering our Place in Nature*, Allen & Unwin, Sydney, 1997, p. 38.

11   Luther Standing Bear, 'My People the Sioux' in Suzuki & McConnell, p. 78.

12   Quoted in Vivianne Crowley, 'Wicca as Nature Religion' in Joanne Pearson, Richard Roberts & Geoffrey H. Samual (eds), *Nature Religion Today*, Edinburgh University Press, Edinburgh, 1998, p. 176.

13   Starhawk, *The Spiral Dance: A Rebirth of the Ancient Religion of the Great Goddess*, HarperSanFrancisco, New York, 1979, p. 12.

14   David Suzuki & Holly Dressell, *Naked Ape to Superspecies: A Personal Perspective on Humanity and the Global Crisis*, Allen & Unwin, Sydney, 1999, p. 57.

15   'World Scientists' Warning to Humanity' quoted in Suzuki & Dressell, p. 68.

16   James F. Jarboe, 'The Threat of Eco Terrorism', Congressional Statement before the House Resources Subcommittee on Forests and Forest Health, 12 February 2002.

17   Psalm 36: 5–6.

18   Psalm 65: 12–13.

19   Psalm 37: 11.

20   Psalm 104: 35.

21   Psalm 71: 20–1.

22   Psalm 99: 7.

23   Job 12: 7–9.

24   Quoted in Suzuki & McConnell, p. 156.

25   Deuteronomy 4: 16.

26   Quoted in Raphael Loewe, *Ibn Gabirol*, Grove Wiedenfeld, New York, 1989, p. 126.

27   ibid., p. 145.

Chapter 5 — Reforming Buddhism

1   Jack Kerouac, *Some of the Dharma*, Penguin, New York, 1997, p. 41.

2   ibid., p. 61.

3   Jack Kornfield, *A Path with Heart*, Bantam, London, 1993, p. 244.

4   Shunryu Suzuki Roshi, *Zen Mind, Beginner's Mind*, Weatherill Inc, Trumbull, CT, 1970, quoted in Jean Smith (ed.), *Everyday Mind: 366 Reflections on the Buddhist Path*, Riverhead Books, New York, 1997.

5   Suzuki Roshi quoted in Charles Prebish, *Luminous Passage: The Practice and Study of Buddhism in America*, University of California Press, Berkeley, CA, 1999, p. 72.

6   For the whole story, see Michael Downing, *Shoes Outside the Door: Desire, Devotion and Excess at the San Francisco Zen Center*, Counterpoint, Washington DC, 2001.

7   Michael Roach, *The Diamond Cutter: The Buddha on Strategies for Managing Your Business and Your Life*, Doubleday, New York, 2000, p. 44 et seq.

8   ibid., p. 5.

9   ibid.

10   Charles Prebish, *Luminous Passage: The Practice and Study of Buddhism in America*, University of California Press, Berkeley, 1999, p. 262.

Chapter 6 — Renewing Judaism

1   Stephen Kent, *From Slogans to Mantras*, Syracuse University Press, Syracuse, 2000.

2   Rodger Kamenetz, *The Jew in the Lotus*, HarperSanFrancisco, New York, 1994, pp. 78–9.

3   ibid., p. 87.

4   David Cooper, *God is a Verb: Kabbalah and the Practice of Mystical Judaism*,
     Riverhead Books, New York, 1997, p. 3.

5   www.eletchayyim.org/jewish-found.html

6   Cooper, p. 132.

7   ibid., p. 133.

8   ibid., p. 69.

9   Lawrence Kushner, *The River of Light*, Jewish Lights Publishing, Woodstock, VT,
     1990 (1981), p. 71.

10   ibid., p. 71.

11   ibid., p. 72.

12   ibid., p. 72.

13   Shimon Shokek, *Kabbalah and the Art of Being*, Routledge, London, 2001, p. 69.

14   ibid., p. 69.

15   Rabbi Bachya Ibn Paquda, *The Duties of the Heart*, quoted in Shokek, p. 95.

16   Bachya, op. cit., quoted in Shokek, p. 96.

17   www.rickross.com/reference/Kabbalah 06/02/01.

18   Rodger Kamenetz, 'What I Know From Kabbalah', in
     www.beliefnet.com/story/95/story_9574_1.html.

19   Michael Berg, *The Way: Using Kabbalah for Spiritual Transformation and Fulfillment*,
     John Wiley & Sons, New York, 2001, p. 38.

20   ibid., p. 41.

21   Rodger Kamenetz, *Stalking Elijah*, HarperSanFrancisco, New York, 1997,
     pp. 49–50.

22   Berg, p. 44.

23   ibid., p. 213.

Chapter 7 — Re-Souling Psychology

1   Sigmund Freud, *New Introductory Lectures on Psychoanalysis*, trans. W.D. Robson-
     Scott, rev. & newly edited James Strachey, Anchor Books, Garden City NY, 1964
     (1927), Chapter 7.

2   Sigmund Freud, 'Obsessive Acts and Religious Practices', in *Collected Papers*,
     trans. under supervision of Joan Riviere, Basic Books, New York, 1959, vol. 2,
     pp. 25–35.

3   David Bakan, *Sigmund Freud and the Jewish Mystical Tradition*, Beacon Press,
     Boston, 1958, p. 27.

4   Carl Jung, 'Sigmund Freud in his Historical Setting', in Frank Cioffi, *Freud*, Macmillan, London, 1933, pp. 50–51.

5   Sigmund Freud, *Civilization and its Discontents*, W.W. Norton, New York, 1962 (1930), p. 19.

6   Paul Heelas & Rachel Kohn, 'Psychotherapy and the Techniques of Transformation' in *Beyond Therapy: The Impact of Eastern Religions on Psychological Theory and Practice*, ed. Guy Claxton, Wisdom Publications, London, 1986.

7   Carl Jung, *On the Nature of the Psyche*, Princeton University Press, Princeton, 1960 (1946), p. 188.

8   Robert Sardello, *Freeing the Soul From Fear*, Riverhead Books, New York, 1999, p. 4.

9   Mordechai Rotenberg, *Dialogue with Deviance: The Hassidic Ethic and the Theory of Social Contraction*, Institute for the Study of Human Issues, New York, 1983, pp. 71–2.

10   Sardello, p. 104.

11   *The Zen Teachings of Bodhidharma*, trans., Red Pine, North Point Press, New York, 1997, p. 47, quoted in Sardello, p. 87.

12   Jack Kornfield, 'Psychotherapy and Mediation' in *A Path With Heart*, Bantam, London, 1993, p. 249.

13   Gabriel Lafitte & Alison Ribush, *Happiness in a Material World: The Dalai Lama in Australia and New Zealand*, Lothian Books, Melbourne, 2002.

14   Freud, *Civilization and its Discontents*, p. 26.

15   Sigmund Freud, 'Analysis of a Phobia in a Five-Year-Old Child', *Standard Edition of the Complete Psychological Works of Sigmund Freud*, trans. and ed. James Strachey, Hogarth Press and Institute of Psychoanalysis, London, 1958, vol. 10, p. 23.

16   Mark Epstein, *Thoughts Without a Thinker*, Persus Books, New York, 1995, p. 115.

17   Sigmund Freud, 'Recommendations to Physicians Practising Psychoanalysis', *Standard Edition of the Complete Psychological Works of Sigmund Freud*, trans. and ed. James Strachey, Hogarth Press and Institute of Psychoanalysis, London, 1958, vol. 12, pp. 111–12, quoted in Mark Epstein, *Thoughts Without a Thinker*, Persus Books, New York, 1995, p. 115.

18   Sigmund Freud, 'Remembering, Repeating and Working Through', *Standard Edition of the Complete Psychological Works of Sigmund Freud*, trans. and ed. James Strachey, Hogarth Press and Institute of Psychoanalysis, London, 1958, vol. 12. p. 147, quoted in Mark Epstein *Thoughts Without a Thinker*, Persus Books, New York, 1995, p. 166.

19   Thomas Moore, *Original Self: Living with Paradox and Authenticity*, HarperCollins, Sydney 2000, pp. 72–3.

20   Thomas Moore, *Meditations: On the Monk Who Dwells in Daily Life*, Hodder & Stoughton Australia, Rydalmere, 1995, p. 43.

21   ibid., p. 31.

22   Bede Griffiths, *Return to the Centre*, Collins, London, 1976.

23   Christopher Lasch, *The Culture of Narcissism*, W.W. Norton, New York, 1978.

24   Quoted in Robert Coles, *The Secular Mind*, Princeton University Press, Princeton, 1999, p. 28.

25   Robert Coles, *The Secular Mind*, Princeton University Press, Princeton, 1999, p. 40.

Chapter 8 — Removing Morality

1   Neale Donald Walsch, *Conversations with God 1*, Hodder, Sydney, 2001 (1996), p. 1.

2   ibid., p. 200.

3   ibid., p. 28.

4   ibid., p. 17.

5   ibid., p. 39.

6   ibid., pp. 40, 42.

7   Friedrich Nietzsche, 'Human, All too Human' in *Genealogy of Morals and Ecce Homo*, Vintage Books, New York, 1969. pp. 169–70.

8   Ibid., 'Ecce Homo', p. 234.

9   ibid., 'Why I Write Books', p. 264.

10   Civilus, in Tacitus, *Histories*, c. AD 115.

11   Don Cupitt, *Solar Ethics*, SCM Press, London, 1995, p. 46.

12   ibid., p. 36.

13   D.H. Lawrence, *Cambridge Edition of the Works of D.H. Lawrence*, Cambridge University Press, Cambridge, vol. 3, p. 35 quoted in Don Cupitt, *The New Religion of Life in Everyday Speech*, SCM Press, London, 1999, p. 73.

14   Neale Donald Walsch, *Communion with God*, Hodder & Stoughton, London, 2000, p. 120.

15   ibid., p. 125.

16   From William Wordsworth, 'Lines Composed a Few Miles Above Tintern Abbey'.

17   From Elizabeth Barrett Browning, 'Aurora Leigh', book VII.

18   Walsch, *Communion with God*, p. 103.

Chapter 9 — Reclaiming Moral Sense

1   Augustine, *City of God*, vol.1, p. 20, trans. Demetrius B. Zema & Gerald G.
     Walsh, Catholic University of America Press and Consortium Books,
     Washington DC, 1977.

2   Thomas Aquinas, *The Summa Theologica*, ed. and trans. the English Dominican
     Fathers, Bensinger Bros., New York, 1918, Part 1, Question 64: 1.

3   Andrew Linzey & Dan Cohn-Sherbok, *After Noah: Animals and the Liberation of
     Theology*, Mowbray, London, 1997, pp. 38–42.

4   D.N. Jha, *The Holy Cow*, Verso, London, 2001.

5   See website www.koko.org/news/1996

6   Frans de Waal, *The Ape and the Sushi Master: Cultural Reflections of a Primatologist*,
     Basic Books, New York, 2001, p. 312.

7   ibid., p. 339.

8   Frans de Waal, *Good Natured: The Origins of Right and Wrong in Humans and
     Other Animals*, Harvard University Press, Cambridge, MA., 1996, pp. 75–77.

9   Mark Henderson, 'Orang-utans watch table manners', *The Times*, reprinted *The
     Australian*, Jan 4–5, 2003.

10   ibid.

11   Edward Westermarck, *The Origin and Development of the Moral Ideas*, Books for
     Libraries Press, Freeport, 1971 (1906).

12   Frans de Waal, *The Ape and the Sushi Master: Cultural Reflections of a Primatologist*,
     Basic Books, New York, 2001, p. 338.

13   Frans de Waal, *Good Natured: The Origins of Right and Wrong In Humans and
     Other Animals*, Harvard University Press, Cambridge, MA., 1996, pp. 178–80.

14   Leviticus 22: 17–19.

15   Hosea 6: 6.

16   Amos 5: 21–4.

17   James Q. Wilson, *The Moral Sense*, Free Press, New York, 1993, p. 43.

18   Luke 16: 19–31.

19   Luke 16: 31.

20   Charles Darwin, quoted in *The Columbia History of the World*, eds John Garraty
     & Peter Gay, Harper & Row, New York, 1972, p. 957.

21   Michael Shermer, *How We Believe: the Search for God in an Age of Science*, W.H. Freeman & Co., New York, 1999, p.72.

22   J.S. Haldane, quoted in Stephen J. Gould, *Rock of Ages: Science and Religion in the Fullness of Life*, Ballantine, New York, 1999, p. 91.

23   ibid., p. 92.

24   Mary Midgley, *Beast and Man* (rev. ed.), Routledge, London, 1995, pp. 119–27.

25   ibid., p. 124.

Chapter 10 — Redeeming Religion from Itself

1   Denis Diderot, quoted in Will Durant, *The Story of Philosophy*, Washington Square Press, New York, 1961, p. 231.

2   Sydney E. Ahlstrom, *A Religious History of the American People*, Yale University Press, New Haven, 1972, p. 804.

3   Washington Gladden, quoted in Peter J. Theusen, 'The Logic of Mainline Churches', in Wuthnow, *The Quiet Hand of God*, University of California Press, Berkeley, 2002, p. 42.

4   Walter Rauschenbusch, *A Theology of Social Gospel*, Macmillan Co., New York, 1917.

5   Richard Niebuhr, *Social Sources of Denominationalism*, Meridian Books, New York, 1957.

6   Albert Schweitzer, in *Out of My Life and Thought*, Meyer & Bergel, eds, *Reverence for Life*, Syracuse University Press, Syracuse NY, 2002, p. 120.

7   ibid., p. 121.

8   Ibid.

9   ibid., p. 273.

10   ibid., pp. 132–3.

11   Ibid., p. 121.

12   Dr Umayma Jalahma, 'Blood Libel: US War on Iraq Timed to Coincide with Jewish Holiday Purim', MEMRI, 15 April 2003.

13   Yigal Carmon, 'Harbingers of Change in the Antisemitic Discourse in the Arab World', 23 April 2003, www.memri.org/bin/opener_latest.cgi?ID=IA13503

14   Robert Wistrich, *Muslim Antisemitism: A Clear and Present Danger*, American Jewish Committee, New York, 2002, p. 17.

15   Albert Speer, cited in Wistrich.

16   Ira A. Lapidus, *A History of Islamic Societies*, 2nd ed., Cambridge University Press, Cambridge, 2002, p. 88.

17   Tariq Ali, *The Clash of Fundamentalisms: Crusades, Jihads and Modernity*, Verso, London, 2002, p. 295.

18   Salman Rushdie, 'No More Fanaticism as Usual', *New York Times*, 27 November 2002.

19   E.B. White, *Here is New York*, Little Bookroom, New York, 1999 (1949).

Chapter 11 — Rethinking Rigid and Romantic Religion

1   Peter Cameron, *Fundamentalism and Freedom*, Doubleday, Sydney, 1995.

2   'Enron Inquiry Bogged Down', *Cape Cod Times*, from the *Dallas Morning News*, 31 July 2003; Scott Lindlaw, 'Enron-itis: SEC Chairman says he hopes "We've seen the Worst of it"', redding.com, 22 July 2003.

3   'Ebbers Out at WorldCom', *CNN Money*, 30 April 2002, money.cnn.com; 'WorldCom Malfeasance Revealed', cbsnews.com; 10 June 2003, cbsnews.com/stories.

4   Robert Darden, 'An Interview with Ken Lay', *The Door*, May–June 2002; Cary McMullen, 'Charges Facing CEOs at Odds With Faith', *Courier* (Houma LA), 14 July 2002.

5   McMullen, op.cit.

6   Babylonian Talmud, Tracate Shabbat 33a.

7   *War Cry* magazine, 4 January 2003.

8   Richard Sipe, *Sex, Priests and Power: Anatomy of a Crisis*, Cassell, London, 1995.

9   Hillary Mayell, 'Thousands of Women Killed for Family "Honour"', *National Geographic News*, 12 February 2002.

10   *Koran*, trans. Muhammed Marmaduke Pickthall, George Allen & Unwin, London, 1976 (1930).

11   Thomas Moore, *The Soul's Religion*, HarperCollins, New York, 2002.

12   Thomas Moore, interview, 30 March 2003.

13   Hillary Mayell, 'Thousands of Women Killed for Family "Honour"', *National Geographic News*, 12 February 2002.

14   Charles Birch, *Biology and the Riddle of Life*, University of New South Wales Press, Sydney, 1999, pp. 92 et seq.

15   Jared Diamond, 'New Guineans and Their Natural World', in Stephen Kellert & E.O. Wilson, *The Biophilia Hypothesis*, Island Press, Washington DC, 1993.

BIBLIOGRAPHY

Ahsltrom, Sydney E. *The Religious History of the American People*, Yale University Press, New Haven & London, 1972.

Akbar, M.J. *The Shade of Swords: Jihad and the Conflict Between Islam and Christianity*, Routledge, London, 2002.

Ali, Tariq. *The Clash of Fundamentalisms: Crusades, Jihads and Modernity*, Verso, London, 2002.

Aquinas, Thomas. *Summa Theologica*, edited and translated by the English Dominican Fathers, Bensinger Bros, New York, 1918.

Bakan, David. *Sigmund Freud and the Jewish Mystical Tradition*, Beacon Press, Boston, 1958.

Batchelor, Stephen. *Buddhism Without Beliefs: A Contemporary Guide to Awakening*, Bloomsbury, London, 1997.

Bauer, Bruno. *Christ and the Caesars: The Origin of Christianity from Romanized Greek Culture*, translated by Frank Schact, A Davidonis, Charleston House, Charleston S.C., 1998.

Baum, Frank L. *The Aberdeen Saturday Pioneer*, 25 January 1890.

—— *The Wonderful Wizard of Oz*, with pictures by W.W. Denslow, G.M. Hill Co, Chicago & New York, 1900.

Berg, Michael. *The Way, Using the Wisdom of Kabbalah for Spiritual Transformation and Fulfillment*, John Wiley & Sons, New York, 2001.

Birch, Charles. *Regaining Compassion for Humanity and Nature*, University of New South Wales Press, Sydney, 1993.

—— *Biology and the Riddle of Life*, University of New South Wales Press, Sydney, 1999.

Blavatksy, Helena Petrovna. *Isis Unveiled: A Master-key to the Mysteries of Ancient and Modern Science and Theology*, Theosophical University Press, Pasadena CA, 1972 (1919).

Blee, Kathleen M. *Inside Organised Racism: Women in the Hate Movement,* University of California Press, Berkeley CA, 2002.

Brockelman, Paul. *Cosmology and Creation: The Spiritual Significance of Contemporary Cosmology*, Oxford University Press, Oxford, 1999.

Bultmann, Karl Rudolf. *Faith and Understanding*, edited by Robert W. Funk, Fortress Press, Philadelphia, 1987.

—— *Jesus Christ and Mythology*, Scribner, New York, 1958.

Cameron, Peter. *Heretic*, Doubleday, Sydney, 1994.

—— *Fundamentalism and Freedom*, Doubleday, Sydney, 1995.

Campbell, Joseph. *The Hero With a Thousand Faces*, Princeton University Press, Princeton NJ, 1990 (1949).

——'Forward' to Marija Gimbutas, *The Language of the Goddess*, Harper & Row, San Francisco, 1989: xiii–xiv.

Campbell, Joseph, with Moyers Bill, Betty Sue Flowers, (ed). *The Power of Myth*, Doubleday, New York, 1988.

Capra, Fritjof. *The Tao of Physics: An Exploration of the Parallels Between Modern Physics and Eastern Mysticism*, Shambala, Boston, 2000.

Carlyle, Thomas. 'The Hero as Divinity. Odin. Paganism: Scandinavian Mythology', lecture delivered 5 May 1840, published in *On Heroes, Hero-Worship and the Heroic in History*, Collins Clear Type Press, London and Glasgow, 1840.

Cioffi, Frank. *Freud*, Macmillan, London, 1933.

Coles, Robert. *The Secular Mind,* Princeton University Press, Princeton, 1999.

Collins, Paul. *The Good Earth: Religion if Matter Really Mattered,* Harper CollinsReligious, Melbourne, 1995.

—— *From Inquisition to Freedom: Seven Prominent Catholics and the Struggle With the Vatican*, Simon & Schuster, Sydney, 2001.

Cooper, David. *God is a Verb: Kabbalah and the Practice of Mystified Judaism,* Riverhead Books, New York, 1997.

Crossan, John Dominic. *The Historical Jesus: The Life of a Mediterranean Jewish Peasant*, Collins Dove, North Blackburn, Vic, 1991.

Crowley, Vivianne. 'Wicca as Nature Religion' in Joanne Pearson, Richard Robert & Geoffrey H. Samuel (eds.) *Nature Religion Today*, Edinburgh University Press, Edinburgh, 1998.

Cupitt, Don. *The New Religion of Life in Everyday Speech*, SCM Press, London, 1999.

—— *Solar Ethics*, SCM Press, London, 1995.

Currott, Phyllis. *Book of Shadows*, Broadway Books, New York, 1998.

Darden, Robert. (ed.) *The Door*, Trinity Foundation, Dallas TX, June/July 2002.

Diamond, Jared. 'New Guineans and Their Natural World' in Stephen Kellert & E.O. Wilson (eds.), *The Biophilia Hypothesis*, Island Press, Washington D.C., 1993.

Downing Michael. *Shoes Outside the Door: Desire, Devotion and Excess at the San Francisco Zen Center*, Counterpoint, Washington DC, 2001.

Eisler, Riane. *Sacred Pleasure*, HarperSanFrancisco, New York, 1995.

Epstein, Mark. *Thoughts Without a Thinker*, Persus Books, New York, 1995.

Ericksen, Robert P. *Theologians Under Hitler*, Yale University Press, New Haven, 1985.

Foster, Barbara, Foster, Michael & Durrell, Lawrence. *The Secret Lives of Alexandra David-Neel*, Overlook Press, New York, 1998.

Fox, Matthew, et al. *Creation Spirituality*, Millennium Books, Sydney, 1991.

Freud, Sigmund. *Totem and Taboo*, trans. A.A. Brill, Routledge and Sons, London, 1919.

—— *New Introductory Lectures on Psychoanalysis*, trans. W.D. Robson-Scott, rev. & newly edited, James Strachey, Anchor Books, Garden City NY, 1964 (1927).

—— *The Future of an Illusion*, trans. James Strachey, Anchor Books, Doubleday, Garden City NY, 1964 (1927).

—— *Moses and Monotheism*, trans. Katherine Jones, Vintage Books, New York, 1939.

—— 'Obsessive Acts and Religious Practices' in *Collected Papers*, authorised trans. under supervision of Joan Riviere, Basic Books, New York, 1959, vol 2.

—— *Civilization and its Discontents*, W.W. Norton, New York, 1962 (1930).

—— 'Analysis of a Phobia in a Five-Year-Old Child' in *Standard Edition of the Complete Psychological Works of Sigmund Freud*, ed. & trans. James Strachey, Hogarth Press and Institute of Psychoanalysis, London, 1958.

Funk, Robert. *Honest to Jesus*, Hodder and Stoughton, Sydney, 1996.

—— 'The Incredible Christ', talk given at Uniting Theological College, Sydney, 7 May 2000.

Funk, Robert, Hoover, Roy W. & The Jesus Seminar. *The Five Gospels: The Search for the Authentic Words of Jesus*, Maxwell Macmillan International, Sydney, 1993.

Gabay, Alfred J. *Messages from Beyond*, Melbourne University Press, Melbourne, 2001.

Gaia, thea. 'Goddess/Witch/Woman' in Doug Ezzy (ed.) *The Witch's Craft*, Allen & Unwin, Sydney, 2003.

Godbeer, Richard. *Sexual Revolution in Early America*, Johns Hopkins University Press, Baltimore, 2002.

Goodison, Lucy & Christian Morris. *Ancient Goddesses: The Myths and the Evidence.*' University of Wisconsin Press, Madison WI, 1999.

Gould, Stephen J. *Rocks of Ages: Science and Religion in the Fullness of Life*, Ballantine, New York, 1999.

Griffiths, Bede. *Return to the Centre*, Collins, London, 1976.

Habel, Norman. (ed.) *The Earth Bible*, Vols I, II, III, Sheffield University Press, Sheffield, 2000, 2001.

Hebblethwaite, Margaret. *Motherhood and God*, Geoffrey Chapman, London, 1984.

Heelas, Paul & Kohn, Rachael. 'Psychotherapy and the Techniques of Transformation' in *Beyond Therapy: The Impact of Eastern Religion on Psychological Theory and Practice*, ed. Guy Claxton, Wisdom Publications, 1986.

Henderson, Mark. 'Orang-utans Watch Table Manners', *The Australian*, 5 Jan 2003, reprinted from *The London Times*.

Houston, Jean. *A Mythic Life: Learning to Live our Greater Story*, HarperSanFrancisco, New York, 1996.

—— *A Passion for the Possible: A Guide to Realizing Your True Potential*, HarperSanFrancisco, New York, 1997

Houston, Jean with Rubin, Margaret. *Manual for the Peace Maker: An Iroquois Legend to Heal Self & Society*, Quest Books, Madras/London, 1995

Huntington, Samuel. 'Clash of Civilizations', *Foreign Affairs*, Summer, vol. 72, no. 3, Council on Foreign Relations, 1993.

Huyler, Stephen. *Painted Prayers*, Rizzoli, New York, 1994.

Jarboe, James F. 'The Threat of Eco Terrorism', Congressional Statement before the House of Resources Subcommittee on Forests and Forest Health, 12 February 2002.

Jung, Carl. *On the Nature of the Psyche*, Princeton University Press, Princeton, 1960 (1946).

Kamenetz, Rodger. *The Jew in the Lotus: A Poet's Rediscovery of Jewish Identity in Buddhist India*, HarperSanFrancisco, New York, 1994.

—— *Stalking Elijah*, HarperSanFrancisco, New York, 1997.

—— 'What I Know From Kabbalah' in www.beliefnet.com/story/95/story_9574_1.html

Kent, Stephen. *From Slogans to Mantras*, Syracuse University Press, Syracuse, 2000.

Kerouac, Jack. *Some of the Dharma*, Penguin, New York 1999 (1997).

Khouri, Norma. *Forbidden Love*, Random House, Sydney, 2003.

Kirsch, Jonathan. *King David: The Real Life of the Man who Ruled Israel*, Allen & Unwin, Sydney, 2001.

Klausner, Joseph. *Jesus of Nazareth: His Life, Times and Teaching*, trans. Herbert Danby, The Macmillan Company, New York, 1925 (1922).

—— *The Messianic Idea in Israel, from its Beginning to the Completion of the Mishnah*, trans. from 3rd ed. by W.F. Stinespring, Macmillan, New York, 1955.

Kornfield, Jack. *A Path With Heart*, Bantam, London, 1993.

—— *After Ecstasy, the Laundry*, Bantam Books, New York, 2000.

Kornfield, Jack & Feldman, Christina *Soulfood: Stories to Nourish the Spirit and the Heart*, HarperSanFrancisco, New York, 1996.

Kung, Hans. *Global Responsibility: In Search of a New World Ethic*, Continuum, New York, 1993.

Kushner, Lawrence. *The River of Light: Spirituality, Judaism, Consciousness*, Jewish Lights Publishing, Woodstock VT 1990 (1981).

Lafitte, Gabriel & Ribush, Alison. *Happiness in a Material World: The Dalai Lama in Australia and New Zealand*, Lothian Books, Melbourne, 2002.

Lapidus, Ira A. *A History of Islamic Societies*, 2nd edn, Cambridge University Press, Cambridge, 2002.

Lindemann, Albert S. *The Jew Accused: Three Anti-Semitic Affairs — Dreyfus, Beilis, Frank, 1894–1915*, Cambridge University Press, Cambridge, 1991.

Linzey, Andrew & Cohn-Sherbok, Dan. *After Noah: Animals and the Liberation of Theology*, Mowbray, London, 1997.

Mackey, Brendan. 'The Earth Charter and the Catholic Church' in *Compass: A Review of Topical Theology*, vol. 37, Autumn 2003: 17–23.

McMullen, Cary. 'Charges Facing CEOs at Odds With Faith', *New York Times Regional Newspapers, Courier, Houma*, Los Angeles, 14 July 2002.

Masson, Jeffery. *When Elephants Weep*, Delacorte, New York, 1995.

Mayell, Hillary. 'Thousands of Women Killed for "Family Honor"', in *National Geographic News*, 12 February 2002.

Midgley, Mary. *Utopias, Dolphins and Computers: Problems of Philosophical Plumbing*, Routledge, London, 1996.

—— *Beast and Man*, rev. ed., Routledge, London, 1995.

Moore, Thomas. *Meditations: On the Monk Who Dwells in Daily Life*, Hodder & Stoughton, Sydney, 1994.

—— *Original Self: Living With Paradox and Authenticity*, HarperCollins, San Francisco, 2000.

—— *The Soul's Religion: Cultivating a Profoundly Spiritual Way of Life*, HarperCollins, New York, 2002.

Niebuhr, Richard. *The Social Sources of Denominationalism*, Meridian Books, New York, 1957.

Nietzsche, Friedrich. 'Human, All Too Human' in *Genealogy of Morals and Ecce Homo*, trans. Walter Kaufmann & R.J. Hollingdale, Vintage Books, New York, 1969 (1878).

Ofshe, Richard & Watters, Ethan. *Making Monsters: False Memories, Psychotherapy and Sexual Hysteria*, Andre Deutsch, London, 1994.

Ibn Paquda, Bahya ben Joseph. *Duties of the Heart: The Gate of Trust*, trans. Avraham Yaakov Finkel, Yeshivath Beth Moshe, Scranton PA, 1998.

Paton, Alistaire. 'Getting Back to Nature and God: On Top of the World' in *War Cry*, Salvation Army, Burwood, Victoria, 4 January 2003.

Prebish, Charles S. *Luminous Passage: The Practice and Study of Buddhism in America*, University of California Press, Berkeley CA, 1999.

Rainbow Spirit Elders. *Rainbow Spirit Theology: Towards an Australian Aboriginal Theology*, HarperCollins Religious, Melbourne, 1997.

Rauschenbusch, Walter. *A Theology of Social Gospel*, The Macmillan Co., New York, 1922.

Renan, Ernest. *The Life of Jesus*, trans. Charles Edwin Wilbour, Michel Levy Freres, New York, Carleton, Paris, 1864.

Roach, Geshe Michael. *The Diamond Cutter: The Buddha on Strategies for Managing Your Business and Your Life*, Doubleday, Sydney, 2000.

Rotenberg, Mordechai. *Dialogue With Deviance: The Hassidic Ethic and the Theory of Social Contraction*, Institute for the Study of Human Issues, New York, 1983.

Rushdie, Salman. 'Islam's Words Are Not Enough: Muslim Leaders Must Prove to the World that They do Not Support Evil', *The Age*, 3 July 2002.

—— 'No More Fanaticism as Usual,' *New York Times*, 27 November 2002.

Sardello, Robert. *Freeing the Soul From Fear*, Riverhead Books, New York, 1999.

Schweitzer, Albert. *The Mystery of the Kingdom of God: The Secret of Jesus' Messiahship and Passion*, trans. Walter Lowrie, Prometheus Books, Buffalo NY, 1985 (1914).

—— *Philosophy of Civilization*, Beacon Press, Boston, 1962.

—— *Out of My Life and Thought*, Henry Holt & Co, New York, 1990, in Meyer & Bergel eds, *Reverence for Life*, Syracuse University Press, Syracuse NY, 2002.

—— *The Quest for the Historical Jesus*, trans. W. Montgomery, Johns Hopkins University Press, Baltimore, 1998 (1906).

Seth, Vikram. *Beastly Tales*, Phoenix, London, 1991.

Shermer, Michael. *How We Believe: The Search for God in an Age of Science*, W.H. Freeman and Company, New York, 1999.

Shokek, Shimon. *Kabbalah and the Art of Being*, Routledge, London, 2001.

Sipe, Richard. *Sex, Priests and Power: Anatomy of a Crisis*, Cassell, London, 1995.

Smith, Jean. *Everyday Mind: 366 Reflections on the Buddhist Path*, Riverhead Books, New York, 1997.

Spong, John Shelby. *Rescuing the Bible From Fundamentalism: A Bishop Rethinks the Meaning of Scripture*, HarperSanFrancisco, New York, 1992.

——*Why Christianity Must Change or Die*, HarperSanFrancisco, New York, 1998.

—— *A New Christianity for a New World*. HarperCollins, Sydney, 2002.

Stanton, Elizabeth Cady. *The Woman's Bible*, Bell & Bain Ltd, Glasgow, 1985 (1898).

Starhawk. *The Spiral Dance: A Rebirth of Ancient Religion of the Great Goddess*, HarperSanFrancisco, New York, 1979.

Strauss, David Friedrich. *The Life of Jesus Critically Examined*, ed. Peter C. Hodgson, trans. George Eliot, SCM Press, London, 1975.

Suzuki, David with McConnell, Amanda. *The Sacred Balance: Rediscovering Our Place in Nature*, Allen & Unwin, Sydney, 1997.

Suzuki, David with Dressell, Holly. *Naked Ape to Superspecies: A Personal Perspective on Humanity and the Global Crisis*, Allen & Unwin, Sydney, 1999.

Suzuki, Roshi Shunryu. *Zen Mind, Beginner's Mind*, Weatherhill Inc., Trumbull, CT, 1970.

Tacey, David. *The Spirituality Revolution*, HarperCollins Publishers, Sydney, 2003.

Theusen, Peter J. 'The Logic of Mainline Churchliness: Historical Background since the Reformation', in Robert Wuthnow (ed), *The Quiet Hand of God: Faith Based Activism and the Public Role of Mainline Protestantism*, University of California Press, Berkeley, 2002.

Thic, Nhat Hanh. *Living Buddha, Living Christ*, Riverhead Books, New York, 1995.

Torjesen, Karen Jo. *When Women Were Priests*, HarperSanFrancisco, New York, 1993.

Vermes, Geza. *Jesus the Jew*, Collins, London, 1973.

—— *Jesus and the World of Judaism*, Fortress Press, Philadelphia, 1984 (1983).

—— *The Religion of Jesus the Jew*, SCM Press, London, 1993.

—— *The Complete Dead Sea Scrolls in English*, Penguin, London, 1998 (1992).

—— *The Changing Faces of Jesus*, Allen Lane, The Penguin Press, London, 2000.

de Waal, Frans. *The Ape and the Sushi Master: Cultural Reflections of a Primatologist*, Basic Books, New York, 2001.

—— *Good Natured: The Origins of Right and Wrong*, Harvard University Press, Cambridge MA, 1996.

—— *Chimpanzee Politics: Power and Sex Among Apes*, rev. ed., Johns Hopkins University Press, Baltimore, 1989.

Walsch, Neale Donald. *Conversations With God: An Uncommon Dialogue*, Book 1, Hodder & Stoughton, Sydney, 2001 (1996).

—— *Conversations With God*, Book 2, Hodder & Stoughton, London, 1997.

—— *Conversations With God*, Book 3, Hodder & Stoughton, London, 1998.

—— *Communion With God*, Hodder & Stoughton, London, 2000.

Warner, Marina. *Monuments and Maidens: The Allegory of the Female Form*, Picador, London, 1987.

Weldon, Fay. *Godless in Eden*, Flamingo, HarperCollins, London 1999 (1976).

Westermarck, Edward. *The Origin and Development of the Moral Ideas*, Books for Libraries Press, Freeport, 1971 (1906).

White, E.B. *Here is New York*, The Little Bookroom, New York, 1999 (1949).

Wilson, James Q. *The Moral Sense*, The Free Press, New York, 1993.

Wistrich, Robert. *Muslim Antisemitism: A Clear and Present Danger*, American Jewish Committee, 2002.

Wolf, Rabbi Laibl. *Practical Kabbalah: A Guide to Jewish Wisdom for Everyday Life*, Three Rivers Press, New York, 1999.

DOCUMENTARY FILMS

Jews and Buddhism: Belief Amended, Faith Revealed, Chayes, Bill & Solotaroff, Isaac, Chayes Productions, 1999.

Buddha Realms East: The Delusion of Permanence, Edmondson, Mark and Kohn, Rachael producers, Australian Broadcasting Corporation, 2001.

Buddha Realms West: All is Change, Salgo, Steven & Kohn, Rachael producers, Australian Broadcasting Corporation, 2001.

INDEX

ACKNOWLEDGMENTS

This book would not have been possible without the many inspired individuals whom I have interviewed over the years for *The Spirit of Things*, and the supportive environment of the ABC's Radio National network. These include the former Editor of Radio National, Amanda Armstrong, who first endorsed this writing project; Florence Spurling, the Executive Producer of Religion programs for ABC Radio National who is a true professional in all that she does; and Geoff Wood with whom I have had a great working relationship producing the program since its inception in 1997. They of course bear no responsibility for the views expressed in this book, which lie wholly with me. I am most grateful for the careful attention to the manuscript of my editor, Amanda O'Connell, who has been a delight to work with. The writing of this book would not have been nearly as enjoyable without the support and interest of my husband, Tom A.E. Breen.

Excerpt from *The River of Light – Special Anniversary Edition: Jewish Mystical Awareness* © by Lawrence Kushner (Woodstock, VT: Jewish Lights Publishing). Permission granted by Jewish Lights Publishing, P.O. Box 237, Woodstock, VT 05091 www.jewishlights.com.

Excerpt from *The Clash of Fundamentalism* © by T. Ali, 2002, reproduced with permission from Verso, London/New York.

Excerpt from *The Way* © by Michael Berg, 2002, is used by permission of John Wiley & Sons, Inc.

Excerpt from *Jump Time: Shaping Your Future in a World of Radical Change* © by Jean Houston, 2000, Tarcher, is reproduced with permission from Penguin Putnam Inc, 375 Hudson Street, New York, NY 10014.

Excerpt from *Conversations With God Book 1* © by Neale Donald Walsch, 1996, Putnam Adult, is reproduced with permission from Penguin Putnam Inc, 375 Hudson Street, New York, NY 10014.

Dr Rachael Kohn received her Hon BA in Religion and Sociology in 1975, her MA in New Testament and Rabbinic Studies in 1977, and her doctorate in Religious Studies in 1985 at McMaster University, Canada. She was awarded the Leverhulme Post-Doctoral Fellowship, which she held at the University of Lancaster in 1985–86. She has lectured in religious studies in Canada, Britain and Australia, and taught in the Departments of Religious Studies and Semitic Studies at the University of Sydney. In 1992 she joined the Australian Broadcasting Corporation where she produces and presents *The Spirit of Things* and *The Ark* on Radio National. She has made documentaries on the Dead Sea Scrolls, Spirituality and Animals, and Buddhism for ABC TV, and has won World Gold Medals for her work. She lives in Sydney, Australia.